CW01640581

ET GY

Ethnographic Theology

An Inquiry into the Production of Theological Knowledge

Natalie Wigg-Stevenson

palgrave
macmillan

ETHNOGRAPHIC THEOLOGY

Softcover reprint of the hardcover 1st edition 2014 978-1-137-39043-1

First published in 2014 by PALGRAVE MACMILLAN® in the United States—a division of St. Martin's Press LLC, 175 Fifth Avenue, New York, NY 10010.

Where this book is distributed in the UK, Europe and the rest of the world, this is by Palgrave Macmillan, a division of Macmillan Publishers Limited, registered in England, company number 785998, of Houndmills, Basingstoke, Hampshire RG21 6XS.

Palgrave Macmillan is the global academic imprint of the above companies and has companies and representatives throughout the world.

Palgrave® and Macmillan® are registered trademarks in the United States, the United Kingdom, Europe and other countries.

ISBN 978-1-349-48261-0 ISBN 978-1-137-38775-2 (eBook)
DOI 10.1057/9781137387752

Library of Congress Cataloging-in-Publication Data

Wigg-Stevenson, Natalie.
Ethnographic theology : an inquiry into the production of theological knowledge / by Natalie Wigg-Stevenson.
pages cm
Includes bibliographical references and index.
1. Christianity and culture. 2. Ethnology—Religious aspects—Christianity. 3. Theology—Methodology. 4. Knowledge, Theory of (Religion) I. Title.

BR115.C8W53 2014
261.5—dc23 2014028628

A catalogue record of the book is available from the British Library.

Design by Scribe Inc.

First edition: October 2014

10 9 8 7 6 5 4 3 2 1

For my friends at First Baptist Church, Nashville

Contents

Acknowledgments

My first thanks go to my teachers and mentors: I am thankful for all the ways Alison McQueen, John Robertson, Siobhán Garrigan, Serene Jones, Paul Dehart, and John Thatamanil have both encouraged and challenged me in my scholarly work. I am especially grateful for the significant support offered by Graham Reside, Christian Scharen, and Ted Smith at crucial moments in this book's development. Most of all, I am indebted to Ellen Armour, my doctoral supervisor, for her wisdom, care, and friendship.

Conversations with my doctoral colleagues, the inaugural cohort of Vanderbilt's program in Theology and Practice, are the heart of this project: Jin Young Choi, Angela Cowser, Sean Hayden, Asante Todd, and especially Kate Lassiter. I am grateful for the formative influence our work together has had on my own thought. Thanks are also due to Samantha Cavanagh who helped breathe new life into this work as it came to its end. Travis Ables and Steve Jungkeit have seen this project through from start to finish. I am deeply thankful not only for their gracious willingness to read—and reread and reread—the manuscript in whole and various parts along the way but also for their friendship throughout the whole process.

A number of communities have been willing to engage and support this work, foremost of which is Dr. Frank Lewis and First Baptist Church, especially the necessarily anonymous members of the Sunday night classes where this theology was constructed. The Ecclesiology and Ethnography Network, particularly Mary McClintock Fulkerson and Pete Ward, offered generous feedback to my presentation of an earlier version of Chapter 2. A revised version of that presentation provided material for "Reflexive Theology: A Preliminary Proposal" in *Practical Matters*, issue 6 (Spring 2013). The Lilly Endowment and Vanderbilt's program in Theology and Practice also provided generous funding not only for my education but also to cover costs related to manuscript preparation. Thanks are due as well to Burke Gerstenschlager at Palgrave for his enthusiastic support, and to my research assistant at Emmanuel College, Robert

Timmins, who has provided much help and humor in the editing and preparation of the manuscript.

My deepest thanks are reserved for my family. My mum, dad, and beautiful sister, Danielle, as well as my wild and wonderful nephews Will and Danny, have made my move back home to Canada a joyous gift. My husband Tyler is my partner, love, and friend. I am the only person who has read these pages more times than he has. His insight into both theology and to me has kept me to a rigorous standard of pursuing truth in these pages. Along with our new daughter, Georgia Lil, he has been the home that has held this work together. Thank you.

Introduction

Making Space

I am pleased that the guys enrolled in the class know what to do. By now I have made more than a few official work orders and verbal requests that our Sunday night, adult-education classroom in the church basement be set up in seminar style, but they seem to have gone unheard. Facing all the chairs forward toward a podium from which I, the teacher, am expected to pronounce theological wisdom simply cannot foster the types of vibrant theological conversations we enjoy engaging together. So a subgroup from our small group of church insurgents has arrived early to undo and remake our space together. As I shut off the lights at the end of each night, I wonder who comes in and puts our room back to the lecture style we are—for various reasons—resisting.

This was my third Sunday night teaching adult-education theology classes as the main component of a yearlong ethnographic study I conducted in 2010.[1] The location is at First Baptist Church (FBC), Nashville, where I was an active member from 2006 to 2011.[2] Prior to my study's beginning, I had also spent a year in a discernment process with the congregation, which culminated in my ordination by them in May of 2009. I thus carried out my theological fieldwork in a community within which I held both membership and leadership positions prior to and subsequent to my study's duration.

I conducted this fieldwork (in a Southern Baptist church, politically and theologically moderate for the denomination) for my doctoral dissertation in Theological Studies at Vanderbilt Divinity School (a distinctly progressive mainline theological institution in Nashville, Tennessee, often dubbed "the school of the prophets"). While I detail the content of the Sunday night classes that were a part of this fieldwork more later in the text, in brief, they sought to bring these two disparate worlds I embodied together through the practice of theological conversation. In each course, we tackled a particular Christian doctrine together across its historical development: Christology and soteriology in the spring semester of 2010 and "God as Trinity" in the fall semester of the same year. By teaching these classes, I wanted to see what could happen when the goods of academic theology intervened in ecclesial conversations so that, in turn, the goods of the ecclesial environment might be able to interrupt conversations in academic theology.

While most ethnographic theologies study churches or communities that are not the theologian's own, I wanted to try something a little different. By studying my own people, I sought out the forms of theological knowledge that are inherent within and produced by practices of belonging. Embedded within my field of study as a member and a leader, I wanted to see what would happen when I deployed my particular theological agency—which is shaped by ecclesial and academic, as well as other fields of practice—within the community to stimulate theological conversation. Rather than reflect *on* Christian community or *on* Christian practice, I sought to do theological reflection *in* Christian community *as* Christian practice. I wondered, "What happens when we bring together everyday and academic theologies into a reciprocal conversation? What types of theology can be produced out of their coherence and clash with each other?"

This particular form of theological fieldwork means that three types of story converge in my writing. The first is a story of a community of Christian practitioners trying to pursue wisdom together. I tell this story to contribute to the growing body of literature that reveals the everyday theological wisdom to be found in the "fascinating grain of the ordinary," as Mary McClintock Fulkerson puts it.[3] I therefore tell this community's story somewhat in the mode of testimony; I suppose some small part of me still believes that academic theologians should try to point to the places where the Divine opens herself to us. For a few short years, she opened herself to me in a Southern Baptist congregation, and that is a story strange—to me, wondrous—enough that I think it's worth sharing.

Given this personal investment in the process, the second story I am telling is my own. This is the story of a theologian who is less interested in doing theologies of, about, or for the church and more interested in trying to do theology as a spiritual practice within a particular Christian community. It is therefore a story about refusing to stand a safe distance away from a community in order to speak to it. By necessity, then, my personal story eschews bold pronouncements, ironic detachment, and the ability to make abstract claims. Theologians writing about the church or, better, churches rarely write about themselves, perhaps because then we would have to admit that we often struggle to like the communities we claim to love. So this is, in many ways, a story about my own failings as a church member, a minister, and an academic theologian. As much as it is a story about belonging, it is also a story about alienation and the theological possibilities inherent to each.

A third story thus erupts out of the ways the FBC community and I, as a member of it, pursued our wisdom together. This is a story about how we can open up theological thought and action for revision and reaffirmation through practices of vibrant theological conversation. But it is also a story about the ways each of us in the church can fail in this task and about the ways in which we make ourselves palatable to each other so that we can maintain the social cohesion required to enable any conversation across difference. It's not a story about an idealized community of peace, justice, and harmony. Nor is it a story about an idealized academic theologian who manages to disrupt an ecclesial system's status quo to reveal fresh new possibilities for Christian living—though I wish it were. It is, rather, in many ways, a story about the strategic compromises we make without even realizing it, the regimes to which we unknowingly and knowingly submit, and the tiny untruths we uncomfortably tell so that we can maintain relations across all the ways that difference marks us. This is a story about actual life together. It's a fraught love story, but a love story nonetheless.

First Baptist Church

Of course, these Sunday night practices took place within a broader ecclesial system that requires expounding. While the third chapter will construct a fuller ethnographic ecclesiology of FBC to situate our Sunday night group, for now a few historical and social details about the church are worth mentioning. In 1820, in Nashville, Tennessee, in true Baptist fashion, 35 members of Mill Creek Baptist Church splintered off to form First Baptist Church. Less than ten years later, doctrinal differences led a group that maintained the First Baptist name to leave its building and pastor to found a new—or, depending on one's perspective, to preserve the original—community. In 1844, FBC's African American members, a mix of freed and enslaved persons, began the slow process of moving to independence, which culminated in their founding their own self-governing body in 1865, now First Baptist Church Capitol Hill.[4] In the interim, when the Southern Baptist Convention (SBC) split from northern Baptists in 1845, largely over the issue of slavery, FBC became a founding member.

The marks of these origins still remain; like the majority of churches in the United States, FBC is racially homogenous.[5] It is composed of mostly middle- to upper-middle-class, white, educated professionals. In the 1950s and 1960s, however, when other wealthy, white churches were moving their campuses out of the downtown into the suburbs, FBC stayed. Even so, most of its members commute in from those more affluent neighboring suburbs for church activities. Any racial and class diversity can therefore be observed primarily through the church's outreach programs for the economically disadvantaged and socially marginalized people living on the streets of Nashville's downtown core.

As an original member of the convention, and with the SBC denominational offices and publishing company stationed just a few blocks away (many of the church's members work at the latter), FBC is so thoroughly proximate to and rooted in SBC life that it can forge an identity both in distinction from and in relation to the larger communion. Such a balance between affiliation and autonomy is not atypical in Baptist life, however. As Stephen Warner puts it, despite the "conservative ascendancy" in the SBC, which indicates a strong overarching denominational presence, local church autonomy is "not just a symbol."[6] Indeed, Arthur E. Farnsley points out that Southern Baptists tend to be "fiercely loyal Congregationalists, preferring to think of themselves first as members of particular local churches who co-operate—to whatever degree—with others under the auspices of the SBC."[7] Whether or not this claim can be made across the board for Southern Baptist congregations, it does seem to be true at FBC. Everyone I interviewed said that they joined the congregation because of its kind and welcoming atmosphere. No one mentioned joining because of doctrinal reasons or because they were looking for a specifically Southern Baptist congregation. In fact, a number of the members of our Sunday classes mentioned joining *in spite* of the fact that it was Southern Baptist, noting how important its moderate nature in relation to the larger communion was to them.

People join because of this sense of welcoming love, a core mark of how the church frames its identity. FBC's motto, "Loving God, Loving People," emphasizes our movement toward God and toward each other over God's movement toward us. It thus focuses on our own activity, putting the congregants' desire for emotional bonds with

God and with each other front and center in our life together. As with any community, FBC exhibits implicit and explicit exclusionary practices that create problematic borders around who can gain entry to the shared emotional bonds. Even so, cultural objects like posters and worship bulletins emblazon this motto all over the church's campus, reminding everyone who does find themselves able to enter not only that our love for one another grows out of (or, at least, should grow out of) our love for God but also that love itself is (or, at least, should be) our defining characteristic.

LIFE CHANGE UNIVERSITY

Each year, FBC offers a roster of Sunday night adult-education classes, spread across a spring and fall semester, in what we call our Life Change University (LCU). I found a home in this program for sharing both my ministerial and academic gifts with the church. It is also where I learned as much, if not more, about the theologies constructed in church life than any other ecclesial activity with which I was involved. Prior to the fieldwork conducted for my dissertation, I cotaught a well-attended class called "Citizens in the Kingdom of God" at LCU that sought to highlight the social justice aspects of Jesus's ministry. This led me to develop a series titled "Topics in Theology," wherein I taught "Topics in Theology: Jesus Christ and Salvation" in spring 2010 and "Topics in Theology: God as Trinity" in fall 2010.[8] This series continued after the close of my research period with "Topics in Theology: Worship."

In these courses, we studied historical surveys of each doctrinal focus. Across both classes, we engaged the Gospels, Paul, Justin Martyr, Origen, Arius and Athanasius, Augustine, Gregory of Nyssa, Anselm, Abelard, Aquinas, Beatrice of Nazareth, Marguerite Porete, Luther, Calvin, Descartes, Pascal, Kierkegaard, Kant, Schleiermacher, Hegel, Karl Barth, Karl Rahner, Gustavo Gutierrez, James Cone, Rosemary Radford Ruether, and Elizabeth Johnson—perhaps not your typical church class, and certainly not typical for a Southern Baptist theology class! I situated each theologian within their cultural context and lectured briefly on their writings, but discussion occupied the bulk of the class.

The theologians we studied provided stimulus for our own theological reflection. They opened up theological questions, revealing how doctrines had shifted and changed across time. In this way, everyday and academic theological discourses came together in a shared practice of conversation. In essence, I brought the goods of academic theology into the room for all of us to share while we all drew on our everyday theological wisdom to make sense of those goods. Class members brought personal stories, ideas gleaned from books they had read, and references to movies and television shows—all everyday theologies they reasoned out of the contexts of their daily lives. They also brought insight into more local histories and traditions, those particularly related to FBC, the SBC, and life in the South—many of which, as a transplant to the south and to Southern Baptist life, I did not know, but was very curious to hear.

Mine were not the only courses taught on a Sunday night, of course, and their relationship to the others matters for considering who was in attendance at them. In the semester that I taught "Topics in Theology: Jesus Christ and Salvation," other offerings included the following: "Griefshare," a seminar and support group for people who have lost a loved one; two women-only classes using material by Beth Moore on "Christian Freedom" and the biblical book, *Revelation*;[9] Ken Hemphill's *The Prayer of Jesus*, which focused on living "a kingdom adventure every day";[10] "The Truth Project," which followed a DVD-based curriculum focused on living life with a biblical worldview;[11] and "The Family Life Cycle," which dealt with negotiating standard types of transition in family.[12]

In the semester when I taught "Topics in Theology: God as Trinity," other course offerings included the following: "Bridges: Christians Connecting with Muslims," a class that used the "Crescent Project" curriculum;[13] "5 Conversations You Must Have with Your Daughter," which is based on a book by Vicki Courtney that affirms traditional gender roles;[14] and "Praying to Make a Difference," which seeks to establish "a meaningful and consistent prayer life." Beth Moore's study of Revelation was also repeated, and Pastor Frank (our senior pastor) taught "Servant Warriors" followed by "The Man God Uses," which is a combined men's fitness and Bible study course that he runs every few semesters.[15]

Courses therefore covered various topics, meeting the needs and desires of a cross-section of the community's theological, practical and lifestyle interests. At the same time, they mostly followed Southern Baptist and more broadly evangelical curricula and themes. As will become clear throughout this book, the courses I taught departed from this model in various ways. That they were offered thus begins to reveal one of the ways in which academic theologians might be able to try to impact Christian social practices, specifically ecclesial ones, a core theme of this book.

TEACHING INSTINCTS AND TEACHING FANTASIES

Even with such a seemingly simple activity as making our space together each week, I find myself torn between conflicting emotional responses. As a non-Southerner, I am frequently frustrated by the awkward dance that ensues when I try to open a door for a man who is wrestling the handle from my clutches in a display of good manners. In general, chivalry annoys me. Or, at least I think it does, because when I arrive to find the tables and chairs already arranged to my liking, my instinctual response, to my surprise, is not so much frustration at these men trying to take care of me. Rather, a smile escapes my lips, and I happily grin a sweet "Thank you!" to them for it. There is something different happening here than the confused wrestling at the doorway. Indeed, there's actually something quite pleasurable in seeing the seeming opposites of my feminist pedagogy and their chivalry coinhere as we create our space together.[16]

The three narratives I mention previously—of self, others, and the relationship between us all—converge in these stories about how our Sunday night group would make our space together. Each begins to reveal the joys and tensions, pleasures and frustrations that marked the ways in which we all moved within our shared space together. These brief allusions help illustrate the moods, motivations, dispositions, and instincts, for example, which we all embodied via the different social positions available in our community and the particular ways in which each of us took them up.

For example, my desire to arrange the room in seminar style, in a nonhierarchical way, grew out of an instinctual feminist pedagogy that had been inculcated into me by my various feminist teachers throughout my formal academic education. My body feels strange when spatial arrangements force me to sit at the head of a table to teach, let alone stand at the front of the room at a podium. If people can't see each other, then I find it difficult to imagine them accessing a bodily sense that their contributions to our shared conversation are all as valid and valued as I understand them to be.[17] Yet in a Southern Baptist church where feminism can often be treated as a dirty F word, there is something deliciously jarring about my slipping stealth feminist practices into our shared space. Perhaps these small interventions will create larger effects, I find myself hoping, as they contribute to shifting the ways we in our community think and act around gender norms. Even if their chipping at our patriarchal codes is slight, the chipping brings me a modicum of pleasure nonetheless.

Most (but not all) of those who came to the classes I taught would not use phrases like "feminist pedagogy" and "nonhierarchical space," but they did share my desire for robust conversation, and they knew that sitting like an audience waiting to be fed by me wouldn't get us there. Or, at least, this is what I told myself as the men moved around the tables so that I didn't have to. I tried each time to ignore the nagging suspicion that the real reason these guys had begun showing up before I even arrived was because they wanted to protect me from doing "men's work."

Perhaps part of the reason our divergent motivations managed to converge in this shared practice of making space was because we were able to join in common labor to try to disrupt a larger ecclesial system from which we almost all felt a little alienated (even as we also called it home). The classes I taught drew out church members who themselves were a little atypical within the broader church community. Most of them were self-described liberals. As one of them put it, referring to her and her husband's political party affiliation, "We're that D word you don't say around here." They were a group more interested in questioning the status quo—albeit to a certain degree—than upholding it, even as the status quo would mostly engulf our labor into its own institutional machine, as we will see in Chapter 3. As a number of them described it to me in interviews, they were excited for a Sunday night class that taught them to question theological answers rather than memorize them.

Lest this picture get too rosy, however, I should acknowledge a tension that lies within it. Each of our self-understandings as liberal or radical was always defined in relation to the norms (patriarchal, heteronormative, middle class, etc.) of the larger group. Each of us could only stray so far from home—and only desired to stray so far—before we got lost in the woods, so to speak. Inasmuch as the group could be frustrated with the church's broader conservatism, then I could get frustrated with our group just the same—and it's true that I fairly consistently encountered colleagues back at Vanderbilt whose eyebrows would raise in a statement of mistrust at having a Baptist (a Southern Baptist, no less) in their midst. Most Baptists who enroll at the "school of prophets" quickly cease to be a Baptist, gravitating instead toward more mainline or sacramental traditions. Nevertheless, while we would all find ourselves straining against the limits of the systems within which we each had chosen to live, we could never find ourselves wholly dismantling them.

FBC is a racially homogenous, politically and theologically conservative community that is organized largely around the lifestyle of traditional, middle- to upper-middle-class nuclear families. While, like the majority of FBC members, I experience significant cultural privilege as a middle-class, cisgendered person with a postsecondary education, my identity and social practices also depart from our majority norms in some significant ways. For example, I am a biracial, multiethnic, theologically progressive woman engaged in feminist and queer politics, practices, and advocacy. I recycle and compost. While I would give my church family hints regarding these nonnormative aspects of who I am—or, at least, who I understand myself to be—in moments when I felt they could hear them, I can't say I ever fully "came out." And this marks a level of dishonesty or, at least, a lack of self-disclosure for which I still harbor guilty regret—particularly when I have to face the fact that one significant reason I didn't come out was because I was protecting my own privilege. So in the frequent moments when our worlds clashed rather than cohered, I felt my imagination slip my body straight into that pulpit—drunk with and protected by the power with which I imagined it imbuing me—to lecture to a captive audience about our racialized biases, the stifling nature of our heteronormativity and frequent gender policing, and the reasons God really doesn't like our Styrofoam cups and exploitative coffee. In other words, sometimes I had these utopian fantasies in which I completely failed to recognize my own forms of complicity, privilege, and just how smug a liberal yuppie I can be.

Occasionally, when I allowed these utopian fantasies to unfold in my imagination, everyone began working for peace and justice and campaigning for same-sex marriage rights, while a fringe group started up a book club reading queer theology and began questioning whether or not same-sex marriage only perpetuates the hetero- and gender normativity of our broader culture anyway. I saw the youth group planting a rooftop garden to supply our neighbors living in a food desert with fresh veggies. In other words, I projected my own fantasies of church as an ideal theopolitical community as the appropriate, even possible, ends to my own teaching activity. But most often, these hero fantasies ran out of steam quickly because I knew such outbursts would be largely unintelligible within a community that has not self-generated them. If I am not intelligible to them, I cannot be one of them. I cannot be one of us.

Because the truth is, even as these utopian fantasies inspired my labor, they also exhibited a strange form of authoritarianism in the end. Their imagining required excluding from the community anyone who disagreed with me and depended entirely on my hierarchical elevation as the teacher—an elevation I was supposedly consciously trying to resist. Each time my imagination was so swayed, I would struggle to bring the fantasy to a close. In so doing, I would make one of those small decisions so many of us frequently make in church life—decisions to our detriment and perhaps to the detriment of others but that keep our social fabric intact: I would keep my mouth shut. These moments of self-censorship and silence pervade this text, each one offering a different configuration of my desire for community, for transformation, and my failing nerve. Each one thus offers the chance to reflect on the glory and brokenness, and perhaps most of all the fragility, of life together.

In sum, these tensions that exist between my desires and the desires of those with whom I was in conversation, as well as between my various teaching instincts and teaching fantasies, reveal why we needed to arrange our tables so that we could see each other. As much as those men who arranged the tables were seeking to protect me from work they thought I could not—or, perhaps, should not—handle, I was seeking to protect them from the same. "Even if they could hear what I really think," I thought, "do I want to deal with the fallout? Won't pushing them too far too fast undermine my credibility to teach them anything?"

In our frantic, often paternalistic, protection of each other, we each embodied complex, well-intentioned but fraught motivations for doing so. The space we created together provided space for each of us to speak even if that speech remained constantly constrained by the parameters that produced it. I wanted to be heard, but I also wanted to hear. We reached toward each other without ever fully reaching each other. My conversation partners expressed a desire to learn from me, but also from each other, just as I had something to learn from each of them.

Ethnographic Theology

One particular research question guides the theological experimentation of this work: "How can ethnographic methods help us foster the already organic relationship between everyday and academic theologies in order to bolster their shared production of theological knowledge?" Therefore, the ethnographic theological methods outlined in the first section of this book, and the constructive theologies that demonstrate the fruits of those methods—outlined in the second section—are all articulated specifically in relation to this question. As a result, the proposal being made here is not for how ethnographic theology in general should be done. Rather, I propose that ethnographic theological methods—like sociological or anthropological ethnographic methods—should always be geared to the particular research question(s) at hand. The research question thus guides both the mode of inquiry and the type of knowledge that inquiry can produce.

In order to begin unpacking the methods of this text, Chapter 1 draws a theological map of my field of study. As with any cartography, the particular type of map drawn over a terrain is related to and intended to produce the particular type of activity the person who consults the map wants to perform therein. We use a road map to drive from Seattle to Vancouver, a topological subway map to negotiate station transfers on the London Underground, scribbles on the back of a bar napkin to lure a potential lover to our home, or an orienteering map to run wildly through the woods. Likewise, how we imagine theology spatially shapes the mode and destination of our theological movements. Theological fieldwork necessitates being able to map the field of study *and* the academic theologian's role within that field; otherwise, we mistakenly imagine ourselves to have a God's-eye view on the action, failing to see our implication in it. In Chapter 1, I argue for a map of theology that explicitly locates the academic theologian inside it, drawing on interview data with my conversation partners at FBC and on Kathryn Tanner's notion of theology as a postmodern cultural practice.

Having drawn this theological map, my second task is to articulate how I as the academic theologian used it. While ethnographic theologians have focused much-needed attention on the particularity of ecclesial and everyday practices for theological reflection, the role played by particular academic theologians within our fields of study has remained largely undertheorized. But if we do not bring reflexive attention to the precise and personal connections between our fields of study and ourselves, then we likewise are unable to understand how we might influence Christian practice, as Tanner and others would have us do. It is not enough to map the theological terrain; we also have to understand the relationship between the terrain, the map, and our bodies' movements—a relationship we often negotiate intuitively. In Chapter 2, I critically engage work in reflexive and carnal sociologies—Pierre Bourdieu, Sherry Ortner, Michel de Certeau and Loïc Wacquant, in particular—to argue that the academic theologian who is socially embedded in her field of study as a member and leader is shaped by that field with a particular bodily knowledge that guides her activity therein. Moving and acting from that bodily knowledge, she is able to participate in producing forms of theological knowledge that are communal yet fragmented; local yet humble; and, often, illuminative precisely where they fail.

The second section of the book offers some constructive theological insights that arose from the community's shared theological work, each in dialogue with a particular emphasis of the ethnographic theological method I have articulated. These revised doctrinal theologies function in the mode of knowledge just mentioned: they are fragmented, messy, and in a constant state of undoing themselves. They testify to a community's attempt to reach toward the Divine together, as they are also marked by the human foibles inherent to such an endeavor. The first constructive theology, "A Reflexive Theology of Ecclesial Change," tests Tanner's idea—and my intention—that academic theology can bring about social and theological change within Christian social practices. Tracking the power dynamics that constellate around community formation practices, I demonstrate how our small community of liberals nevertheless supported, rather than disrupted, the broader ecclesial institutional equilibrium. Having thus chastened our understanding of what a conversation between everyday and academic theology can accomplish, Chapter 4, "Carnal Theologies of Friendship, Sex, and Suffering," looks specifically at the role played by embodiment in theological construction processes. The final constructive chapter, "A Performance Theology of Sanctification," teases out some of the aesthetic dimensions of this ethnographic theology. Using performance art to critically expand Tanner's description of the academic theologian as *bricoleur*, I analyze the conversational dynamics by which our community constructed theology together. The book concludes with some reflections on how theological normativity functions in these various ethnographic theological methods.

THEOLOGY IN THE BELLY OF THE BEAST

The three stories being told here, of an ecclesial community, an academic theologian, and their integration, are deeply personal stories. I have been asked again and again by family, friends and, even, random strangers in airport bars, "Why this church?" Perhaps an answer is in order here or, at least, I feel the desire to give one as I close this introductory chapter.

I had entered my doctoral program wanting to do theology ethnographically in large part because I had so enjoyed my brief forays into qualitative methods in my MDiv Liturgical Theology class, taught by Siobhán Garrigan at Yale Divinity School. Therein, I saw the possibility for qualitative research to connect academic theology to the lives of concrete churches and communities. At the same time, my own intellectual preferences guided my interest toward studying some alternative form of Christian community. I wanted to discover something new, the one thing no one else had written about yet (perhaps a distinctly academically constituted desire). I wanted to stretch the possibilities for what might be considered faithful Christian living (a desire that echoed the ways my own academic training had expanded the possibilities of my personal faith life). And so searching for what I perceived to be unique and other, I toyed first with studying a community I had visited whose worship life was explicitly shaped according to the philosophical movement known as deconstruction, and then with studying an underground Christian community I had heard about that participated together in both worship and BDSM practices.[18] A little like the early anthropologists, I wanted to travel far from home, perhaps to find myself anew—and also like them, I had not yet adequately considered the sociopolitical and ethical implications of studying "others."[19]

In this project's early stages, therefore, it did not occur to me that I might study my own Southern Baptist congregation, which I perceived as exceedingly normal, mainstream, and even intellectually boring. Perhaps this oversight occurred because my own ecclesial and academic lives were stretching apart from each other, becoming more and more difficult to reconcile. Indeed, part of the personal aspect of this project entails my desire to knit the two back together in some loose configuration. In a way that I found surprising and a little unnerving, the deeper I got into First Baptist's life, the more I felt the lure to make it the focus of my study.

At the same time, the reflexive ethnographies I was studying as part of my doctoral coursework, previously mentioned, were complicating my understanding of participant observation. As a result, particularly while reading Wacquant, I began to wonder how I might deploy my own ministerial vocation within the FBC community as my primary research tool. At FBC, one of the chief deployments of my ministerial vocation occurred in the capacity of Christian education. In this way, this particular aspect of my vocation (i.e., teaching Sunday night theology classes) loosely integrated the ways in which my ecclesial and academic roles shaped my own theological agency—that is, the same theological agency that gives rise to my academic theological writing.

What friends, family, and strangers struggle less with is why I would want to study this church but more of why *this* church is even *my* church to begin with. The answer to that question matters for this project, too. I think I remember the moment when I decided to become an academic theologian, which is deeply connected to a moment when I decided not to abandon a conservative Christian church that I was beginning to find stifling. Naming one's origins is a tricky task; I have inevitably forgotten more about this process than I remember. But I think some form of its beginning happened here: I was in my second year of divinity school, sitting in that same liturgical theology classroom, and two of my friends were giving a presentation on a set of feminist and womanist texts. The two had paired up for the assignment for a particular reason. As I remember it, they saw themselves as sociopolitical-theological opposites, one self-describing as conservative and the other as liberal. And they perceived the ground between them as one that could be mapped by a conversation about a worship experience they had experienced differently than each other but, nevertheless, together. What they didn't know as they presented their work was that I was trying to find my place in that in-between space.

As each had tried to integrate the stuff of her study with her religious life, each had found a fruitful spiritual discipline in the practice of struggling consciously against and within the structures of Christian worship that they inhabited. In this particular presentation, they embodied this struggle beautifully through their conversation across their differences. These two women sunk into real concretion with their descriptions. They narrated and renarrated their paths of struggle within particular divinity school community worship services that the majority of our Liturgical Theology class members had also attended and could thus recognize. Their stories overlapped each other, as they intersected with each of ours. These two women were—still are—brilliant, creative theologians, and their insights stirred us all as we each found ourselves relating with both of them in different ways. Their willingness to be vulnerable with each other and with us opened up the classroom to new forms of risky conversation in which the personal, the political, and the theological converged.

My two friends closed their presentation by turning analysis back onto the rest of us. By this point, we—or at least, I—felt so implicated in the story they were telling that their question, "Why stay? Why stay in congregations that appear to have no room for us as we are, let alone as we are becoming?" caught me up and demanded my response. Their journeys had intersected with mine. I too was at the crossroads that might well be one of the goals behind the design of divinity school curriculum: first year, dismantle the religious self; second year, flounder; and third year, hopefully, get put back together.

By this point in my education, I had moved through feeling liberated from the evangelical religion that had brought me to divinity school on little more than a whim, a prayer, and some sense of God's calling, into feeling alienated instead. I was looking for that third step.

Alienated from my faith formation, however, my grasping toward new religious forms felt equally unsatisfactory. On the one hand, there was a particular shape to my yearning for home's transcendence that could not be fulfilled by a journey to elsewhere. I could assent intellectually to more so-called liberal or progressive Christian practices, but they felt unnatural to my particular faith constitution; they could not stir me. I wonder now if I would have grown into them over time. But doing so felt pointless at the time, as I found that no matter how progressive the congregation or set of Christian practices I tried to engage, they remained also unable to fulfill the yearnings my academic study was now creating in me. Sexism, shallow thinking, homophobia and transphobia, racism, closed-mindedness, fear of the body, and just plain meanness are able to traverse the whole spectrum of Christian and, indeed, all social practices. And so I became less interested in the struggle's matters of degree and more interested in the struggle itself.

Looking back on my moment of decision to stay, I sometimes wonder now if I simply should have admitted my growing sense that Christianity might be a bust. Perhaps my decision to stay was caused by a failure of imagination; I simply could not conceive of any other place to go. Such possibilities haunt the fringes of the life I have chosen. Even so, I remain convinced that my decision to stay with Christianity in general, and with the types of churches where Christianity had become my home in particular, in fact grew out of some nascent realization that no matter who we become, we can never escape who we are.

And so stay I did, and stay with a renewed sense of commitment to the life of faith as a spiritual discipline of struggle. *Let's take this commitment to the belly of the beast*, I remember thinking. One decision thus forged two distinct, yet intersecting paths: I began discerning a call to ordination that culminated in the Southern Baptist congregation where I conducted this study, and I began discerning a vocation in the theological academy.

This question of struggle remains at the heart of this book, however. I might have settled in FBC simply because I have a scrappy personality that likes to find admission to clubs from which I otherwise feel excluded. FBC offered a rare path into ordination in a denomination that on the larger scale, outside of the autonomy of rare, local congregations, is fundamentally opposed to women in such roles. But framing my belonging in this way allows me an ironic detachment from it that exposes only the most fragmented version of the truth. I settled in FBC because in the fullest sense of what it means to claim a place as home—a place to which we can never really return once we have left but that surprises us with moments of belonging that sink deeper than we knew possible—FBC felt like home. Not intellectually, not theologically, and certainly not politically, FBC connected with some form of the faith so deep in my bones that I can hardly articulate it when I try. It was a community that could help me hold on to my faith and, in this way, FBC provided the anchor for a few years of struggle to understand that faith, to go as deep into it as I could, to reclaim it again and anew for myself, precisely so I could try to share its gifts with others.

The marks of this struggle are evident throughout this text. It is, in many ways, an exercise in understanding why I might call this community home. The anxiety and ambivalence I feel at my own, indeed, pleasurable sense of belonging leave traces in each story I tell about the community. These traces threaten to disrupt not only my insistence that I belong but also my insistence that I do not. They risk undermining the reader's trust in me, precisely because they mark the places where I do not entirely trust myself. The question "why this community, and not another?" therefore also haunts the text. And perhaps the most honest answer I can give is simply the text itself and my desire to write it—both of which are marked by my enduring conviction that of all the locations in which theology needs to find itself, a place some might call the beast's belly, but which yet others call home, remains one.

Part I

Chapter 1

Making Space

Constructing the Theological Field

Most academic theologians would agree that theology is always already culturally located. Indeed, as theology's foundations in reason, revelation, or notions of the self have all been shaken by the critiques extending throughout modernity, *culture* has become the omnipresent factor that has bearing on the content and form of what and how we know. As a result, cultural studies—the modes of inquiry that help us analyze cultural practices—has become a crucial companion discipline to theologies created in academic institutions.[1] Despite this wide agreement that theology is culturally located, however, the ways in which we map that location tend to differ.

In this chapter and the next, I contend that those of us using cultural theory and ethnographic methods to engage lived Christian practice should, as we participate in this theological cartography, theorize carefully the relationship between ourselves and our fields of study. Lack of such reflexive self-awareness leads us to employ methods that are laden with unarticulated and unrecognized assumptions. This, in turn, can lead us to misrepresent the dynamics of the field and our role as cultural producers within it, and worse, to make ethical mistakes within it.[2] In the first part of this chapter, I engage critically with Pierre Bourdieu's concept of *field* as a semiautonomous social space made up of networked social relations in order to stake out the space within and around which an ethnographic theologian might conduct her work.

As Kathryn Tanner's theology of culture has well demonstrated, academic theologians are already implicated in the everyday social practices that shape the questions we ask and seek to answer.[3] We are not standing outside the borders of everyday theology's territories brandishing our papers to get in. Of course, we might wander off the beaten path sometimes. But the intrinsic connection between everyday and academic theologies means that the relationship between the two, embodied by each ethnographic theologian in her own particular way, cannot be severed. How this intrinsic connection shapes what forms of knowledge ethnographic theology can produce is explored more fully in the next chapter. Here, our main interest is in how these everyday and academic theologies coconstitute each other as they compose the larger theological field of practice. Bourdieu's notion of field as social relations thus helps us imagine the theological field as being shaped and reshaped by theological conversations taking place in multiple modes and locations across time.

Having employed Tanner's theological continuum to emphasize the ethnographic theologian's location within a theological field of practice, I narrow my attention to my own particular field of study in the second part of this chapter. Here I draw on conversations with my research partners to sketch maps of three distinctly different spatial imaginations for the theological field of practice, any combination of which could be operative within our classroom conversations at any given time.[4] These maps chart the locations in which people who think, write, speak, and act—all along the theological continuum—might do so in relation, competition, and cooperation with each other. The first map is temporally and spatially grand, plotting the broad geographic and historical movement of expanding institutions. The second is small and intimate, attending to how theologies become mapped onto our bodily ways of being in the world. The third bridges these two, pressing for a theology done in the mode of not only thinking or talking but also of acting.

A Field Guide for Theological Conversation

Put most simply, for Bourdieu, "to think in terms of field is to *think relationally*."[5] For English speakers, as Patricia Thomson points out, the metaphor of *field* tends to conjure the agricultural space of a meadow or a field of wheat. But this is an accident of translation of Bourdieu's term, *le champ*, which is more specifically related to the social space of practice in which relations marked by competition are played out (e.g., the field on which a game is played).[6] In this way, a *field of practice* does not highlight an actual physical space, but rather it demarcates an interrelated network of social positions that different agents can take up in different ways.

Like the field on which a game like soccer, for example, is played, certain behavior-governing rules are in effect before the players even arrive. By the very act of showing up in the game, players enter into an implicit contract to honor these rules as they play and as each stakes out different positions that will allow each to shape or, hopefully, contribute to winning the game.[7] The desire to win, or at least to compete, crucially marks these social relations for Bourdieu, perhaps because class struggle functions as one of the dominant paradigms by which he interprets social relations. Competition thus trumps cooperation as the characteristic of how he sees social change catalyzed, a characteristic I challenge in my own experiments with conversing across theological difference later in the text.

Bourdieu uses the concept of field to analyze fields of practice as diverse as those related to education, gender relations, kinship practices, aesthetics, law, literature, religion, housing, television and more. Each of these is much too complex to be fully described according to a precise set of governing rules, as is possible with a game like soccer. And so, field, for Bourdieu, also transcends this one key example for understanding it. Unlike a game, he argues, a social field "is not the product of a deliberate act of creation" because it "follows rules or, better, regularities, that are not explicit and codified."[8] Therefore, whereas the rules for a soccer game are explicitly articulated and can be consulted and imposed, the regularities at play in a social field are more implicit. Players learn them slowly and then know them tacitly on an intuitive or dispositional level, without necessarily being able to bring them to words.[9] Take the academic field, for example, in which it can take years to figure out the path to success, if one ever figures it out at all. The rules of play are certainly not printed somewhere, available for dissemination to agents as they enter the field of practice. Indeed, the competition of a social field constitutes and is constituted by different people jockeying for the chance to shape and reshape those tacit regularities for their own benefit. Social norms are constantly in flux, as they can be deployed strategically much more readily than they can be imposed overtly.[10] In this way, agents can conform their behavior (consciously or unconsciously) to social norms, but they can also (again, consciously or unconsciously) work creatively with and from these norms, thereby creating new strategies of thought and action.

Doxa in the Field

These tacit regularities are related, for Bourdieu, to the ways in which knowledge is produced within a particular field of practice, and this is key for thinking about how everyday and academic forms of theological knowledge might work together to create new patterns of thought and action for Christian living. As sets of "pre-reflexive, unquestioned opinions and perceptions," these tacit regularities determine what is taken to be "natural" for agents participating in any given field.[11] Bourdieu refers to this regulating form of prereflexive knowledge as doxa—that is, the type of knowledge essential to any given field that "*goes without saying because it comes without saying*."[12] In other words, doxa—while structured by the practices of the field, and continually contributing to the structuring of those same practices—appears to be so natural and self-evidently true that it eludes articulation. It does not need to be brought to words or even imposed because almost everyone who participates in a given field takes it to be *the way things really are*. In a theological field, doxa might be composed of anything from the unarticulated metaphysical or cosmological presumptions required to hold together a particular soteriology to naturalized assumptions about how gender, family, and sexual norms undergird particular concepts of sin and redemption.

Doxa entails a form of symbolic power for Bourdieu precisely because it is so difficult to recognize accurately, let alone question or disrupt—either by those subjected to it or by those who benefit from or exert it. Part of the sociological project, for Bourdieu, entails bringing doxa to light in the hopes of questioning and even replacing it in various social fields: "The critique which brings the undiscussed into discussion," he argues, "has as the condition of its possibility objective crisis."[13] When "the social world loses its character as a natural phenomenon," and the self-evidence of doxa is thus undone, then social facts can begin to be questioned.[14] According to Bourdieu, crisis is necessary for social change because it can lead to the articulation of doxa as heterodoxy—that is, the explicit questioning of previously unquestioned social norms by which those norms are challenged and transformed. But while it is necessary, crisis is nevertheless not sufficient for social change because it can also lead to orthodoxy—that is, as the assertion of doxa as dogma and the more explicit imposition of what were a social field's previously unquestioned assumptions.[15] Unlike heterodoxy, orthodoxy loses the innocence of doxa while nevertheless preserving it. Indeed, the process of change is driven by the ways in which crisis creates a battle between heterodox and orthodox views within a particular field of practice or power. Consider, as an expansion of one of the examples previously mentioned, not only the pseudoscientific defenses of creationism against changing scientific knowledge but also the political and cultural movements that accompany them.

Nevertheless, given the crucial catalytic role played by crisis in this model for how knowledge and social transformation are produced in a given social field of practice, we might then ask how such crises can occur. For Bourdieu, multiple fields of practice intersect with each other in any given social space. For example, at FBC, embodying the social positions of both minister *and* academic theologian, I negotiate a theological field that intersects with a field of religious practice *and* an academic field. These are certainly the most significant fields of practice to recognize for the project at hand given that my research interest is in how everyday and academic theologies might work together to create new patterns of Christian thought and action. But as this text unfolds, we will also pay attention to the ways in which fields related to gender, family, sexuality, economics, media, and more also come to bear on my ethnographic practice. All these multiple fields therefore come together and, for Bourdieu, actually compete, within a more extensive field than any one given field of practice: what he calls, the *field of power*.

The Field of Power

As David Swartz points out, Bourdieu's field of power functions primarily as a "sort of 'meta-field' that operates as the organizing principle of differentiation and struggle through *all* fields." But it also functions as a way of describing the "dominant social class."[16] The relative levels of dependence and semiautonomy of various fields in relation to each other,[17] as well as the forms of capital (economic, symbolic, etc.) each produces, impact the ways in which the struggle between them plays out. At the same time, those able to deploy more capital—that is, the dominant class—within the field of power have greater access to reproducing the social field and its related knowledge (doxa, orthodoxy, heterodoxy and so on) in ways that benefit them. And so the field of power designates another social space with dynamic, permeable borders within which complex networks of relations struggle and contest implicit and explicit forms of knowledge and practice.

Indeed, this notion of struggle and contestation is central to Bourdieu's thinking. The relationship between fields of practice within the field of power is hierarchical for him, as are the relationships between social positions within particular fields and the various ways agents come to inhabit and embody those social positions. The Jesuit theologian T. Howland Sanks has demonstrated creatively how a field of struggle and conflict shaped Roman Catholic theology in the latter part of the twentieth century. He recognizes the roles played by the *Ressourcement* movement of the so-called *Nouvelle Théologie* and the praxis-orientated, Marxist-informed movements of Liberation Theology in unseating neoscholasticism from dominance within Catholic traditions.[18] In so doing, Sanks demonstrates how new (or a reclamation of old) sources and foundations can disrupt the doxa of a theological field. Yet his acceptance of Bourdieu's focus on hierarchy and struggle leads him to shape the theological field with the same markers. Just as Bourdieu overlooks the possibility that social relations can produce new avenues of thought and action through cooperation—not just competition—so too does Sanks.

In the next section, I expand our understanding of a theological field beyond the debates that take place in academic theology—Catholic or otherwise—to include also the types of reasoning that Kathryn Tanner calls "everyday theologies" and activities she calls "everyday Christian practices." In so doing, I endeavor to shape a theological field that not only is marked by hierarchy and struggle in the contestation of doxa and other forms of theological knowledge (although it will certainly include a fair amount of contestation and competition) but also includes cooperation and collaboration. It is the task of the remainder of this book to establish what types of theological knowledge such collaboration might yield.

Patterns and Regularities in the Theological Field

Mapping a theological field is not just a theoretical activity; it has practical implications as well. It helps me locate not only myself in relation to my field of study but also those with whom I partner for theological work within that field. By extension, it shapes the social space out of which the practical activity of my ethnographic theological methods arise. Thus, by mapping out a theological field, we find ourselves able to begin naming the types of theological knowledge that can be produced in theological community, thereby beginning also actually to produce them.

The theological field, I want to argue, contains social positions structured by both everyday Christian and academic theological (as well as other) practices within it. Kathryn Tanner's model for theology as a cultural practice in fact situates academic theologians in the ebb and flow of Christian social practices, among which various theological conversations might happen. Indeed, Tanner argues that academic theologians interested in practice too often imagine themselves as positioned external to the ebb and flow of this action, untainted by it, as second-order reflectors on supposedly first-order events. When we make this error, we also begin to make too sharp a distinction between everyday Christian social practices and our theoretical reflection on them without acknowledging how the latter might have shaped our perception of the former.[19] A false vision of coherence thus eclipses the internal messiness of the practices we study. In other words, we mistake the map of the land for the land itself. If a road has been temporarily or permanently closed, we endeavor to forge on regardless, unable to acknowledge that an alternative route is required and that our map might need to change.

Postliberal theologies perhaps offer the best example of this error. As Tanner points out, these theologians "dig underneath the messy surface of Christian practice" to unearth "some underlying body of rules or patterned order to which the theology of practice conforms despite its messiness."[20] In so doing, they impose a supposedly neutral scriptural logic that "validates the conclusions of the theologian while disqualifying the people and practices it studies from posing a challenge to those conclusions."[21] Following Bourdieu's understanding of field-specific doxa, we might say that the symbolic power that accrues to the academic theologian allows her to articulate an orthodoxy against which nonacademic voices are silenced. Tanner argues that the construction of Christian identity and, correlatively, Christian knowledge is a matter of engagement, not agreement. It is a "hybrid, relational affair."[22] Whatever map I attempt to draw must therefore remain open to revision by all of us who might use it. For this revision to occur, so too must conversation across theological difference. Everyday Christians and academic theologians must, in fact, talk to each other if we seek to clarify, expand, or even simply recognize and articulate our shared doxa.

While endeavoring to conform practice to supposedly regulatory patterns is thus a problematic move for academic theologians, simply recognizing patterns at play in everyday Christian practice is not. The way I see it, recognizing such regularities helps us see how Christian theological histories and traditions come to be embodied, somewhere beneath the organizing principles of cognition, as the disparate elements that make up the faith in our bones. Faith and theological knowledge are produced and carried not simply in the mind but in the whole, embodied, mindful, and communally constituted self. In fact, this faith that we carry in our bones—academic and nonacademic bones alike—is not naïve and simple. Rather, it comes loaded up with a chaotic panoply of prior thought and action, both explicitly Christian and not. Access to this thought and action might only be granted to many of us at this level of prereflexive, embodied knowing (i.e., at the level of the way each of us comes to embody a field's doxa). Our bodies are like reliquaries, housing communities of saints therein, bone to our bone, flesh to our flesh, buried within us all in messy, often inaccessible ways. Our contemporary practices always embody traces of their prior performances.

Everyday and Academic Theologies

Even though we bear all this weight of prior performances, however, the fact remains that most Christians do not need a detailed theological understanding of their religious practices to participate fully in them, as Tanner points out. This is why doxa goes unarticulated. Indeed, as many academic theologians and seminary graduates already know, too detailed an understanding can actually impede one's ability to enjoy complete immersion in the practices of church life. Instead, "everyday theological investigation," because it embodies patterns of Christian histories and traditions more than it articulates them, functions largely by instinct: a culturally ingrained, perhaps unconscious "sense for the game, a feel for the possibilities of Christian living."[23] When walking through our neighborhoods, we don't need a map because we already know our way around, even if we've long forgotten the names of the streets.

These everyday theologies, as Tanner calls them, are thus composed of all sorts of ad hoc responses to context-specific activities. Seemingly random configurations of multiple embodied faith forms dwell close to the activities that produce them, indirectly perpetuating their own continuance via those activities, albeit with constant moments of slight slippage and change. Everyday theologies keep the faith moving in all its forms, not only perpetuating logics that might now be out of step with a broader cultural landscape, but also unconsciously adapting to that culture, creating new faith forms without necessarily recognizing the inventiveness as it happens. Indeed, as Tanner points out, and in an echo of Bourdieu's notion of different fields of practice competing within a larger field of power, the borders between so-called Christian and non-Christian cultures are fluid and porous, easily ruptured and traversed. And this means that social and theological change can be generated and sustained by practices engaged both within and beyond the borders of what anyone might recognize or name as Christian. Because we live across multiple fields of practice at once, the faith in our bones is mixed together with our economics, gender performances, class consciousness, family and kinship networks, and eating practices, for example, all sedimented in the marrow.

Everyday theologies thus feel natural, even though the process by which they come to feel natural is held together and produced by a complex, multifaceted social machinery. Sometimes the cultural adaptations don't run so smoothly and the machinery is unable to keep up. The logic holding together the "sense for the game" then breaks apart, and what felt natural comes to feel alien. In these moments of crisis, which parallel those described by Bourdieu, we begin to talk past and fail to understand each other. Faith forms long forgotten might rise to the surface of individual consciousness or group articulation. Others might slither out of sight, quietly absent until they are needed again. Still others might long for a transformation, a tinkering that can make them work anew, if only we had the right tools for the mending. And it is in these moments of crisis when the academic theologian becomes a most helpful conversation partner, according to Tanner's model.

Tanner argues that "specialized theological investigation should be placed on a continuum with theological activity elsewhere as something that arises in an 'organic' way out of Christian practice."[24] Because the work we do with our academic specialized theologies is "less episodic" and "more cumulative" than processes of everyday theological investigation, academic theologians are better able to see the intrinsic relationships that held the fragments of practice together, either tightly or loosely, before they broke apart. As Bourdieu points out, sometimes "the intervention of professional practitioners" is required to accomplish "the symbolic work needed in order to break out of the silent self-evidence of *doxa*."[25] Academic theologians can see—and, importantly, help draw—the map of that familiar space once again, but in a new way. There is, therefore, continuity between these everyday and specialized forms of theological reasoning. Both seek to influence their shared Christian practice, sometimes together, sometimes in competition, but always in conversation with each other.

Unlike a postliberal theologian, for example, who might use a predetermined and supposedly neutral pattern to reassemble these broken pieces, the academic theologian in Tanner's model sits willingly, even gleefully, with the broken pattern until a new aesthetic coherence can be generated from within. Patterns understood this way do not provide rules that bind theological reflection; rather, as with Bourdieu's scheme, they expose the regularities of the field, thereby offering tools, themes, images, and conceptual links that can be configured and reconfigured in a wide variety of ways. The academic theologian does not excavate an old path just to impose its use in a place where it no longer works. But an unearthed network of crumbled pathways might reveal a location where a new way of walking can be tried. In this way, theological patterns are not *normative for*, but rather are *productive of* theological reflection. Far from falling into false caricatures of academic theology as a decontextualized "ivory tower," the mode of discourse, then—that is, the academic theologian's ability to turn "practical answers to practical problems" into "intellectual answers to intellectual problems"—is precisely what enables her to be of service when Christian living feels conflicted.[26]

Tanner is not, in essence, describing a new way of doing theology. She is, arguably, calling our attention to a nuanced version of one of the ways theology has historically been done. Consider Augustine's *City of God* or Calvin's *Institutes* and Barth's *Church Dogmatics* or Althaus-Reid's *Indecent Theology*. All these texts record abstracting moves made by their authors out of the particular religio-cultural practices in which they participated (practices always already embedded in a broader set of cultural practices). They articulated the doxa of the theological field in which they lived, creating new ways to disrupt and reconfigure Christian life together. These academic theologians systematized, thematized, and criticized what people were doing, thinking, and saying in the concrete communities where they lived. Each did so, for better or for worse, with some intention toward responding to crises of faith within those communities while also inspiring their more faithful living. In each situation, the texts were made intelligible by their continuity with other Christian (and nonspecifically Christian) intellectual traditions in ways that simultaneously reorganized the context out of which their concerns initially arose.

To summarize with an expansion of our cartographic metaphor, imagine a GPS map. This interactive techno-cartography allows me to zoom in close to my position to help me negotiate the precise spot at which I am standing. The map moves with me, so I can hold a constant vision of my changing but immediate vicinity. I cannot, however, see the broader context in which each of these immediate locales is situated, and unless I track them carefully, I am unlikely to recollect all the transitions between them or fully predict the path to where I am headed. This zoomed-in map functions much like the discourses of everyday theology: they provide and produce local and context-specific knowledge but with a relationship to the bigger picture—the fuller theological field of practice—that remains obscured. At the same time, zooming out to encompass the larger field with my GPS map might aid my perspective, giving me a sense of myself within a larger terrain. But I end up losing clarity on my local position because the names of the streets closest to me can no longer be read. In the same way, academic theology needs to step back from the everyday if it is to offer historicizing and systematic insights. But the further it steps back and the longer it stays away, the less chance it has of reconnecting in a way that is intelligible to the local context.

Indeed, it should be noted that academic theology also has its own doxa specific to its own necessarily distanced perspective. Moreover, everyday theological discourse can be crucial in stimulating the crises that reveal and reform academic theologians' unarticulated assumptions as well. Bourdieu argues that the history of educational institutions, as well as each scholar's personal history of implication in the practices of those institutions, converge in a host of unspoken assumptions that condition the very nature of how and what we are capable of thinking. For example, the way in which scholars tend to overemphasize the differences between different fields of practice in order to offer detailed analysis of their workings can lead us to obscure both the larger field of power and the dynamics of concrete human activity.[27] Because scholars are "freed from the direct sanction of reality" in his understanding, we have the room to play and can have the possibility of "seeking and trying out solutions in conditions of minimum risk," but we also face the concurrent risk of losing our bearing on that divested reality.[28]

With what she characterizes as a "division of labor," then, Tanner draws on this model to argue that academic theologians possess the necessary skills for helping everyday Christians negotiate their reinvestment in broken practices with a fresh sense for Christian living (even as the academic theologian's sense of Christian living is derived largely also from her own participation in it). Yet, at the same time, I argue in these pages, because of the ways in which her own scholastic doxa can make Christian living feel less natural to the academic theologian, her relationships with everyday Christians must be understood as mutually reciprocal. Everyday and academic theologies need each other in Tanner's model because while everyday theology's concretion suffers from a loss of broad, systematic, and historical perspective, academic theology's broad, systematic, and historical perspective suffers from a lack of concretion. Each thus has the potential to share with the other what it lacks out of its own abundance. Each has the potential to disrupt the other's doxa. When this exchange works well, we create the potential for moments of insight that can bring about significant reforms in the way faith is lived that are not only intelligible but also reproducible in the concrete contexts where that faith is lived.

Tanner's model thus maps out the types of relationships that hold together a theological field of practice. These relationships are marked by tension and love, competition and cooperation, agreement, and disagreement and compromise. They facilitate the conversations by which theology plays out as a *hybrid, relational affair*, the ebb and flow of which requires participation from both everyday and academic theologies. For Tanner, however, these relationships hang in the background of theological construction, providing perhaps helpful disruptions to the academic theologian's prereflexive or early stage awareness of the theological issues she wants to tackle.

For ethnographic theologians, however, these relationships are central to our research. They make up the theological field we want to bring into view. We therefore turn the volume on these conversations up so that they become the focus rather than the background noise.

My own ethnographic theological research demonstrates that even when those of us who occupy social positions of everyday Christians or academic theologians see ourselves as inhabiting a shared social space, the spatial imaginary for construing that field of practice nevertheless may differ. By attending to additional dynamics such as class, age, gender, education, and more, this research also points to how a broader field of power has the potential to shape how one perceives, participates in, and even produces a shared field of practice—that is, we come to see how the broader field of power makes possible certain agents' social positions, as well as the options for their ways of taking up those positions.

Three Ways of Mapping the Theological Field

Tanner's model outlines an intellectual abstraction of a practical activity, but not the practical activity itself. Theory follows practice even as it seeks to reinform that practice. But as I've already noted, we fall into error when we imagine theory to provide a neutral pattern that we can then apply to or impose on practice. Recognizing the conversational dynamic of theology, through which theology can be a common project of communal creation, likewise means recognizing that academic theological arguments alone also should not dictate the terms of that conversation. Such arguments matter, of course. Nevertheless, it always puzzles me how often academic theologians talk to each other to construct methods to facilitate what we can do *for the church* without much consultation around what people who attend churches would actually like from us and to do with us.

While I cannot speak to any abstract notions of *The Church* and what it might want from us, I can offer a little insight into what my conversation partners wanted out of our shared work together. Everyday theologies, I found in my study, are rich and dynamic enough not only to warrant ethnographic attention but also to withstand and be able to push back against such academic theological interventions into them. Despite all the sociological and theological methods with which I girded my loins to enter the field, once therein my conversation partners consistently challenged the ways in which I would participate in constructing theology with them. This is evident throughout the constructive chapters of this text. While ethnography in general can help academic theologians engage concrete Christian practices for deeper understanding and reflection, the particular ecclesial teaching methods I engage here can take us a step further into partnership with our communities of Christian practice for social and theological construction and change.

So what kinds of maps did my conversation partners draw for understanding the relationship between everyday and academic theologies? Before my second class began, I conducted interviews with members of the first class to explore this question. In each interview, I described my project loosely as an exploration of the relationship between theologies created in the church or by nonacademics and theologies created in the academy.[29] I then asked some variation on the following questions: "How do you think theologies created by people in church should interact with academic theologies?" and "Do you have any advice for me on this topic?"

Every one of whom I asked these questions agreed that academic theology had an important role to play in churches, but no one thought that their everyday theologies should be treated as a *source* for academic reflection[30] or that academic theology could provide them with the "right answers" to questions they might have about belief and practice. Their reflections did not divide out or prioritize the work of the academic theologian in relation to everyday Christian practices with such clarity. Rather, each of the three examples I offer here—each of which resonates with answers from others—implies that a mutual, reciprocal relationship between academic theologians and their everyday theological conversation partners not only should, but already does, exist.

Each of the conversations examined later in this chapter—with Peter, Ann, and Joan and Harlan—is grounded in a different spatial imaginary, each of which offers an alternative perspective on the academic theologian's modes of traversing its terrain. By extension, each different map and mode of movement facilitates the coproduction of a slightly different theological good.

Peter's story is grand in scope; it occludes particularity by invoking sweeping historical gestures, moving from coast to coast of the continental United States. In this story, everyday Christians and academic theologians fall out of and into relationship with each other, finding each other as need arises. It is a story about, among other things, academic theologians trying to figure out where they stand in relation to the production of theological knowledge. Ann's story is much more local, mapping the grander theological terrain onto her own bodily way of being in the world. She does not shy away from theology's personal dimensions, revealing the way broader social systems touch our hearts and shape our souls. In her story, theology helps us interpret the structures of what we all as Christians believe so that we can believe it confidently. Finally, Joan and Harlan bring this theologically mapped body to life and reimmerse it in the cultural landscape that constituted it, as they insist that theology is less about belief and more about action. Theology, they argue, should help us all to live better.

From Frontier to Institution: Taking Up Positions in the Theological Field

Peter began his career as a Baptist minister. After finding himself burned out by church leadership sometime in the late seventies and early eighties, he started working for the Southern Baptist Sunday School Board (now LifeWay Christian Resources) on "family and marriage enrichment" curricula.[31] While most Christian projects that use keywords like *family* and *marriage* sound quite conservative to contemporary ears, Peter's descriptions of his work actually come across as progressive for their time and place. Like a number of the retired people at FBC, whose Baptist commitments were formed before the culture wars of the late 1970s and following, Peter resists the conservative political leanings of the denomination in its current form (evidenced in part by the fact that he was willing—delighted, even—to take a theology class from an ordained woman).

Given changing societal norms around gender, especially around gender and work outside the home, Peter's resources tried to help families negotiate—not resist—their lives together in this new world so that each family member could flourish. Peter describes the foundation of the resources he created being the notion of "marriage as a partnership between equals." This foundation was fine until the conservative resurgence in the Southern Baptist Convention, after which Peter began to receive numerous complaints about his work and was eventually ousted from his job. "My snide comment is," he noted, "once you decide that man is the head and the woman is submissive, there really isn't that much to do after that." So his department was dissolved, and Peter finished his career as a pastoral counselor in various settings.

The way in which Peter embodies a theological field of practice—as mapped by Tanner's scheme—is thus complexly hybrid. He has an MDiv, which he obtained for the purpose of practicing ministry, but he is not shaped by the distinct practices associated with a vocation in the theological academy. He negotiates various Christian roles, such as former minister, former pastoral counselor, and now, by practice, layperson. But he does not negotiate the role of academic theologian. Versions of his type of complex theological identity are not uncommon in ecclesial life in general and, in particular, are especially not uncommon at FBC. We have many retired ministers as members, as well as many current and former employees of LifeWay Christian Resources and other SBC institutions. Peter thus reveals the complex textures of practice and identity that give rise to the theological discourses in church and everyday life.

One afternoon, I visited Peter in his home in Brentwood, a wealthy suburb just outside of Nashville (a part of town where many FBC members live). He seemed to get a kick out of referring to his bright, efficient, and airy digs (complete with granite kitchen countertops, a walk-out deck and a sprawling backyard, hardwood floors, and full-sized, beautiful windows) as "a basement apartment in my son's house." His son and daughter-in-law, who both live upstairs, built the apartment for Peter and his wife to move to after they retired. After a brief tour of the space, we settle into an efficiently organized office that Peter refers to as his "man cave," the room in which he conducts his study both for fun and for what he describes as "a desire to never stop learning."

The darkest room in the home, the office space does have a masculine feel with its large, deep brown leather chairs. Books are the chief mode of décor in the room, and Peter gestures to them often while telling stories, even sometimes springing out of his seat so that he can pull one from the shelf to make a point. These books are primarily theological in theme but also historical. He has books written by popular theologians and books written by academic theologians for a popular audience, as well as books that are more narrowly academic in nature and related to Baptist life, left over, probably, from his formal theological studies. There are some novels as well and texts related to one of his hobbies of tracing his family genealogy. When my recording device malfunctions, Peter grabs his for me to use; it is much nicer than mine. I'm not the only one who conducts interviews: Peter serves on FBC's "historical committee" and records for the church's archives the memories of members who have played some significant role in its life.[32]

Peter speaks with confidence and authority in this space and out of it, and he loves telling stories, especially historical ones. So he tells the story of theologies rising out of church, academy, and everyday life as a historical, geographical narrative back and forth between what he calls frontier and institutional theologies. As the United States expanded west, he tells me, frontier Christians left institutional, academic theologians behind on the east coast. He notes that "having left academia, they evolved a kind of cultural, adaptive theology of their own . . . They didn't worry about 'theoretical stuff' or doctrine." In a sense, academic theology was not welcome on the frontier. It did not know how to fit in with that gritty form of life. So, as he tells it, there was a tangible, spatial divide between frontier and institutional theology for a while.

This divide was not a problem at first according to Peter. The academic theologians were happy, "cloistered away in their ivory towers" to think about God, and the frontier Christians ticked along just fine with their contextual, everyday ways of negotiating faith.[33] Indeed, we can imagine that separated by distance in this way, the theologies produced by the frontier Christians were as grounded in and shaped by their frontier practices as the academic theologians' theologies were grounded in and shaped by their academic practices. But the further apart they stretched, the more the memory of each other's resources faded, each becoming isolated in its own distinct practices, perhaps languishing without the other.

The result, Peter continues, was that on the frontier "different movements began to stir and the people were not prepared to discern . . . they just went with their guts—what seemed to be right to them." Slapping his knee to punctuate his story's end, "someone could come along with a powerful sermon and they'd be like, 'oof, wow!'" meaning that they were easily swayed by anyone with a good story. I can't help but grin at his dramatic gestures. Peter is good at this and I wonder to myself what it would be like to see him preach. "They weren't rootless," he continues, leaning forward in his chair, "but they had been removed from their roots." He gestures his hand quickly, and I can almost see the plants being yanked from the ground as he mimes it. In other words, the greater the distance between the frontier people and the resources of academic theology, the easier it was for them to be swayed by preachers with emotionally moving stories.

For Peter, when our theology is immediately adaptive to its cultural context, in close proximity to the practices that shape it, and with little critical distance on those same practices, it also lacks the critical distance to resist a seductive line of thinking that can lead into lived error. That is, everyday theology works fine until crisis erupts. Peter's description resonates well with both Bourdieu's and Tanner's models. When just going "with their guts" ceased to work for them, the frontier Christians needed to develop skills of discernment to think carefully through their embodied faith. Meanwhile, the academic theologians, languishing in their retreat from the world, needed to find a way to reenter it to aid in this task.

While Peter's story outlined that academic theologians could be helpful in this way, his final word ended up emphasizing another aspect to the narrative: "I think the crisis brought a strong emphasis on doctrine . . . Institutions began to grow . . . academia began to establish itself again," he added. With that, he shrugged his shoulders, gave a grin, and then with a knowing little pout recrossed his legs and sat back in his chair. Story over. Academics can therefore indeed be helpful in times of crisis, helping people think through what they really believe and want to believe. But times of crisis also produce the conditions that enable academic theology to flourish. Theological institutions followed the gritty lives of everyday Christians; they did not lead the way westward. As Peter tells it, we could imagine there would be no seminaries in California if it weren't for manipulative preachers on the frontier.

Peter is, of course, making a historical claim that may or not be accurate. The veracity of his story seems less relevant, however, than how its claims are situated within his own narrative—and spatial—understanding of how academy, church, and everyday life interrelate. His story provides a framework for understanding what role he wants (or at least expects), academic theologians to play in the everyday practices of Christian life. According to Peter's narrative, academic theologians' retreat from the frontier effected their exclusion from it. They could not find a home there until crisis erupted to make space for them and until they could find a way to fit in with what was already going on. From this perspective, the academic theologians' desire to help is revealed as their own personal desire to feel useful or to have a purpose. And in this way, everyday Christians might need academic theologians in moments of crisis about the same amount that academic theologians need them to have those crises.

Tanner's model is not naïve in this regard. She acknowledges that academic theologians do and must care about the perpetuation of their own discipline. Peter's story fleshes out what this might look like in practice with real people and thus its relational, emotional dimensions. Affirming the idea that the church needs the academy to hold onto the roots of the faith for the sake of the faith, he also reminds us—to extend the tree metaphor—that roots require ever-budding leaves to live. As academic theologians, we rely on the faith's continued everyday practice for the very exercise of academic theology. Peter thus stops us from imagining that theological reflection moves along Tanner's continuum in one direction (from the everyday to the academic) by also demonstrating the reverse direction: from institution to frontier, and then back again, and again, and again as this network of social relations and positions together construct the permeable borders of a theological field of practice—as Bourdieu's concepts help us to see. Somewhere between the roots of the faith and the life of the faith seems to be, for Peter, where the growth happens.

Doctrine and Indoctrination: Theology as Embodied Awareness

Like Peter, Ann's story also demonstrates how mutual cooperation between everyday Christians and academic theologians has the potential to help us all resist corruption, engage our beliefs more deeply, and find ways to live the Christian life more faithfully. Whereas Peter mapped a grand historical narrative with vast geographical scope, Ann narrated from where these grand movements are mapped onto her own personal experience. Their stories do not invalidate each other; rather, they demonstrate how different ways of mapping similar topics within shared communities of practice can produce different theological goods. While the notion of a field of power cannot explain all these differences—nor would we want it to—it can help us engage some of them a little more deeply.

Peter, a wealthy, ordained Baptist preacher, spoke from his man cave library, placed his story in the past, and gave it historical scope. He thus allowed himself a distance from the narrative that imbued it with an air of objectivity and authority—even though it probably is not factually accurate or, at least, he spent no time substantiating its claims. Ann also had theological training but achieved an MRE (master of religious education) rather than MDiv. She desired ordination, but never felt she could access it. As she put it, in those days you could get an MDiv as a woman if you wanted to, but "it was frowned on."[34]

Ann and I began our meeting in the intensely intimate, gendered space of a wife's bedside care for a dying husband, before moving it to the public space of an Indian restaurant. Unlike Peter's story, hers felt subjective, tinged with much emotion—particularly anger and frustration—even though the facts that hold it in place are, also unlike Peter's story, likely true. Despite the fifty or so years between us, our conversation has the tone of girlfriends chatting. We laugh and joke, our humor even having playful sexual overtones at times. We complain about men. We share a good meal. Like my conversation with Peter, this is still a conversation about everyday and academic theologies. But the shifts in personal, relational, and even gendered dynamics simultaneously shift the ways in which the theology comes to life.

One Nashville-hot summer evening, I met Ann at the hospice care center where her husband, Bill, was living with and dying from a degenerative disorder that seemed to elude specific diagnosis. With the television on in the background, we fed him and tried to participate in the delusional conversations that had become his chief mode of communication. I usually visited Bill by myself, so it felt strange to occupy the space with Ann in it too. I found myself unsure of how to react, feeling nervous to reveal the ways I might do things differently than her when I was in her husband's room. The fact that on this night Bill's verbal streams of consciousness were marked by a joyful demeanor, rather than the sense of fear and panic that equally often characterized them, took the edge off this feeling somewhat. At least for me, his cheery disposition meant I didn't have to feel guilty as I whisked his wife away for what she described as a much-needed evening out.

Not having tried Indian food in her eight decades of life (I had chosen the restaurant), Ann described her tastes and I attempted to order a meal that we could both enjoy. She laughed uproariously as she tried to figure out which colors in the food bore more spice: "*What* are you trying to do to me, Natalie?!" she exclaimed more than once. No matter how many times I said, "the colors are just colors. Just because green is spicy in the sauces, doesn't mean it's spicy in the spinach!" she kept searching for the underlying color to heat ratio scheme. Ann, I realized, enjoys finding these underlying patterns to things; looking for them bolsters her enjoyment of them, even when she gets them wrong and has to begin again. Indeed, her laughter became so contagious that our young waiter began to flirt playfully with her whenever he was at the table, suggesting she should take some time and go to India with him. When I ribbed her about the waiter's playful advances, she responded, laughing again with wild abandon, "Oh Natalie, he can do that. I'm old. I'm no threat!" She had me in stitches laughing most of the night. At some point in our hours together, I asked her this question about the relationship between everyday and academic theologies.

Ann likes to resist authority. One of her expressed reasons for enrolling in and then sticking with the class I taught was because it affirmed her sense that "you don't have to believe what you're told to believe." In an interview setting, this kind of feistiness, one of my favorite things about Ann, meant that she also continually reframed my questions, challenged my categories, and refused to respond to my queries on my terms. Whereas I wanted to highlight the idea that everyone does theology in some way, she was interested in naming the ways people do not, in fact, do theology, and that this is a problem for the church. "I don't know if most people do an everyday theology," she argued in response to my question, voicing her concern that many people in the church just "spill off, this is what Baptists believe."

Less interested in the distinction between everyday and academic theology, Ann was concerned with the difference between the practice of simply absorbing and regurgitating "beliefs" or "doctrines" and the practices of engagement by which one might come to genuine understanding of them. The idea that one could regurgitate beliefs rang true to me; I was often frustrated at FBC by how people seemed to me to be overly concerned that Christians believe "the right things," as Ann put it, in ways that seemed to flatten out our statements of belief into facts that had to be memorized (another concern she expressed that I tend to share). But the way she used the language of "doctrine" puzzled me.

To begin with, *doctrine* is not a commonly used word around FBC, and to me, at least, it connotes something more complex than flattened facts presented for cognitive assent. But at another point in our conversation I learned that "Doctrines" was a required class in Ann's MRE. The "Doctrines" class did not invite deeper reflection, but rather simply presented a particular checklist of orthodoxy. "Theology" classes, on the other hand, went deeper, but were available primarily to the men pursuing the MDiv. The women in the MRE program were "supposed to take arts and crafts," Ann noted, which was when, "I knew I had a problem on my hands."

Theology is therefore a practice from which the clash between Ann's gender and denominational affiliation has long excluded her, while it has also been a practice that lures her, perhaps in part because of a mix of its forbidden status and her resistance to people telling her what to do. "Theology," she waxed, "is deeper. It's going deeper to find the basis for those [beliefs] we would list—those things that make us different from Christians who would call themselves Methodist or Fundamental Baptist or whatever." It should be noted that Ann's desire to understand these denominational distinctions is not about aggression against those who differ from her. She noted numerous times, in fact, how much she enjoys learning from other denominational beliefs and practices. For Ann, theological engagement with difference, therefore, helps us understand ourselves more deeply; it is what you do when you "work out a puzzle or struggle through an idea yourself." Claiming the right to practice theology like the male MDiv candidates thus gave Ann access to the gift she imagined they possessed: the ability to affirm their own beliefs with confidence.

Whereas understanding the distinctions between different types of Christians more deeply helps to bolster faith, however, Ann admits that theology—in distinction from doctrine—can also be scary. But such fear itself can cause problems: "I think that people in the churches I've been in are scared of the word 'theology,'" she offered, "but they're not scared of the word, 'doctrine.' And I think that's one reason why people who want to in*doctrin*ate find ripe fields for in*doctrin*ating people." On this topic, Ann's physical expression of her emotions became pronounced: her face became flushed, she became more animated in her gestures, and she spoke in rapid disconnected, flustered fragments as she tried to tell a story about a contemporary preacher from the religious right who had recently held a rally in Nashville. In Ann's telling, this preacher was so "conceited" and "prejudiced" that it seemed his whole career was spent imposing his own self-interested agenda on others. Knowing that I was her kindred spirit on this topic, she let herself speak freely: "Oh I never got so sick! Turned my stomach he was the most conceited . . . [*she trails off, looks around the table, then finds her words*] He was supposed to speak on the family. All he spoke on was [himself]."

It is true that this particular preacher invokes ire in many who encounter his pronouncements, myself included. Yet the escalation of Ann's anger in this moment was intense enough to indicate a deeper well of pain on which she drew. The preacher seemed to encapsulate the arrogance of so many others who had sought to impose their agendas on her throughout her life, limiting what and who she could be—sexist teachers, unsupportive colleagues, her own father—all of whom appeared in her stories in similar modes of dishonesty, self-promotion, and self-importance, and all of whom were described with similar types of language. In her narrative, it thus seemed that this preacher bore the brunt of all the anger she had accumulated against all these people. Placing the preacher beyond the reach of influence over her enabled her to place everyone else who threatened her there with him.

Ann's concern about such dangerous preachers therefore differs from Peter's. He worried that these charismatic itinerants would lead people into false belief and lived error. Put on the defensive by the tension between her tenuous social position and robust theological desires, Ann's chief concern was that those who listened to the preacher would be swayed by his lie, "you have to believe, this, this, this and this, or *you aren't a Christian*." The emphasis is slightly different here. Both types of preachers in these stories tell lies, but Peter's male—as well as other forms of—privilege affords him the confidence that he stands firmly within the borders of orthodoxy he wants to protect. Ann's gendered disadvantage, however, makes her social position feel less secure. She wants to preserve the freedom to construct her own beliefs and practices, but she also wants to feel the confidence that when she does so, the borders of orthodoxy remain wide enough to contain her.

Her own powerful experiences with thinking theologically thus inspire Ann to be concerned for those Christians who do not practice the same—the very people whom she believes largely populate today's churches. Here is where, having redefined my terms, Ann begins to answer my question about what role academic theologians in such communities might play. People like the religious right preacher are not theologians, and their language is not theology in Ann's view; they are indoctrinators and their language is doctrine. Her implication, then, is that academic theologians can help people in churches be less afraid of theology—that is, academic theologians can help people in churches be less afraid of engaging and interrogating their beliefs and practices intellectually. We are to do this, in Ann's telling, not to hold onto the roots of the faith, as Peter would have us do, but to bolster the confidence of the faithful. The academic theologian helps Christians see a broader understanding of their own, personal theology and, more important, helps them feel safe doing so.

Ann's understanding of theology and of the ways academic theologians might involve themselves in church life is marked much more explicitly by emotion than Tanner's or even Peter's. Her story locates the scope of everyday theology at the site of the individual embodied self it constructs, marking out a place of real need to which academic theologians might be able to respond. Faith is a riskier business for some than others; the faith Ann practiced produced frequent assaults on her sense of self that required rebuffing. Academic theologians can thus help people know why they believe what they believe when their confidence is undermined by unjust causes. Yet at the same time, the personal and emotional dynamics Ann introduced enriched our theological conversation overall. They pressed us to listen to each other carefully, and in turn enabled the types of back and forth reasoning we engaged together to challenge where each other stood. The emotional connections made us persist until we helped each other into speech and refined our language carefully so that we could get at the meaning each intended. Who knows if we got there? But the conversational process achieved something like what Ann was seeking: a deepened reaffirmation of the places from which we both began.

Not Talking Theology, but Acting Theology: Putting the Pieces Back Together

A few days after my interview with Ann, I was scheduled to meet with a married couple who took the class together, Joan and Harlan. Joan and Harlan worked for years together in ministry in Manhattan, but they retired to a condo in Nashville to be closer to their children and grandchildren shortly after Harlan was diagnosed with Parkinson's disease. They invited me to their home to be interviewed, and we scheduled our meeting for just a few days after the annual church BBQ, an event I had to miss because I was out of town for a conference.

At the BBQ, Harlan took a nasty fall. While I was away, I received updates on his condition via email from other people who had been in our class. Despite his injuries, Joan and Harlan did not want to cancel the interview. I too was eager to get round to their house and check on how he was doing. I had to work hard not to overreact to his bruised and battered face. While I had learned in my few short years of knowing Harlan how to slow down in conversation to allow space for his speech to make it past his bodily tremors, witnessing the effects of these tumbles was new and upsetting. Indeed, the tumbles themselves were new and upsetting, and I had the distinct sense while interviewing him that Harlan was nearing the end of his life.

People around the church looked to Joan as a source of inspiration in what seemed to us to be unwavering care of her ailing spouse. Joan addressed this topic herself in the midst of our conversation, noting how embarrassing and upsetting it is to her to hear such accolades: "You don't see me when I'm not so kind or when I am impatient, when I lose my cool," she insisted. Her willingness to be vulnerable and admit her own limitations made me wonder if her friendship with Ann had deepened since Ann too came to find herself caring for a husband with a degenerative disease. What I did learn about their friendship, though, was that Ann had given Joan the scoop on what kinds of questions I would be asking. When Joan admitted this halfway through her interview, I teased her affectionately for trying to "cheat at something that wasn't a quiz."

Like Ann, Joan also expressed the idea that theology not only transforms belief and practice but also helps us more deeply affirm what we know to be true, both for ourselves and as a guard against manipulation by others. Here she made explicit reference to one of the topics of discussion in the "Jesus Christ and Salvation" class, noting that our conversations about sanctification in particular did not change her beliefs, but rather helped her to understand more fully why she believed them. But a deepened understanding, she indicated, must also always then connect what we believe more deeply with what we do. Joan noted passionately, in praise of her fellow churchgoers, and punctuating important words by drawing them out slowly, "I think that *many* in our church are interested in and involved in *acting out* their theology . . . To me that is theology—*not talking theology, but acting theology*!" To this Harlan added, "Yes, I think the theology term gets used when we might better speak of an enfleshment of our belief."

This enfleshment was spatially grounded for Joan and Harlan. In telling their life stories, transitions between events were most often framed in relation to a particular geographic move, whether from Maryland to New York or New York to Nashville or any of the smaller moves in between. Their choice of FBC for their Nashville church home was founded on their sense that it was "Yankee friendly," and thus somewhere to where they could take friends when they visited from up North. They didn't want a church that was so "steeped in Southern culture," as Joan put it, that they couldn't fit in with their own embodied Northern tendencies. Places and, more so, places of belonging mattered deeply to Joan and Harlan in their sense of who they are and how they fit into their communities.

Whereas Ann worried that churchgoers spend too little time thinking about their faith, Joan and Harlan were explicitly concerned with what the thinkers did with their thought. As Joan put it one time, laughing while she explained her understanding of the Transfiguration to me, the disciples wanted to stay on that mountain and keep contemplating and make themselves "an ol' boys' club." But Jesus said no. "Those boys have got to get back down the mountain and get to the business of helping the people." In an echo of Peter's concerns about academic theology, Joan's story presents disengaged, cloistered away, and prolonged thinking as ineffectual. Such practices reify themselves into exclusionary institutions (i.e., the ol' boys' club). A little contemplative thought is good, but as soon as Jesus departs from that thought, it only distracts us from the work of justice according to Joan.

The story of the mountaintop not only is gendered, with its reference to the boys' club, but also implies the need to be on the move.

When it came to my question about everyday and academic theologies, just as with their telling of their own life stories, most of Joan and Harlan's examples placed their theological reflection in particular times and locations. Circumstances of time and place give rise to theological illumination for Joan and Harlan. They referenced how various neighborhoods in Nashville were impacted by the 2010 flood, and how this was a time when people from our church "used their skills to get out there and help people" as an enfleshment of faith. They told stories of their ministry in New York, and how they would go to listen to James Cone's public lectures to gain a deeper sense of how to enact their urban ministries.[35] Harlan's first exposure to something he could name as theology happened in conversation with a young Catholic man in a department store where the two worked as stock boys. The otherness of this man's faith opened Harlan's ears to hear that they were talking about more than just belief.

Furthermore, as people who had lived their lives on the move, following God's voice to wherever they discerned it calling them, their sense of theology's goods related primarily to how theology helps us stay on the move. When I asked them what the good in theological thinking was, Joan talked about the need for Christians to be challenged in what they believe. "I don't think we should ever become comfortable," she argued. When I asked why, she continued, using explicitly bodily language that juxtaposes stillness and movement: "You become lethargic. There's no standing still in any subject. In life, there's no standing still. You're either learning or you're falling back. Even as—whatever age you are—I think no matter what age you are, you continue to learn."

Acting theology, rather than just talking it, keeps us on our toes and keeps us moving. As Harlan nodded along with his wife's interpretation, it became clear that thinking new thoughts in their view is helpful inasmuch as it destabilizes us from complacency and opens us to what God would have us do next, where God would have us next go.

Joan and Harlan add yet another layer to our mapping of theological terrain. Yes, conversations between everyday Christians who do and do not have academic theological training can help us all avoid manipulation, respond to crises, understand why we believe what we believe, and more reflectively affirm the beliefs we have. These conversations all take place within and across the lands and institutions that make up our lives, just as they all are mapped onto our bodily ways of being in the world. As theological conversations guide our practices, simply by being one of those practices, they move us from simply being confident with our position in the world and into acting boldly from that confidence. Joan and Harlan's narratives take the confident, constituted self and reimmerse it into the lands, institutions, and locales of its activity. As Joan and Harlan rightly point out, reflection and enfleshment are thus intimately linked. Thinking leads to doing leads to thinking leads to doing and so on. In this way, Joan and Harlan capture the spirit of what practices of theological conversation across everyday and academic theologies might produce.

Peter, Ann, and Joan and Harlan together provide a rich, multilayered, and complex map of what should happen in those conversations that both resonates with but also tweaks what Tanner proposes by insisting that it actually be a conversation and that the conversation be located in a shared community of belonging.

Making Space for Conversation

Peter's spatial imaginary located academic theologians temporarily outside the places where everyday Christians congregate and then criticized that model. His narrative, like Tanner's theological model, calls academic theologians to a vigilance regarding where we understand ourselves to be positioned in relation to the Christian social practices we study and seek to serve within a larger field of theological practice. As I have already noted, reflexive sociologists—Bourdieu included—are particularly concerned with this careful attention to self in relation to the field of study. In the next chapter, I therefore engage reflexive sociology to highlight the reflexive dimensions of ethnographic theology in response to Peter's model. In Chapter 3, I use this reflexive theology to chart a course through my field of study that produces reflections on how social change might and might not happen in ecclesial contexts.

As Ann and I refined our ideas in relation to what the other had said, our second story in particular showed us the generative possibilities of everyday and academic theology competing and cooperating with each other via conversation. At the same time, the differences between Peter's and Ann's spatial imaginaries helped us see the different positions made available to agents within a theological field and the different ways agents might take those positions up. Whereas Peter's various forms of social privilege allowed him to map the theological field itself, thereby instilling his description with an air of objectivity, Ann offered a seemingly more subjective view by demonstrating the ways in which that field gets mapped on to us as embodied beings—what Bourdieu might describe as "a habitus inhabited by the world it inhabits."[36] In the next chapter, I unpack this type of bodily, theological knowledge by critically engaging Loïc Wacquant's carnal sociology to emphasize the bodily dimensions of ethnographic theology in response to Ann's story. In Chapter 4, I use this carnal theological method to explore the ways in which theologies are produced and borne on bodies.

Finally, Joan and Harlan's story showed us that awareness of and confidence with one's social and theological position must give way to action or what they referred to as *acting theology*. Here, the relationship between belief and practice (what we say and what we do) was especially important. In Chapter 5, we play with this notion of *acting* theology by using the metaphor of performance art to expand Tanner's image of the theologian as a bricoleur. This expanded metaphor helps us ask questions not only about the relationship between belief and practice, between thought and action, but also about the relational interactions that make up theological conversation. In so doing we endeavor to avoid idealized notions of theological creativity to take seriously dynamics of power and privilege in processes of theological knowledge production.

In closing, I should note that when I asked people to think about the relationship between everyday and academic theologies, no one responded that academic theologians should write texts for lay people to read—or even that we should train ministers well in seminary or write texts that ministers could read and then incorporate into their preaching and teaching. The call for populist texts and the assertion that academic knowledge follows a trickle-down effect remain two key ways that academic theologians imagine our work to connect with Christian social practices. The absence of these techniques from my conversation partners' discussions is therefore important. Quite a few of my conversation partners do actually read such texts, so I am not negating their importance. People in the classes I taught cited academic theologians, church historians, and biblical scholars they had read, mentioning Barth, Bonhoeffer, Karen Armstrong, Marcus Borg and Amy-Jill Levine (the latter being a particular hometown favorite in Nashville, as she teaches at Vanderbilt University and speaks regularly at local churches) as contributors to their own spiritual development. More to the point, the creation of such texts enables academic theologians to continue our particular conversation with each other, as well as to contribute to the formation of ministers, thus impacting congregational life but in a somewhat muted way.

Even so, the overwhelming response I got from people I interviewed was that the good that academic theologians could offer to local churches involved participating in Christian social practices directly.

Whether we do this by providing direct instruction in local churches or simply participating in ongoing interpersonal conversations with everyday Christians seemed to matter less to my interviewees than the fact that we do it in an intentional, sustained way. This insight shifts the way in which we imagine the goods of professional theological training or academic theological education to relate to everyday Christian social practices within a larger theological field of practice. Christian social practices are not merely a source for academic theological reflection. Neither (and this is critical) are everyday practices merely the site where academic theologians can dispense their wisdom to the church. Rather, Christian social practices are the location in which the academic theologies participate in partnership with everyday theologies. Consequently, as I mentioned in the opening pages of this book, rather than reflecting ethnographically *on* Christian community or *on* Christian practice, the method I construct here seeks to do ethnographic reflection *in* Christian community and *as* Christian practice as a particular method of attending to the intersection of everyday and academic forms of theological knowledge. This method therefore demonstrates that the practical dimensions of a theological text can occur in its construction rather than its application.

What is challenging about this conclusion is that it calls everyday Christians and academic theologians (who also occupy the social position of everyday Christians in many cases) into a joint venture whose success cannot be determined by either party alone. I am not saying that this is a venture in which all academic theologians should engage, although it is also a practice in which many of us already engage, both within our own particular communities of worship and as guest lecturers, preachers, and teachers in communities that are not intimately our own. Therefore, I name it as one site from which the academic theologian already working in both church and academy can serve with more reflexive intention and, I hope, joy. The classroom in and from which I did such work implicated not only my research partners but also me. It is the place in which we all together became my research subject.

Chapter 2

Making Theologians

Deploying a Theological Habitus

The night I interviewed Miriam and Gary, a married couple in their midthirties who enrolled in both classes, we met at their house for dinner. Gary, a documentary filmmaker, is out interviewing someone for his most recent project, so Miriam and I start without him. We are cooking dinner together—a common shared activity given that Miriam and Gary are two of my husband, Tyler's, and my closest friends in Nashville. Miriam and I laugh at the addition of my recording device to a familiar routine. Both she and Gary are comfortable with such equipment, though, as they both used ethnographic methods in their own PhD dissertation projects in social science areas. Miriam is now a tenure-track professor at a local university. They teach the Sunday School class that Tyler and I attend, and we all engage conversations about our faith—conversations I would call "theological"—frequently.

Before Gary joins us, I begin asking Miriam my questions about the relationship between everyday and academic theology. In her response she notes, "I think that was a funny moment . . . when you essentially made us all theologians for a moment saying, 'What do you really think?'" Her answer takes me by surprise; somewhere between her academic credentials and theological experience, I don't expect Miriam to imagine herself to need a word from me to be *made theologian*. The process by which someone is *made* theologian, I think, certainly begins somewhere beyond their conscious awareness of it, but then I imagine most of us become aware—to some degree and at some point—of our everyday theological activity. For example, Miriam, like all of us who participated in our Sunday night theology classes, reasons and responds daily to her social world in various theological modes. She doesn't need me to make her a theologian because she already is one.

Indeed, as we saw in the first chapter, a theological field of practice is integrated with various other fields of practice within a larger field of power, each of which integrates with and disrupts the others as they together construct our social worlds. It feels to me then that Miriam ascribes too much power to my question by indicating that it *made* her a theologian. My question, rather, invited her to draw on the hidden well of knowledgeable agency by which she had already been made a theologian of the everyday, simply by virtue of her participation in the everyday Christian practices that contribute to making the theological field. My question simply invited her to articulate what was already there.

Perhaps it is only in such a moment of conscious articulation that Miriam finds she can claim a particular identity, like theologian, as her own, however. That being said, here I am less interested in how *theological identities* are claimed, and more interested in how *theological agencies* are embodied and performed, with or without our conscious awareness of them—that is, the types of social wisdom or embodied agency that are, by now, commonly described by academic theologians using the concept of *habitus.*[1] In this chapter, I engage critically with reflexive sociologist Pierre Bourdieu's recent revival of this ancient concept, less to study the embodied theological agency of those within my field of study, however, and more to deploy it as the grounds for my own ethnographic theological methods. This critical engagement helps me unpack how the particular nature of my belonging at First Baptist Church (FBC)—as an ordained minister and academic theologian—shapes my own theological agency, the ethnographic theological methods made possible by that shaping, and the types of theology that can be produced by those methods.

As I sought to exercise my theological agency as a minister and academic theologian at FBC in a way that could integrate everyday and academic theologies into a shared production of theological knowledge, the practice of teaching adult-education classes felt like a clear and obvious option. Throughout my ordination discernment process with the church, we had discussed my vocation as a teacher, which I articulated consistently as a desire to be a "minister who taught ministers." My role as an adult-education teacher at the church had also been initiated by a congregant who requested that I be put to work in that capacity; as she had put it, "I figured, if we've got a theologian in the congregation, we should get her teaching theology!" Teaching theology on Sunday nights thus became a way for me not only to channel my academic skills into my ministry at FBC but also to guide theological conversations that could integrate everyday and academic modes of theological reasoning for—I hoped—their mutual flourishing.

This chapter explores the theoretical underpinnings and practical processes by which my role as a theology teacher at FBC was constituted, as well as the ways in which that role facilitated my ethnographic theological methods. Put simply, our classrooms functioned a little like a lab. Together we would experiment—sometimes in ways more controlled and other times, ways more chaotic—with deconstructing and reconstructing our own theological presuppositions. I would articulate historical theologies that had contributed to our embodied faith, and they would articulate the hidden histories of our shared place, all of us doing so in ways that began revealing the doxa holding all of our particular practices and beliefs together. What "goes without saying because it comes without saying" was brought to voice as we sketched our vast and local histories together.[2] In faith together, then, we sought understanding, as we tried also to imagine new possibilities for Christian thought and action in dialogue with what Christians in our place and beyond had been thinking and doing for centuries before us.

Everyone in the class gave informed consent for me to use our conversations for my academic research. They knew that I was gathering data not only from what they believed as individuals—most of them were bemused by this fact—but also from what sprung forth from our shared conversation. As I digitally recorded and transcribed all these conversations, kept detailed field notes, and conducted follow-up interviews after the close of each of the two theology courses, the ethnographic component functioned somewhat like a mix of group and individual interviews within an action research methodological framework.[3] This type of immersive ethnographic activity, done in conjunction with forms of interviews as well, is typically referred to as participant observation. The epistemological problems and possibilities of participant observation have been thoroughly questioned and critiqued by Bourdieu, among others, and I follow those critiques here. Throughout this chapter I argue for a form of theological fieldwork that is less participant observation and more objectified participation. This distinction will become clearer as I tell my story.

HABITUS: A DEFINITION

As sociologist Karl Maton has pointed out, *habitus* is not only the most popular and most cited concept from Bourdieu's lexicon, but it is also the most misunderstood and misused.[4] It is therefore with some trepidation that I add my voice to a potentially off-key chorus. According to Maton and others, it is most crucial that we not use the concept of *habitus* in distinction from that of *field*, which we explored in the previous chapter.[5] Doing so abstracts the concept not only from the context of its meaning but also from the arena in which it can do its work.[6] Described by Bourdieu as the "schemes of perception, conception, and action common to all members of the same group or class," habitus limns a site where the "objective structures" that generate a field of practice and a subject's knowledgeable agency meet with and coconstitute each other.[7] Put simply, habitus describes the types of embodied, knowledgeable agency any of us derives from participation in social practices. Bourdieu's conceptual tools of field and habitus thus give weight both to the ways in which theological context shapes theological knowledgeable agency and to the potential for that knowledgeable agency to reconfigure the context that situates it. Shaped by context and practice, the type of theological agency that the notion of habitus helps us see is therefore one that is less than fully conscious of its act or intention but nevertheless is still active and knowledgeable.

To offer a simple example from FBC, we always dim the lights for baptisms on Sunday mornings, and almost exclusively dim them only for baptisms. My own baptism as an adult had happened in what we might think of as a Baptist style (full immersion accompanied by testimony), though not in a Baptist church (rather, it happened in an independent evangelical church that I attended through some of my teenage years). It had been a powerful experience for me, and so I tend to feel more emotionally invested in baptismal moments than I necessarily do in other typically Baptist liturgical events (like baby dedications, or communion services where trays of crackers and juice are passed around). In essence, I love baptisms; whether it is font or immersion or infant or adult, I experience a deep emotional connection when witnessing that moment that crystallizes belonging in the body of Christ. I think, therefore, that I might tend to pay attention when I join a new church as to what the cues are that a baptism is on its way.

The first time I ever experienced lights dimming at FBC, I recall wondering what the heck was going on. But over the following years, that cue trained me to respond. If I am distracted or disengaged, dimming lights immediately draw my attention to the tank at the front and center of the sanctuary. It is not as though the lights dim and I think consciously, "Oh, it's time for a baptism. I had better look front and center now so that I can see the baptism." But more so, when the lights dim, I find myself instinctively leaning slightly forward in my pew for a better view before I have even had time to register what has happened. Moreover, in that moment of instinctual bodily movement, I also experience a dispositional movement; in general, a sense of joyful anticipation and wonder erupts somewhere inside me, as I wait to see who will descend into the water. From that wonder, I frequently find myself uttering small prayers for the person in the tank, feeling myself connected to them emotionally, even spiritually, even if I have never met them before. And even though I tend to think that (for a community that does not affirm pedobaptism) FBC simply baptizes some children too young, as soon as those lights dim, even if it is a child in the tank, I am still right there with them, celebrating the moment, and often getting a little choked up.

The notion of a theological habitus does not pin in place the precise reasons why or causes of how liturgical repetition creates this prayerful, excited, connective set of bodily gestures, dispositions, and actions. But because all knowledge "presupposes a work of construction" that has "nothing to do with intellectual work," as Bourdieu argues, the notion of a theological habitus does help tell a story about how that liturgical repetition has made me competent to read the logic of worship time flowing within worship space.[8] And because that construction of bodily knowledge "consists of an activity of practical construction, even of practical reflection, that ordinary notions of thought, consciousness, knowledge prevent us from adequately thinking," the notion of a theological habitus operating with a particular field of practice also helps tell the story of my body knowing instinctively not only when to lean forward in my seat but also how to open myself to something I would describe as sacred once I'm in the lean.[9] Before I even begin negotiating what I think about baptizing children in light of other ecclesial practices, for example, my leaning is itself a theological act, as are the dispositions it produces. And these dispositions tell me something about what I believe, even if I am unable to articulate it. My lean, my wonder, and my prayer all therefore come together to form the beginning places for any theological reflection I will do on the act and nature of baptism.

Acknowledging that action and knowledge are only possible within, because of, and from one's various habitus certainly helps us envision a rich complexity not only to human activity but also to human reasoning. It turns our ethnographic attention away from focusing solely on articulated beliefs to the more complex interplay of beliefs, practices, and their integration in "socially informed bodies."[10] Furthermore, while the relationship between my forward lean and prayerful, hopeful disposition captures the immanence of my personal practice, it also gestures toward the transcendent theological field that gives that action meaning. Indeed, in a particularly lovely turn of (albeit translated) phrase, Bourdieu argues that "it is because agents never know completely what they are doing that what they do has more sense than they know."[11]

This prereflexive knowledge, carried in my flesh and blood and bones, waits for me to reflect on it. Some of it, of course, will always remain nascent, a mystery to me, even as it is wrapped up in the doxa of the communities to which I belong. But the ways in which my particular theological agency—as minister and academic theologian—can nurture such processes of reflection, both my own and those of others, come into clearer view through engagement with three core defining aspects of habitus: (1) habitus teach embodied histories that are (2) transposable across fields and (3) through which social reproduction and change are generated.

Habitus Teach Embodied Histories

Even a liturgical action so seemingly simple as dimming the lights bears within it what Bourdieu calls, an "implicit pedagogy," one that is able to "instill a whole cosmology."[12] Because this act of sinking into slight darkness is not just practically constructive but also practically reflective, it gently teaches me at least aspects of the logic of a whole theologically constituted universe—even though I might not be readily capable of articulating those logics. Habitus is, Bourdieu argues, "embodied history, internalized as second nature and so forgotten as history" such that it is, for the one it possesses (because it possesses us as much as we possess it), "the active presence of the whole past of which it is the product."[13] Our bodies thus carry the wisdom (and folly) of more than our own personal histories; they carry the wisdom (and folly) of a whole—albeit, fragmented whole—theological history we cannot necessarily recall but can nevertheless enact.

It is doubtful that any of us at FBC knows where the practice of dimming the lights for baptism first began in our community or which other practices gave rise to it. Perhaps the act is programmed simply with the theatrics of stage lighting. And certainly, some aspect of that association is probably at play when I feel my anticipation build. But who knows what lingers in the logic of our practice from Anabaptist persecution and the sense that we might want to dim the lights to hide what we're doing? What logic might be implicit from our reformed roots and the practice of candlelight vigil baptisms on the night before Easter? Does the positioning of the pew from which I lean relate somehow to a history of evangelical camp meetings, an eagerness to witness conversion, or a sense for the possible?

The dimming of lights teaches my body dispositional responses that bear whole histories of theological practice and meaning, none of which I could trace with precision or necessarily put into words in the moment, but each of which intersects multiple fields like those related to gender, sex, politics, and class as well. Indeed, as Marcella Althaus-Reid has provocatively argued in reference to kneeling in particular, the theological histories that shape our bodily practices are always already implicated with and held together by gendered, sexual, class, and colonial histories.[14] Just as Bourdieu argues that the way I learn to hold my knife while eating carries within its movement an entire history of class relations, gendered bodies, domestic practices, and so on, so too does the act of leaning forward in a pew to respond to an ecclesial, baptismal covenant.[15]

So seemingly simple an act as kneeling or leaning or quieting my heart to pray, therefore, makes my body one of the many sites through which a broad history of Christian belief, theology, and practice flows into and out of FBC, as well as into and out of all the other bodies worshipping therein. Together we keep that history alive, even as its intersection with the other histories that constitute us, as well as the ways in which we respond to each, shifts and molds it into something new. This is why moving between different worlds can sometimes feel so difficult; we always carry the weight of our prior worlds in our bones, in our flesh, in ways we don't fully understand.

Everyone who took the classes I taught carries these histories in their bones, histories that surface as bodily intuitions and dispositions more than words (although certainly sometimes as words too). As an academic theologian, however, my formal education taught me how to articulate these hidden histories that we all bear more explicitly; precisely because I have studied the histories themselves, I can discern them in their hiding places a little more clearly. As a result, I could articulate the kinds of social, historical, and theological connections that were less immediately apparent to others in the class but nevertheless, could resonate with them as meaningful or true somewhere deep inside themselves. I could make the implicit pedagogies of habitus construction explicit.

My articulated theological histories are not enough in themselves, however, for creating a communal, contextual theology because my bodily knowledge could not produce the same wisdoms as the bodily knowledge possessed by and possessing my classmates. To begin articulating our shared doxa so that we could likewise begin trying to create new patterns of Christian thought and action required that we all work together, and all from the wisdom shaping and guiding our particular theological agencies. We needed to teach each other.

Such particularity, of course, breeds disagreement, and so it is worth noting that theology done this way is what Kathryn Tanner calls "a hybrid, relational affair."[16] Theology, when done this way, is located in the process of production more than any final, coherent product, as will become clear in the constructive chapters next—each of which composes what we might call, following Tanner, a *hybrid, relational theology*.

. . . That Are Transposable across Fields . . .

Once we begin discerning the presence and pattern of an embodied history in a particular knot of perceptions, intuitions, and dispositions, we can also begin to see how these knots, these bodily wisdoms, are also transposable across different fields of practice. The rich and abiding yet also messy way in which the faith history, as embodied history, lingers in our bones rather than flutters superficially on the surface of the skin explains why habitus can be divorced from their original conditions of creation. As someone whose early childhood faith formation occurred in Catholic school, my theological agency is still shaped by an intuitive, sacramental wonder that is foreign to my current Baptist community. I have carried that wonder in my flesh from one context to another, and it has managed to stay alive despite the transition. Because habitus not only are generated by fields of practice but can also be transposed across them, homologies appear among them across diverse fields that have little or no seeming relationship to each other.[17]

For example, a disposition to try new things, shaped through all the ways a family's life is enriched by emigration to a new country, might be passed down through unfolding generations all living within that same new country. In such a case, the habitus associated with national or class status, for example, might contribute to a theological habitus that is open to experimenting with new beliefs and practices. Likewise, a downturn in family fortunes initiated by a negative immigration experience could create a fear of the unknown, also passed down through generations who are happily transient but unwilling to experiment with eating foreign food or trying a new laundry detergent. This family might produce generations who can travel the world, be exposed to the beauty of multiple and different religious practices, but for whom a theology of salvation in Christ alone feels so natural as to be taken as unquestionably true.

Indeed, perhaps one of the best examples of homologies within the theological field is how the endurance of Anselmian forms of atonement theory tends to reproduce elements of a medieval feudal system context (hierarchical ordering of reality, doctrines of God that focus on the problem of dishonor, etc.) from which they have long been culturally separated. Theological perceptions, apperceptions, and dispositions can therefore be passed on without the agents who embody them ever knowing of their distant, absent genesis.

That we can be not only haunted but also indwelled or even possessed by our theological and other histories indicates the potential for either exorcising our ghosts or affirming long-lost saints in our communities depending on the current, contextual need. Here is where the historicizing and systematizing impulses of academic theology, in particular, are able to participate in the process by which we are all made and remade as theologians. As we help bring those hidden hauntings to the surface in speech—that is, help name them and then help discern whether to banish them or reintegrate them anew into our life together—we bring doxa to light in all the various ways it might be articulated.

. . . Through which Social Reproduction and Change Are Generated

These processes by which we exorcise our ghosts or affirm our saints are what can, in theory, enable social change rather than stasis. A theological field of practice and its related habitus thus work together or battle each other, create or subvert, and make visible or hide the various choices in belief and practice that face agents in their specific contexts.[18] They also work together or battle each other, create or subvert, and make visible or hide the various ways these agents might make such choices.[19] Because we are never fully conscious of our embodied faith, the ways in which we live, move, and have our being, to cite Paul citing Epimenides (Acts 17:28), are teeming with an ongoing production of bodily knowledge that can be opened up for reshaping.

Critics of Bourdieu, however, tend to see his understanding of social change as inevitably maintaining the status quo. As anthropologist Sherry Ortner points out, various French theorists, like Bourdieu, have each in their own way "directed us to see subjects as constructed by, and subjected to, the cultural and historical discourses within which they must operate."[20] Arguing that much is at stake in this choice of language, Ortner notes that the word *construction* is a metaphor for industry. It connotes the weight of immovable structures that are made of iron, steel, or some other tough, unbendable product that keeps the building from falling down. *Construction* thus emphasizes the structures themselves over those who make them.

Given that subjects and structures have a constructive relationship to each other in Bourdieu's scheme, however, the problem here is not so much with the theoretical principles with which he engages the field of practice. Rather, the problem is with where he tends to focus his attention within the dynamic interplay of habitus and field. Bourdieu might make room for flux in the play between the two, but Ortner is right to point out that the very heavy material weight he gives to a field's objective structures tends to "emphasize the role of practice in social reproduction rather than change."[21] Of course, as she adds, "social reproduction and social transformation can never, and should never, be wholly separated."[22] Nevertheless, there are different ways that we can approach the data produced out of our field of study.

We could, like Bourdieu, "do practice analysis as a loop, in which 'structures' construct subjects and practices, but subjects and practices reproduce 'structures.'"[23] While allowing for the possibility that reproduction entails slippage, by focusing on the reproductive loop, Bourdieu nevertheless tends to eclipse those slips. Or we could, like Ortner, choose to "avoid the loop, to look for the slippages in reproduction and the erosions of long-standing patterns, the moments of disorder and of outright 'resistance.'"[24] Focusing on the slippages of power and the disruptions of the status quo by actual agents, she argues, is more in line with feminist and other "subaltern" forms of analysis.[25] This is not to deny that the loop exists. It is rather, to let it fall into the background, drawing on it when it is helpful for illuminating something particular.

Departing from this heavy industry metaphor, Ortner instead lifts up the lighter language of "making," language I have also been using so far in this chapter as I have followed Miriam's word choice. Derived from the less weighty materials of crafts rather than industry, the flexibility of making is better suited for focusing attention on the activity of the agents themselves who make the structures that simultaneously make them. This allows for a more malleable vision of the structures that make and are made—one that, by extension, proliferates the possibility for creating new practices of justice, for example, within them, as well as other new theological practices and ways of theological knowing. This language is better tooled to ethnographic tasks that are capable of "looking at and listening to real people doing real things in a given historical moment . . . to figure out how what they are doing or have done will or will not reconfigure the world they live in."[26]

The different ways that a practice of ecclesial teaching might participate in social reproduction and/or change are perhaps obvious. Indeed, recalling the majority of classes on offer at FBC on Sunday nights that I outlined in the book's introduction, we might note that most of them were directed toward maintaining a status quo—whether intentionally or not. I mentioned how many of the curricula sacralized traditional gender and family norms in the face of changing social mores, while others maintained a narrow and largely evangelical orthodoxy presented as objective truth about reality, for example. While the class I taught probably adhered more closely than others to the topics and figures associated with historical Christian orthodoxy, it nevertheless did so with the intention of opening up our beliefs and practices to critical engagement for the purpose of fresh theological thinking. Discerning whether or not it accomplished that goal will be one burden of this book's constructive theological chapters.

Furthermore, as we learned from Joan in the first chapter, and as the concept, habitus, has helped us see in this section, thinking is always inextricable from doing. My attempts to refine and revise our theological thinking are therefore connected with a desire to revise and refine our social and theological practices as well. In particular, it will be the burden of the next chapter to ascertain the degree to which any types of slippage we managed to create in the loops of our social reproduction were able to give way to genuine social change. But to get into how my ethnographic methods sought not only to *look for* those moments, as Ortner suggests we do, but also to *create* them, we need to understand how Bourdieu frames the relationship of the researcher's various competing and cohering habitus to her field of study.

DEPLOYING HABITUS IN THEOLOGICAL FIELDWORK

We are already moving toward an awareness of how particular configurations of habitus and field can give rise to certain ethnographic foci. When she emphasizes the activity of *real people doing real things* within a field of practice in order to see how they *will or will not reconfigure the world they live in*, Ortner's methods resonate with the way particular ethnographic theories and methods ground my attempts to construct fresh possibilities for Christian thought and action within my own church context. Whereas Bourdieu and Ortner focus on describing and analyzing the habitus constructed and made in and by the fields of practice that they study (whether or not those fields' structures are reproduced or reconfigured), I endeavor to participate directly in—even disrupt—the reproductions and reconfigurations of the theological field of practice. While I too am looking to see, describe, and analyze those moments of slippage, disorder, and outright resistance, I am also looking to participate in them, create them, and nurture them to cocreate fresh theological reflection and practice in community.

As a member and leader at FBC, I therefore relate differently to the habitus/field dynamic of my study than Bourdieu and Ortner would to theirs, for example. Possessing and possessed by the habitus associated with my field, different epistemological possibilities frame my methods than Bourdieu's, even if mine are grounded in a critical engagement with his. Following Bourdieu's understanding of how the ethnographer's reflexive engagement with her field of study should account for her concurrent social and epistemological breaks from it, I argue here for a form of theological ethnography that begins not with participant observation, or even with participant objectification, as Bourdieu describes it, but with *objectified participation* in the theological field of study.

Participant Observation to Participant Objectification

The participant observer is tempted in two problematic directions according to Bourdieu: objectivism and subjectivism. Criticizing ethnographers who "in taking up a point of view on the action, withdraw from it in order to observe it from above and from a distance," Bourdieu argues that they mistake multiple, dynamic, and interrelated, temporally embedded practices for a single, static "object of observation and analysis."[27] In other words, the knowledge they gain in site leads them to presume the capacity to describe *the way things really are*, as if they have attained an external, omniscient view of the working whole. Constructing detemporalized models of what they see, these objectivists eclipse the complex dynamics of actual practice as they fail to account for the ways in which they have become implicated in that practice.

The ethnographic tendency toward subjectivism also arises from a mistaken perspective, as the researcher fails to account for the fact that knowledge of her field of study is produced in, through, and by what we might call her academic or research habitus, not the habitus associated with the field itself. Without belonging to the field, the researcher experiences a social break from it that amounts also to an epistemological break. Any sense that she possesses or is possessed by the habitus of study is only an illusion. Whenever an ethnographer imagines herself to be a true participant in the field, then, for Bourdieu, she has actually unconsciously forgotten the conditions of her research habitus and mistaken her occasional mimicry of site-specific actions for the practical, bodily understanding gained from years of membership: just because you noticed that the lights dimmed, doesn't mean you're excited for the baptism.

Whether the methodological problem lies with a false objectivism or false subjectivism, for Bourdieu the solution is not to seek a more genuine form of membership in the field of study—whatever that might mean. Instead, Bourdieu argues that the ethnographer must perform a reflexive reaffirmation of her research or academic habitus through an explicit accounting for the habitus that she is studying. Instead of participant *observation*, Bourdieu argues, ethnographers must perform a participant *objectification* that brings to detailed light the conditions that construct—or make—the forms of bodily, practical knowledge endemic to the site, while also accounting for their relationship to those conditions. This epistemological reconstruction accounts for, rather than falsely abstracts from or attempts to replicate, the practical wisdom that the ethnographer lacks.[28] It is, in essence, what Bourdieu sees as the task of the ethnographer's reflexivity.

Bourdieu thus takes seriously the effects that an ethnographic approach has on what it produces as its object of study as he accounts for the tempo of practices, the role of the ethnographer, and the open-endedness of the relationship between "objective structures" and all the practicing agents. As Michael Grenfell puts it, Bourdieu's reflexivity in his ethnographic methods leads him to use habitus and field "not only in analysing a particular context, but in analysing the construction of the analysis as it occurs."[29] The ethnographic field is not, for Bourdieu, something to be mined for information. Rather, it is a field of cultural production in which the ethnographer participates by taking strategic account of her own particular relationship to it. This is where Bourdieu's method opens up to ground my own.

Participant Objectification to Objectified Participation

While for Bourdieu the types of cultural production that the ethnographer facilitates must be generated as reflexive analysis of the relationship between her research habitus and her field of study, and not simply from any nascent bodily wisdom gained in site, his student Loïc Wacquant tries a slightly different approach—one that parallels and helps guide my own fieldwork at FBC. In order to study a boxing gym in Woodlawn (a Chicago ghetto) and the social world around it, Wacquant actually trained as a boxer, thus inculcating himself with a *pugilistic habitus*. In this way, he does not shift the conceptual meaning of habitus, as Bourdieu describes it. Habitus is still embodied history, constituted by and constitutive of social fields and practices. While radicalizing habitus, therefore, Wacquant does not follow Ortner's path in focusing on social slippage and change over social reproduction. Rather, he engages a process of apprenticeship by which the social structures of a boxing world become reproduced in his own flesh.

Wacquant describes himself as "repeat[ing] the same exercises to the saturation point," thus constituting not only his body but also his bodily knowledge: his intuitions, perceptions, and dispositions, for example, as a *boxer*.[30] This bodily constitution also facilitates social belonging as Wacquant settles into the community and receives multiple nicknames from his buddies (e.g., Fightin' Frenchman, brother Louie, the French Hammer, and the Black Frenchman), as well as a ring moniker, "Busy Louie." Each name indicates at least some measure of acceptance of him as a copugilist and, in various cases, friend. He even competes in a semipro tournament, "The Golden Gloves," losing the fight but still performing well. While it can be argued that Wacquant—a white, Harvard-educated French sociologist—never completely fits in at the gym; it is certainly the case that he does come to embody the habitus of his field to a startling degree, perhaps more so than any other sociological project has managed or even endeavored to do. So much more than participant observation or even objectification, Wacquant thus affects something more like an *objectified participation*.

Radicalizing the methodological uses of habitus, Wacquant did not just study the culture; he moved into it—fully. Indeed, like me he was (or, at least, was in the process of becoming) a member of his field of study before his study even began. Possessing and possessed by the habitus associated with both academic research *and* our fields of study, Wacquant and I both sought to produce knowledge generated at our competing and sometimes cohering habitus' intersection. In a way that likely worried his mentor, Wacquant therefore risked hurting his project's objectivity by relying heavily on his seemingly subjective knowledge. Loosely integrating his research and field habitus, rather than prioritizing the former over the latter, was risky by the standards of Wacquant's teacher's methodological praxis. Indeed, his risk and Bourdieu's concern are both evident as, in the midst of his fieldwork,

Wacquant writes in his notes: "PB [Pierre Bourdieu] was saying the other day that he's afraid that I'm 'letting myself be seduced by my object' but, boy, *if only he knew*: I'm already way beyond seduction!"[31] The risk, however, pays off. Despite some inevitable problems with Wacquant's ability to balance his various habitus with each other in practice, which I discuss later, his method nevertheless yields rich insight not only into what it is to be bodied boxer but also into the world that the boxer has access to see.

My hope in following Wacquant's path out of the epistemological problems Bourdieu outlines (while keeping Ortner's concerns in view as well) is, in part, to learn from the ways he mitigates that risk. Wacquant guards against the potential for subjective solipsism in his research by trying to avoid hinging his findings on the quality of his membership in the community (even if he does not always succeed at this): "Membership in a category or collective," he argues, "does not by itself make one a good anthropologist of it."[32] Indeed, as I found in my own ethnographic theological fieldwork, belonging to FBC had the potential to cloud my understanding of the community as much as, if not more than, illumine it. Therefore, my membership alone at best made me a good informant, not a good ethnographer.[33] One's social ties to a field of study cannot, therefore, warrant inquiry into it; only "the *theoretical problematic* that animates the inquiry" can do that, as Wacquant argues for ethnographic sociology.[34] In ethnographic theological contexts, I realized in my own theological fieldwork, the theoretical problematic can be intimately linked to the theological problematic, and both are crucial for constructing the modes of inquiry.

On the one hand, the theoretical problematic animating my inquiry related to questions of theological epistemology. I wanted, like Wacquant, to "take full epistemic advantage of the visceral nature of social life," not to do theology "*of* the body (as intelligible social product)," to borrow Wacquant's phrasing regarding his sociology, "but *from* the body (as intelligent social spring and vector of [theological] knowledge)."[35] Rather than mine knowledge out of the site, I sought to produce—or, better, coproduce—knowledge from my embodied location within it. Belonging to the field of study did not authorize my project, but reflexive analysis of that belonging could give rise to the methods I used for it. Here I followed the lineage that Wacquant draws out of Bourdieu's reflexive sociological interest in articulating the relationship between one's own habitus and the habitus associated with the field of study. Like Wacquant, I wanted to act, think, and write in ways generated not only by my research habitus. Despite

Bourdieu's warnings, and also like Wacquant, I wanted to act, think, and write in ways generated out of the habitus of my field of study. In what specific ways, I wondered, could the social roles I played within the site reshape modes of inquiry like participant observation and group interviews? And how does the nature of theology, in its disciplinary distinction from sociology, impact my particular habituation in those social roles?

On the other hand, my inquiry's theological problematic was related to this final theoretical question. I have already mentioned that I wanted to find a way to bring together everyday and academic modes of theological discourse into a conversation to produce fresh theological insights and new possibilities for Christian living. In other words, I sought a constructive theological method that could make visible the communal conversation out of which that theology arose. In terms of theology's practicality, I was more interested in the particular communal theological practices that give rise to theological constructions than any abstracted application of them. And so I didn't just want to create theory by asking epistemological questions about how theology works; I also wanted to put those theoretical findings *to work* to create theology out of a shared, communal practice. Alongside asking how my social roles might produce knowledge within the site, this theological problematic emphasized the coproduction of that knowledge; whatever theologies we created had to be created together and, to put it quite simply, they actually had to be created. (Chapters 3 through 5 provide some humble offerings of these communal theological constructions.)

In this way, and as the first chapter of this book demonstrates, I did not view everyday and academic theologies as comprising and comprised by utterly distinct fields of practice—as the now-proverbial language that articulates the need for theological texts, to "bridge church and academy" so often implies. Rather, I understood them to be different forms of discourse arising from overlapping fields of practice, all of which might converge in one socially positioned body: the academic theologian's or, more specifically, mine. In a more practical sense, I understood them to be words different speakers actually speak to each other, as happened in the classes I taught at FBC.

Objectified Participation in Church and Academy

Our next task, then, in a constructive theology done from my objectified participant position is, quite simply, to outline that objectification.

In this section, I tell two stories that occurred on and around the day I was ordained at FBC, a day that happened eight months before I began my study there. I reconstruct the stories not simply from memory but also out of journal notes I kept at the time both for personal recording and because I thought I might one day write a short piece on ordination. These journals did not reach the level of precision that I later employed in my ethnographic field notes, but they do help me grasp at describing the forms of theological agency I embodied, as well as the social roles I played as my church became my field of study. As will become clear in the second half of the story, I am engaging academic sources quite differently than they are usually engaged in academic writing.[36] Rather than use them in any disembodied way to interpret my experience, they too become embodied and objectified in the narrative. Academic practices, like all practices, are distinctly embodied in their own way. These stories try to capture that.

Your Sons and Daughters

And afterward, I will pour out my Spirit on all people. Your sons and *daughters* will prophesy.

—Joan, Member and Deacon at First Baptist
Church and member of my ordination committee

These words are probably best recognized as the prophet Joel's, but for me they are Joan's. They became hers when she laid her hands on me to whisper them in my ear during my ordination service in May 2009. Tracing the whole process by which my body became minister at FBC is beyond the scope of possibility, let alone this discussion. Still, this ordination service marks the ritual action by which my ministerial theological agency was formally recognized and bestowed. It narrates the way the relationship between my own theological habitus and the theological field is situated in FBC life.

It is my ordination service, and after hearing a number of speakers offer to me traditional "charges" (short addresses exhorting me to the various dimensions of ministry practice), we have arrived at the point in the liturgy where the Holy Spirit is invoked and physically communicated to the ordinand by the ordained clergy in attendance. I have been brought to the front and center in the sanctuary, facing the congregation; my body is in submission on a prayer kneeler, waiting for the hands to come. At FBC, like some other Baptist churches, we lay on hands for clergy ordination but we don't lay them all on at once. Joan is patient, taking her spot somewhere halfway down the aisle filled with ordained clergy (from multiple denominations), deacons, and my ordination committee, all waiting to lay hands on me one by one, and to whisper liturgical secrets in my ear.

This aisle is the same one opened at the end of every Sunday service for the altar call. It is the same aisle that I walked first to join the church and then to declare my call to Gospel Ministry a year and a half later. I have watched bridal processions walk this aisle, as well as processions of families bidding farewell to a loved one now deceased. Indeed, I have walked it to bid farewell in this way myself. We walk it to raise a point or motion for vote at business meetings. It is the aisle down which Pastor Frank carries babies to be dedicated so that everyone can see their cuteness. Many walk it simply to get to our seats on Sunday morning.

All the feet that have trod this aisle, carrying whispers or shouts or declarations of dedication, mourning, and hope have made this aisle sacred. It throbs with memories—not a single conglomerate memory to which the building bears witness but rather constellations of particular memories on, through, and around which an infinity of shared gazes flow. The aisle thus marks the liminal space of becoming in our sanctuary—that is, becoming saved, baptized, dedicated, a church member, or clergy. It marks the space of intention and of declaration that we are starting something new, even if that something new is so simple as attending a regular service.

Bent on my prayer kneeler and facing the gathered, I feel each hand grasp me differently—holding my head and my shoulders and wrapping arms fully around me to whisper words that become secrets in that only I hear them. Some whisper a prayer, some a charge. Others declare a gift they want to see me bring to my ministry. Some simply say, "Thank you." Some pray that justice would flow from my ministry, others pray for a flowing of knowledge and wisdom. One woman from my doctoral program, a Methodist minister, prays in a way I want to describe as *in the power of the Spirit*. Her body unleashes energy into mine in a way I find disarming yet enlivening. One man's lips brush my cheek and ear in a way that would lead a friend to comment later on the shocking intimacy of bodies enclosed together in a small space. Indeed, even without lips and ears and the moisture of breath, all this touch relies on a suspension of norms for bodily interaction that is rare in any form of ecclesial or everyday life.

Overwhelmed, yet on display, I work to hold myself together emotionally. My clergy covenant had included promises that I can no longer articulate with precise memory today but that I hope have become second nature to me, a part of my own embodied history.

I had received ministerial charges from my academic advisor, my spouse, a friend, a member of my ordination committee, and Pastor Frank, evoking altogether the numerous social worlds (academic, familial, ecclesial, etc.) that contribute to my calling. I had been caught up in words, gestures, and touches that delighted, challenged, and called me into a new way of being in the church and in the world. The day was emotionally intense, and yet I held it together. Not yet broken, I felt wholly bolstered by the gathered.

And then came Joan. Joan is in her seventies, yet she moves around the church with a force unparalleled in many of our youth. She is serious about women in ministry. Faith for her is inseparable from justice. Talking about the Transfiguration one time, as I mentioned in the first chapter, she laughed about how the disciples "wanted to stay on that mountain, make themselves 'an ol' boys club.' But Jesus said no. Those boys have got to get back down the mountain and get to the business of helping the people." Friends asked me afterward, "Who was the lady who made you cry?" "She visibly broke you," one commented. "It was like your body crumbled for a moment," said another. "There was no coming back from that."

When Joan leans in to me, at her full height standing not that much taller than me kneeling, I feel the sweat break through my makeup to meet her cheek as it rests on my forehead. A small note is pressed into her palm, which, unlike mine, is not shaking. As a deacon, Joan knows the ritual format well, and she has come prepared. She knows what she wants to say and she knows how she wants to say it: "I will pour out my Spirit on all people. Your sons . . . *and your daughters* . . . will prophesy," she whispers. Emphasizing the word "daughters" over "sons," her words envelop, inscribe, and gender my body with scripture. Her surprisingly performative speech act inaugurates me into a line of women seeking to live into Joel's eschatological promise. Right here. Right now. And then she is gone; the next hands find me.

Before the service, Pastor Frank had warned me not to stand too quickly at the end of this onslaught of hands. I would be emotionally exhausted and a little dizzy from being on my knees for so long. As Joan moves away, I realize how right he had been. The aisle is still full and I wonder if I will make it. Now people start sneaking tissues up in their hands to help me through the weepy, snotty mess my body tends to make in response to the Spirit's influx. At some point, I become aware that everyone who has laid hands on me has been slowly gathering behind me. Tyler, the first whisperer, my husband, and himself an ordained minister, still has his hand on me, now on the space between my shoulder blades, and everyone is connecting to him. The brokenness I experience with each whisper transports the whisperer to this growing shape unfolding from my back. Some fragmented set of imagistic words, scriptural words that must also be already inscribed in my fleshy memory, flashes across my imagination—"But those who hope in the Lord will renew their strength. They will soar on wings like eagles; they will run and not grow weary, they will walk and not be faint" (Isaiah 40:31). And I feel the bodies fanning from my back, stretching out across the sanctuary, as this promise of wings that will bear me up into ministry.

When I stand, that promise is kept. As I mount the steps to the communion table to preside my first Lord's Supper, I sense these wings making me light. I take a deep breath, place my hands onto the table, and feel a jolt of gleeful surprise at the transformation's effect. *My hands feel different.* They feel full of power infused into them by the trail of hands that blessed them to this place. I have been broken, cracked open, to make room for their power to pulse and leap, like sparks of electricity, back and forth between the bread, cup, and my hands—and then back again to those who were, as one friend put it, loaning it to me for this occasion. By submitting to their authority to ordain me, I was made into someone whose preaching and teaching now had authority for them.

Joan's hands participated in ordaining me, but she also subsequently took both of the classes I taught. Indeed, this service was filled with class members. They spoke, laid their hands on, offered the church's charge, and brushed lips against my cheek. The sparks of power that traversed my flesh and then were caught to be held for a moment in my hands did not flow one way. They were passed back and forth among us, gathering energy, coming to life, and functioning differently around our different subject positions and the ways we take them up. Power, indeed, I realized as my hands touched the table, is difficult to pin down.

Bolstered by Brokenness

And yet, for me, it was an experience of being bolstered by brokenness.

—Natalie, Ordained Minister at First Baptist Church
and Doctoral Student at Vanderbilt Divinity School

The day after my ordination, a feminist theologian friend who had helped me discern my call is eager to hear how things had gone. Still feeling emotionally spent, I sit in my favorite chair in my living room and dial her number. We had originally become friends through our shared bond as self-identified former evangelicals who couldn't quite shake all the ways that tradition's traces remain in us—both for ill and for good. I begin to try to explain to her this experience of "brokenness," a language common to both of our former faith lives.

I am aware, I tell her, of the feminist implications of brokenness imagery, especially when it is experienced in such a bodily manner, and especially when it is inflicted on me by a barrage of people who, despite the presence of Joan and a few other women, are mostly a band of white men with churchy authority.[37] Pacing the living room now, I feel my energy return. "And yet," I continue, "it was beautiful." As feminists, we value empowerment, emancipation, and wholeness. Yet despite the various anxieties and ambivalences I feel around my role as a Southern Baptist minister, I would be hard pressed to recall a time when I felt stronger, more free, and more full than I did in those moments that only violent metaphors seem apt to describe. It was, for me, I tell her, a shocking moment of being "bolstered by brokenness."

We toss this "bolstered by brokenness" image around for a few minutes, wondering how as academic feminist theologians we might make sense of these experiences of power in submission that we know with such bodily intimacy.[38] The very set of academic habitus that made me question my experience of submission now come to my aid. Indeed, the academic instincts and dispositions I have come to embody over time are crucial for helping me reconfigure these nascent tensions into a new way of being, as well as into a new understanding of that being.

Michel Foucault has shown us the disservice we do our interpretations of sociality when we imagine power to be located solely in a monarchic figure—like a church's pastor—and not to be constellating between and accruing to myriad subject positions and their ways of being taken up within a social system.[39] And because my academic habitus has made Foucault's vision of constellated power feel second nature to me, when I tell my story to my friend I intuitively imagine those constellations mapped over all the bodies in the sanctuary, mine included. But still, the twin habitus of critical engagement and systematic thinking that get deployed by my academic enculturation both nudged me in tandem: What was it about that submission that brought me *pleasure*? What gave me that jolt of glee? As I hang up the phone, I tiredly amble into my home office, turning to my shelves for an answer.

My fingers traverse the books' spines, resting at a volume by Michel de Certeau.[40] My hands—the power from the communion table still in them, but perhaps fading to a trace, now slowly becoming second nature—begin leafing through pages, searching. Certeau, drawing on

Foucault and Bourdieu, describes the role of power, submission, and desire in the inscription of habitus into a body. Notes I have scribbled in margins over multiple readings draw my eyes' attention. My hands slow down as I reach a section where tentative penciled underlines become punctuated with confident pen: the script of the system that gives us our identity "would have no power if it were not able to support itself on the obscure desire [that one has] to exchange one's flesh for a glorious body, to be written, even if it means dying, and to be transformed into a recognized word."[41] We long to be named by particular social systems, Certeau claims, and so we all—pastors, congregants, and ordinands alike—submit to these systems to let them give us our identity. I begin grafting his words on to the words of my ordination covenant, both now digging into my flesh.

Certeau's language, like mine, is unavoidably violent. The process of being made legible within the practices of a social system requires dying to the possibility—always a delusional possibility—of self-determination outside of that system. But we always belong to multiple communities. I can never perform my ecclesial role apart from my academic, just as my academic role is always shaped by my ecclesial. Both are reaching toward some sort of loose and tense integration or, at least, cooperation with each other. Along with all the other roles I play in life (sister, friend, lover, etc.), these two create tension for subtle forms of resistance in the midst of my submission within various fields of practice. The tension between roles, therefore, does not dissolve; rather, it ignites my desire to continue searching, each role pressing the other deeper into pursuit of an object I cannot quite name. I pull one of Bourdieu's volumes off my shelf and, sitting on my office floor, begin leafing through both texts, comparing underlined passages, finding new ones I hadn't noticed before, and feeling the deep integration of these two writers coming together in my hands.

I find a note I have scribbled that maps Bourdieu's habitus as a middle path between the radically free subjectivism of Jean-Paul Sartre's existentialism and the overly deterministic objectivism of Claude Lévi-Strauss's structuralism.[42] Certeau describes this compromised path as a violent clash because the habitus is written onto, even inscribed into, the flayed flesh of the subject. Freedom is always already shaped by the structures that make, and remake, us. The wisdom of habitus, for which we long, extracts a payment of something like a death to self from us when we receive it. We must be continually broken to be made continually new. Certeau's language appears unapologetically theological next to Bourdieu's. Perhaps this is why he draws my desire closer, especially in this moment when the habitus associated with my ministerial and academic forms of theological agency are demanding answers from each other.

Certeau's insight, when considered in relation to my ordination story, reveals that the ritual in which we all participated could have no power, meaning, or effect if we all did not desire to bear its power, meaning, and effect in our bodies. The hands that the ministers and deacons lay on me carry this power because they were instituted by the community to do so. That power is now transported into my hands, which are now also instituted to carry it further. Named "Reverend" by the ritual, I continue to bear the ordination power back not only to the people who gave it and on to others but also back into the institution itself that grants it. This power "is channeled and instrumented," continues Certeau, helping me see that in this situation—in an echo of my friend's idea that it is loaned to me—the way I hold the power of ordination is always turned into something that the broader ecclesial system can use and then channeled by that system for that use.[43] The institution shapes the power; the institution decides where the power will go.

As I grapple to understand my ecclesial role, my various academic habitus reveal the image I need. Put simply, and utterly unromantically, the institutional machine (of this particular ecclesial community) empowers me to be a cog that enables its own flourishing. Somehow, in the midst of all the ways my desire is constructed and made to want to resist this system, *I also find myself wanting to be this cog*. Belonging to this church in this way creates the space for me to perform my academic role within it fruitfully, precisely because I have the bodily wisdom required to know what the system can and cannot absorb and use. I can participate in and guide conversations that otherwise might not happen. And this realization begins nurturing the seeds that will flower into my ethnographic theological methods.

Still sitting on my office floor, my lower back begins to ache from the hard surface. But I continue to compare texts and marginalia, each of which reveals an outworking spiral of conversation partners: Certeau is not making Bourdieu's notion of habitus more deterministic. No, his descriptions outline a fuller sense of subjective agency than Bourdieu's. I lean back on my elbows to relieve the pressure from my back and take it all in. Perched there, I recall Ortner's critique that in Bourdieu's scheme, agents were mostly seen to reproduce the structures that shaped their habitus in a largely unconscious way, and I lean forward quickly to pull her text down from my shelf too. I am no longer aware of the pain in my back. Indeed, I feel pleasure now at the idea of incorporating Ortner into my process; it does not feel right to let two men alone define the structure of a game inspired by a feminist conversation, no matter how much I love their theories.

Certeau describes the process by which agents experience their reproduction of these structures *and* the way they cause slippage within them, both according to modes of resistance and submission. He writes, "The only force opposing this passion to be a sign," meaning the only force that can disrupt our desires to simply reproduce the power of the institution's meaning in our bodies, "is the cry, a deviation or an ecstasy, a revolt or flight of that which, within the body, escapes the law of the named."[44]

I stand up and stretch, feeling my left hip crack, then I make my way to my desk to grab some paper and a pen. I want to diagram this out by hand before I even consider trying to type coherent sentences. I scan Ortner's pages again: she reminds me that there is a relationship between reproduction and transformation that occurs in moments of difference and slippage. I draw the church on my page, and place myself within it. I try to capture an image of the way its structures shape my various habitus and the way those habitus shape my ecclesial, ministerial role. I draw multiple, densely overlapping arrows from the church directly into my sketch of my body, which is represented by a little blob with an *N* in the center because I'm not all that good at drawing. As I attempt to draw my mutual shaping of the church's social structures, I realize only one arrow, maybe two, is enough for capturing the power of my presence therein. I read Certeau's line again. There is a surplus, a moment of ecstasy, an almost masochistic, involuntary utterance of both protest and pleasure that erupts from the agent's lips as she is wounded by the inscription of habitus into her flesh. "Yes," I think, "that's how I felt it." That's the shocking glee of my hands receiving power.

I move to my keyboard and begin to type. Longing, wounding, ecstasy, and desire come together as the subject is made and remade for the purpose of the institution's use, but also as she resists that making—while one's resistance to being made is always also inextricably wrapped up with one's submission to it. It is this inextricable blend of resistance and submission, as well as the spontaneous cry that erupts from somewhere between the two, that characterizes agency for Certeau and, in some way now, as I read him, for me. Despite my belonging at FBC, there are numerous aspects of who I am that the broader institutional structure would not want to integrate. The tension between the markings of my gender, racialized, sexual, and religious identities—as well as many of my political and theological views—position me as something atypical, an anomaly within a system I have been constituted to serve.

I am an exception helping to prove the rule, and my presence is possible because others with power within the system let it be.

THE MAKINGS OF AN ETHNOGRAPHIC THEOLOGICAL METHOD

My experiences are not normative for other academic theologians, and certainly not prescriptive. By accounting for the processes by which my own ecclesial and academic forms of theological agency became loosely integrated in my own embodiment, I hope that others might find a way to do it better. At the same time, accounting for this process has objectified me—an ordained, academic theologian, committed to and submitted to regimes of both church and academy, shaped in multiple social positions that exist within and beyond a theological field of practice—as a character in this ethnographic theology. Moreover, it has objectified me as a somewhat ambiguous character, one who experiences moments of vocational ambivalence, variously alienated and delighted by my theological tasks. This is an attempt to articulate the utter lack of neutrality with which we academic theologians begin our academic labor. In this section I ask what type of theological agency—and, by extension, which ethnographic theological method—rises from the particular nature of this hybrid ecclesial and academic visceral knowledge.

These stories of ordination and reading demonstrate how both ecclesial and academic fields of practice—each of which intersects with a theological field of practice—constitute my theological agency, as my theological agency also contributes to the constitution of all these fields. As embodied histories, transposable between the two fields, and participant in social reproduction and change within each, the particular hybridity of my agency—the ways in which it is constructed by multiple competing and cohering habitus—makes possible a theological ethnographic method performed through the practice of ecclesial teaching. Such a method has the potential to bring together everyday and academic forms of theological knowledge for the purpose of constructing fresh theological perspectives and new possibilities for Christian living—a potential that subsequent constructive theological chapters will test.

Theological Agency as Embodied Histories of Church and Academy

The inscribing of habitus into flesh takes time. Indeed, I describe the rituals of ordination and academic reading here to capture only snapshots of much longer temporal processes. The practices that produce a habitus, and that a habitus produces, must be repeated until they become embodied history. The hands that trudged the aisle to break me open and make me minister bore their power because each was embedded in a history of shared social and religious practices, as well as a broader history in which those practices make sense. They made me minister because they could bear aspects of our shared social world into me. Much in the same way, the pages of my academic books—which have been read, reread, and filled with competing scripts of marginal notes—compose a textual artifact narrating how I have slowly and, indeed, partially come to embody the intellectual histories contained therein. Each scribble recalled a grappling with the ideas, trying to make them my own by writing my responses along their edges. They offer a textual artifact of the process by which my body has been *made* academic. The touch of hands and pages thus evoke the social, intellectual, and bodily histories of church and academy, and how those worlds have been made incarnate in my flesh.

Moreover, this inscription of habitus into flesh as embodied history brings both pain and pleasure. Wacquant's apprenticeship reveals the willingness to endure discomfort and pain to receive the prize of bodily knowledge. Even in the midst of declarations such as "This is killing me! I can't feel my right wrist or shoulders anymore," he continues to perform painful moves because he knows the pleasure of the "right sound against the mitt" will fill him with the motivating desire to "hit harder next time."[45]

While ordination is not so overtly physical a practice as boxing, as my exhausted submission at the prayer kneeler gives way to a sense of visceral pleasure like rising up on eagle's wings, we see a symbolic reconstruction of how forms of submission to the life of FBC inculcate me with types of knowledge that can relieve, and even bring pleasure out of, the pain. Social conventions of church life, programmed into me through years of participation in it, tell me intuitively that standing up to relieve the physical pain of kneeling will break the aura of the moment. Indeed, standing up never even presents itself as an option to imagination, as that movement would be so foreign to this context and moment. In this world, the willingness to be vulnerable before the gathered can yield blessing, as Certeau reminded me with regards to my baptismal vows: new life is not available without some type of death. Kneeling at the front of the church, or even crouched in front of bookshelves, exacerbating the back problems I have developed through the academic practice of spending countless hours in front of a computer, I endure physical discomfort to win the prize each institution has to offer. In so doing, I come to—and long to—embody the cultural fields in which I participate more deeply.

Finally, the inscription of habitus into flesh as embodied history creates a form of social belonging. Wacquant describes participating in a broad set of cultural practices through which he, as a French, white, Harvard-educated academic, gains access to a predominantly African American, working-class, urban environment. Key to this process of acceptance is the fact that Wacquant originally joined the gym "as a run of the mill trainee, ostensibly to learn the rudiments of the sport."[46] It was not until a year into his training that he decided to begin studying the gym formally, thus requiring his "sociological coming out."[47] By this time, the guys knew him as a buddy, not an objectifying sociological gazer. As Wacquant describes it, they "never really cared and rarely remembered that [he] pursued a research project."[48]

Similarly, I belonged to FBC long before my study began. And while this belonging could not animate the theoretical and theological problematics of my study, it certainly gifted me with the forms of access and trust that were required to pull off the ecclesial teaching practices that composed the bulk of my ethnographic theological fieldwork. Like Wacquant's initial writing about boxing, my diary entries of the ecclesial ritual were recorded primarily for the purposes of personal memory keeping. It is true that I had a vague sense I might one day write a short piece on ordination, but to the best of my self-understanding, the diary was not kept as surreptitious field notes for a large-scale project. Indeed, as mentioned in the Introduction, when I initially proposed using ethnography for my dissertation research method, I had named my fieldwork site as a yet to be determined "alternative" Christian community. I had not considered that I might find an interesting knot of questions to explore in a place I already called home.

And so, like Wacquant, I found the particular bodily dimensions of belonging to open up unexpected methodological possibilities for pursuing my research questions. Suddenly I realized I had the type of access that allowed me not merely to write theory that I imagined could bridge a so-called church-academy divide; rather, because my bodily knowledge already bridged these fields of practice, my bodily agency was able to integrate the two in a communal theological practice.

However, there are also dangers entailed with this belonging and trust, as I discuss throughout the constructive theological chapters of this book. The types of unquestioned trust extended to Wacquant by his gym buddies were also extended to me in my site. For example, when I asked Pastor Frank if I could conduct my fieldwork at FBC, he responded enthusiastically. I tried to explain ethical review boards and the potential for harm when it comes to working with human subjects. But he kindly dismissed my concerns by stating, "It's OK, we trust you." We went back and forth, with me articulating gratitude for that trust while also trying to explain the need for accountability. I tried to tell him how easy it would be for me to mistake my love for the people at FBC as facilitating an automatic link to my awareness of how to conduct myself ethically, but he insisted that everything would be OK: "We trust you," he said, again and again. Looking back, I wish I had had the courage to put it bluntly: "Yes, but I don't know if I trust myself!" My deep belonging in the community therefore gave me a dubious gift: the absolute freedom of ethical self-oversight.

The Transposable Nature of Homologous Habitus

Despite these affinities between Wacquant's methods and my own, there are also some key differences. Previously I mentioned how Wacquant does not shift the conceptual meaning of habitus, but rather shifts the location of the habitus studied to his own flesh. Still bound by an apprenticeship model, however, Wacquant enacts social reproduction more than the social change for which Ortner calls, and that I also wish to pursue in terms of Christian theological knowledge and practice. While Certeau's vision of submission and resistance cautions us against imagining with Ortner too utopian an outcome for any theological method, I should nevertheless account here for how my own apprenticeship in church and academy allows me to take up multiple social positions within a larger theological field of practice with a type of field coherence that is not available to Wacquant in his study.

The reason my methods open onto a possibility not inherent in Wacquant's is not because of any skill on my part (indeed, Wacquant is unquestionably a better ethnographer than I am). Rather, the reason my methods open up in ways that Wacquant's do not is because of a peculiarity of difference between sociological and theological forms of ethnography. Whereas there are few homologies between the habitus related to pugilistic and sociological knowledge, we have already seen—in the previous chapter, and in this one—numerous homologies and potential for organic transposition between the habitus related to ecclesial and academic theological knowledge, both within everyday and academic theological constructions.

Wacquant's reflexive attention to the making of his subjective knowledge objectifies his view of himself as embodying the field of study. Yet this view is not perfect, as critics have observed.[49] As

Richard Lloyd, an expert in urban sociologies, argues, Wacquant tends to overidentify with his buddies in the gym in ways that eclipse his various forms of symbolic, cultural and economic capital. Lloyd's chief concern with these "distortions" is that they gloss over questions of privilege in the site.[50] This is a valid and important critique, but what interests me about this dynamic is how it also glosses over Wacquant's academic role. As Lloyd notes, disruptions to Wacquant's pugilistic regime and gym relationships caused by his academic study of them are rarely observable. Enacting this disappearing act requires more than just hiding the academic role, however; Wacquant actually works to malign it.

One particularly dramatic articulation of his sense of belonging to the community at Woodlawn demonstrates this. Wacquant excerpts the following from his field notes into a prominent textual footnote:

> I'm at the point where I tell myself that I'd gladly give up my studies and research and all the rest to be able to stay here and box, to remain "one of the boys". I know that's completely crazy and surely unrealistic but, at this very moment, I find the idea of migrating to Harvard, of going to present a paper at the ASA, . . . and participating in the *tutti frutti* of academe totally devoid of meaning and downright depressing, so dreary and dread compared to the pure and vivacious carnal joy that this goddamn gym provides me . . . that I would like to quit everything, drop out, to stay in Chicago.[51]

This passage is telling, as on the surface it asserts the primacy—if not exclusivity—of the pugilistic disciplinary regime for producing Wacquant's pleasure. Unwilling to admit any sense of exclusion at the gym, because doing so could undermine the extent to which he fully embodies the pugilistic habitus, Wacquant projects all his feelings of alienation onto the academic field. As a result, the academic disciplinary regime that he already embodies and bears into the pugilistic field is obscured, distorting the text by occluding the positive role that academic embodiment plays in the pleasure he experiences.

Therefore, when Wacquant overidentifies himself as "one of the boys," he eclipses the methodologically interesting ways in which his academic and pugilistic habitus are working together to make his project possible. While boxing reveals the carnal gaps in his academic pleasure, it also seems that his analytical enjoyment of boxing is enhanced by the intellectual pleasures of observing and charting the process of pugilistic submission. The complexity of his theoretical positions, paired with the exuberance of his prose, even when that prose is excerpted from field notes, make it difficult to imagine Wacquant ever wholly thinking of academia as mere "*tutti frutti* . . . totally devoid of meaning and downright depressing." His enjoyment of the gym is inseparable from the academic habitus he brings to it.

The theologian committed to church and academy likely knows this tension of roles well. The clash between my ordination ritual and my feminist theological interpretations of it is intended to reveal the complex overlap of these two social worlds at the site of my own body. And so, like Wacquant, numerous times during my study, I found myself wanting to abandon what felt like rigid academia for my (at times vastly overidealized vision of) church. But as I have already noted numerous times, and as should become more evident in the constructive theological chapters of this book, I also experience alienation at FBC. The hybridity of my belonging allowed imaginative flights of fancy from one field to the other when the other tired me out—or rather, the constitution of my habitus sometimes synced better with and, thus, felt more natural in one field over the other. Like Wacquant, I maintain academia as my primary vocation. Put somewhat crassly, it's what pays the bills. Unlike Wacquant, my longer track record with the church taps me into its brokenness (and my own) in a way he seems not to experience with boxing; my field of study cannot wholly seduce me. Indeed, this is where the methodological possibilities inherent in Wacquant's form of belonging begin to differ from mine, creating a space from which ethnographic theologies might have something to speak back to the sociological ethnographies on which we tend to draw.

In sum, there are no crucial homologies between the academic habitus with which Wacquant enters his field of study and the habitus that he comes to embody within that field. A sociologist and a boxer are two radically different things, as the fields of practice that constitute each social role bear little organic connection to each other. There are, however, crucial homologies among the habitus associated with ecclesial and academic theological communities. Of course, there are divergences, as well. But as we saw in the first chapter, these fields are deeply intertwined historically, socially, intellectually, and practically in ways that create overlap in the moods, motivations, and dispositions each produces. All of us who participated in the classes I taught at FBC are therefore *made* theologian by similar historical trajectories of thought and practice, even as the character of my theological agency is shaped by other intersecting academic practices as well.

Whereas Wacquant describes his gym buddies as utterly confused by what a sociologist does, the people who took the classes I taught at FBC have imaginative space to understand my day job. As Kathryn Tanner argues, academic theology is an extension of everyday theology. Consequently, what I do in the academic field makes some sort of sense to the people with whom I worked in the ecclesial field.[52] Indeed, as we saw in the first chapter, these two fields of practice converge in a theological field that does not fully contain—and is not fully contained by—either one. The people who took the classes I taught at FBC and I are both doing different versions of the same thing. We might even say that I have made a career out of the way we all live.

Therefore, where Wacquant's academic position and privilege risks disrupting his sense of belonging at the gym, so much so that it must be hidden or maligned, the types of academic privilege that have accrued to me can be sanctioned and harnessed by my field of study for its own use—as was evident in my narratives of self-objectification discussed earlier. And because the institution ultimately channels the ways in which I do and do not belong to it for its own use, these disruptions and exclusions need be neither hidden nor maligned. Indeed, they become the fulcrum of my method. The type of ethnographic theology I am doing here is a process that begins in the theologian's own body and, in so doing, it welcomes academic theological practices into the ecclesial theological field (with limitations, of course), with the potential to reshape both.

Social Reproduction versus Social Change

Both Wacquant and I come to embody our fields of study as a form of second nature. Yet because the ways our fields of study intersect with our academic fields differ, so too do the forms of agency that arise from our structured, second nature. To put it simply, whereas Wacquant participated in his field of study as apprentice, I participated in mine as authority. As apprentice, Wacquant was better situated to follow Bourdieu's focus on social reproduction because he needed to submit to the field entirely. As authority—even with that authority granted by those in relation to whom I had it—I was better situated at least to try to follow Ortner's focus on moments of slippage and social change because, as objectified participant, I had the power to create them.

The differences between his academic and pugilistic habitus meant that Wacquant could participate in his field of study first as a novice and later with greater levels of competence. But his academic habitus never afforded him a status of expert or professional within the boxing field. Academic theologians who participate in church life, however, do so with some measure of expert or professional status—even though the validity or significance of that status might sometimes be questioned. In Wacquant's narrative, he submits to an authority to be shaped and molded by it. But Wacquant's training at the gym made him a boxer, not a trainer of boxers or a gym owner. Alternatively, my ordination ritual demonstrates my submission to being shaped by an authority that, crucially, makes me an authority for it. Paired with my academic training, these practices make me into the type of theologian whose teaching has power to contribute to the shape of our communal life. Throughout the remainder of this text, I pay attention to the ways in which that power was qualified, as well as how I exercised it, in order to continue to make visible the types of power dynamics playing out between my research partners and me.

This meant that the ways in which Wacquant and I both experienced a certain sort of "feel for the game" in our fields of study also differed. Wacquant's study by necessity focuses on the reproduction of boxing norms in his own body. Moments of slippage required correction so that Wacquant could adhere more closely to the rules of the game. Indeed, because his field was boxing, when Wacquant failed to follow instructions, he found himself physically hurt. There was certainly some room for improvisation and play within this structure, but not much. The theological field functions, or at least has the potential to function, differently. While slippage can certainly entail pain within the ecclesial field (as anyone who has felt or been exiled from a church home for no longer complying with its core beliefs knows well), in the classes I taught, we strove for expressing and cultivating some measure of theological difference. In most cases, when I asked participants why they enrolled in the course, they would respond with some version of wanting to hear the diversity of what people in the church believed. Debate was valued—within certain parameters, of course—which I explore more in subsequent chapters. Certainly we participated in a reproduction of theological norms, but we also sought to create moments for slippage and change where we challenged each other into something new.

This potential for change was again related to the differences between how Wacquant and I were able to direct practice in our different fields of study. Boxing skills, Wacquant notes, "are handed down like clothes in a large family."[53] The strict hierarchy of expertise values mimesis over creative reinterpretation.[54] Moreover, each boxer knows—or, through practice, comes to know—where their position is in that hierarchy. Once again, the relationship between everyday and academic theology functions—or, at least, has the potential to function—differently. Neither academic nor everyday theology can be seen properly as being in hierarchical relation *over* the other. Rather, as we saw in the first chapter, they compose a field of practices, each of which has goods to offer to the other and their shared work of shaping and reshaping Christian thought and action. Indeed, part of the argument of this book is that academic theologians are in error when we believe that our writings are inherently more valuable than everyday musings, and that they should be passed (or, trickled, as some put it) *down to the pews.* As I frame it here, the role of the professional theologian is not to create ideas that will *trickle down*; rather, as an academic theologian, I endeavored in the classes I taught to use my facility with a theological terrain to help us all negotiate our movement within that terrain together.

Ecclesial Teaching Practices

In closing, I want to outline a little how my ecclesial and academic forms of theological agency were loosely integrated—to varying degrees of success—in the practice of ecclesial teaching. The remaining chapters will outline the kinds of constructive theology made possible by this particular approach to ethnographic theological methods. I have already noted how my academic skill in systematic theology helped me chart pathways within discussions, and how my sense for the FBC game gave me embodied understanding of the terrain within which those pathways could be traversed. This helped me discern which ghosts I thought should be exorcised from and which saints should be incorporated into our community, as I described it previously in this chapter. Perhaps just as important, if not more so, my embodied feel for the ecclesial and academic games (as each came together in the practice of teaching) could raise my awareness when I had done something wrong in the classroom.

For example, on the first night the class met, I forgot to open our time together with prayer. When I arrived in the room, I was quite nervous. I was hoping for eight participants, figuring that I could still teach the class and conduct my research through it if I got five. Less than five, and I would have to abandon my research project. My mind was fixated on numbers as I walked through the door to find more than twenty participants. Seeing all these bodies in chairs, I was simultaneously elated and terrified. As the youngest person in the room, I felt my confidence wane that I could have anything to teach the gathered. My heart fluttering, and palms a little sweaty, I dove straight into introductions and my lesson plan. In other words, in a moment of nervousness, I leaned through my academic theological agency into my practice slightly more than I leaned through my ministerial theological agency.

While everything was running smoothly and everyone seemed to be enjoying themselves, I felt a nagging suspicion that something wasn't quite right. About midway through class, I realized what it was: I had forgotten to open our time together with prayer. In my nervousness, I had lost track of the fact that no meeting, no class, no service, and no meal begins at FBC without a prayer. But my body remembered, producing the sense of a tap at my shoulder, calling me to recall what I already knew. That night, I closed the meeting with prayer, and each night hence, I made sure to invite someone to open us with prayer. My momentary leaning into the space through my more academic teaching instincts—which lead me to start a class with introductions and pithy questions to get to know each other, rather than any invitation for the Spirit's presence—found a deeper integration with the ecclesial.

Despite the ways in which my academic teaching practice occasionally clashed with an ecclesial teaching practice, it was nevertheless crucial for what we accomplished together in the classroom. Beyond simply knowing how to structure a lesson to integrate theory with practice and to make space for personal and experiential exploration, my teaching had a number of less-than-conscious components to it honed through more academic classroom settings, for example. I could unconsciously scan the room to track eye movements, people checking their watches, shifting in their seats, or thumbing through their Bibles distractedly in ways that communicated boredom, frustration, confusion, and shyness. Some intuition usually kicked in during these moments so I could shift us to a new topic, clarify a controversial point or an unclear one, or invite a quiet person into discussion. In most cases, I did not need to think consciously through the steps that needed to be taken to do this. If this intuitive response failed, I felt that failure acutely as I struggled to get us back on track. In these cases, my unconscious checking of the bodies in the space became more conscious.

At the same time, teaching systematic and historical theological topics in the ecclesial, rather than academic, environment revealed the "carnal gaps" in my academic knowledge; it is not that ecclesial teaching is so much more radically embodied than academic teaching, but rather that the personal, concrete specific dimensions of texts that I have primarily read and reread through academic eyes became more evident in this ecclesial milieu. For example, Beatrice of Nazareth's ecstatic practices were reframed for me through the lens of one class member's meditative gardening practices. Neo-Platonic and pseudo-Dionysian trajectories in her writing thus faded a little from my radar as I began to encounter Beatrice as a model for faith rather than a significant figure in the history of Christian thought.

Despite the pleasures of this deepened insight, however, it should be noted that I also found it difficult to teach texts in these ways. I found we would lose a sense of the texts' and figures' systematic coherence, which led me to worry that I was undermining appropriate interpretations of them—perhaps a distinctly academic concern. This happened, for example, when I tried to nuance Luther's view of sanctification in light of his stronger focus on justification. To my dismay, for the rest of the semester class members talked about how "Luther didn't care about sanctification." Each time someone said this I would feel an inward wince. What felt like failures would make me work harder, trying to integrate a more nuanced view of sanctification into class members' everyday understanding of it, and to develop all the integrative dimensions of our conversation so we could create fresh and messy—but perhaps, I was surprised to learn of my own desires, not too messy—hybrid everyday/academic theological insights together.

My teaching practice thus loosely integrates the various habitus I have come to embody through participation in various ecclesial, academic, and theological fields (as well as multiple other habitus related to my class, gender, sexuality, ability, etc.). And in that, it contributes to the ongoing shaping and reshaping of those fields. Moreover, it invites—and, because of the forms of power that accrue to the particular ministerial and academic roles I play, at times directs—the ways in which the class members also contribute to that shaping and reshaping. Yes, Miriam's words from the beginning of this chapter overstate my power somewhat when she says that I made people into theologians by asking a question. Nevertheless, when I asked theological questions in our class, I did participate in their ongoing making and being made as theologians, as they participated in my own processes of the same.

In this way I had the power to interrupt and disrupt the doxa and normative patterns of everyday theology within our shared life, as well as to redirect those patterns toward what I hoped were more flourishing and liberative ends. If this sounds manipulative, I would argue that it is simply a more direct, interpersonal, and even responsible mode of doing what it is that academic theologians imagine the texts we write might do—that is, influence Christian belief and practice. As we see in subsequent chapters, the interpersonal dynamics make my methods ethically fraught at times. But again, I would argue that what they actually do is bring to visibility the assumptions already at play when we hope a text we write will reshape Christian practice. The difference with the more immediate engagement of ecclesial life that my particular ethnographic theological method makes possible is not only that it opens academic theology to be shaped and reshaped by everyday theologies but also that it makes the ways this is already happening in our various contexts more visible. Without the distance afforded by lobbing a textual missive into "the pews"—whether we anticipate that book being read by churchgoers, or whether we anticipate the "trickle down" effect I seek to nuance in previous discussion—our group had to negotiate theological difference between everyday and academic modes of reasoning in community through our shared practice. We had to do it face-to-face.

My academic theological knowledge—by its nature already shaped by similar trajectories that shaped my field of study but also somewhat foreign to it—could help me nurture potential for growth and change already brewing within the community. I could help tease out implications of the more ad hoc, intuitive statements spoken by my conversation partners; draw systematic connections between them; historicize them in ways that both revealed the doxa undergirding them; and open them up for further reflection. This reflection, I hoped, would help us reimagine some of our shared practices together. At the same time, my conversation partners' everyday reasoning and storytelling grounded my flights toward abstraction in ways that not only shaped my Christian living but also enriched my understanding of the theological ideas. It helped reveal to me a different kind of doxa—that is, the academic presumptions by which I treat texts as texts, rather than as artifacts of practical activity. As mentioned earlier, rather than reflecting *on* Christian community or *on* Christian practice, my burgeoning ethnographic theological methods helped highlight the aspects of doing theological reflection *in* Christian community and *as* Christian practice.

Part II

Chapter 3

Cogs in the Machine

A Reflexive Theology of Ecclesial Change

Situated in downtown Nashville, First Baptist Church (FBC) frequently finds itself in the middle of city events. So in the summer of 2009, the church decided to take evangelistic advantage of the annual Fourth of July parades. We printed what is typically referred to as "the plan of salvation" on hundreds of Frisbees, which volunteers then handed out with bottled water to the sweaty masses who passed by our doorstep. While many in our community lauded this salvation strategy, others (myself included) were, for varying reasons, either dubious or even outright disdainful of it. As Miriam put it, "Anything that fits on the back of a Frisbee, it's just not complicated enough to build a life around." A graspable set of rules to order one's existence (something that can fit on the back of a Frisbee) can be attractive to many. We find that desire, or at least one like it, in all churches, organizations, institutions, and even the academy. But the group of thirty-plus church members at FBC who took the Sunday night theology classes that I taught consistently articulated a desire for more than the Frisbee's list (which is, of course, itself a particular theology). Or, better put, they wanted to keep wrestling with what the Frisbee says. As Miriam put it, "We all know the rules, but no one picks apart the rules." The people who came to our Sunday night classes, it seemed, didn't necessarily want to break those rules; they just wanted to pick them apart.

In this chapter, we continue imagining how academic theology can intervene in the everyday to help with this picking apart of the rules, to reassemble them and perhaps, even, to aid the production of something new out of them. To do so, I construct a reflexive ecclesiology—that is, an ecclesiology constructed using the objectified participation methods outlined in the previous chapter. To ensure that reflexivity, I follow Wacquant's work, endeavoring, like him, not to slip into autoethnography, a form of subjectivist ethnography that largely focuses the ends of its research on the internal workings of the researcher herself. Therefore, neither I nor any one of my research partners is the main character of this chapter. Rather, the main character is FBC itself, complete with the complexity of its workings. We pay attention to the ways in which my research partners and I contribute to those workings with our shared labor so that my "socialized body" can provide "a visceral knowledge of the universe under scrutiny."[1]

I also try to maintain appropriate reflexivity by endeavoring to avoid the type of reflexivity that characterizes poststructuralist or postmodern anthropologies. As Wacquant points out, this reflexivity is concerned appropriately with analyzing the researcher's biases, but unfortunately it stops there. Subjectivist anthropologists, he argues, deploy epistemic reflexivity only at the beginning of the project (to isolate bias) or at the end (in the final report's drafting).[2] But a project is only truly reflexive when it is reflexive from start to finish: "From the selection of the site and the recruitment of informants to the choice of questions to pose or to avoid, as well as the engagement of theoretic schemata, methodological tools and display techniques."[3] I seek to understand my own subjective responses and biases in relation to the action I analyze, not merely to evaluate those biases but rather to construct theoretical, theological, and methodological apparatuses that provide me with a "way of elucidating the praxeology of the agents under examination."[4] Expanding our focus beyond the classes I taught in this chapter thus allows me also to position how our Sunday night group functioned in relation to the broader ecclesial system as well.

I therefore describe disagreements and debates in this chapter in which, for the most part, I participated directly during my time at FBC. They are recorded from worship times, prayer meetings I attended, and committee meetings in which I participated, all of which are part of my life as a member of FBC *and* my inquiry for my research. This means that my telling of these narratives is far from disinterested. In interviews, people frequently knew where I stood on issues and, given that most of the people who took the classes I taught stood in similar camps as me, our conversations would sometimes take on the tone of conspiratorial planning. Each of us clearly loved our community, even as we also saw multiple ways we wanted it to be reformed and wanted to contribute to that reformation. This also means that the ecclesiology articulated here looks little like what we usually expect from doctrinal reflection about "The Church" in academic theology. As *ethnographic* theological reflection, this ecclesiology is not a general reflection about the nature of an abstracted or conceptual idea of Church; rather, it is particular reflection from within a particular church: FBC Nashville. It aims to show the body of Christ not just glorified but broken. Similarly, it shows a church not just as it should be but as it is in all its beautiful and sobering reality.

The question that animates this ecclesiology, then, relates to how social and theological reform might happen in an ecclesial context. Here, I test Kathryn Tanner's idea that academic theology can bring about such change in everyday theological contexts. I argue that the intervention of academic theology in the everyday has the potential to contribute to a number of context-specific goods. But despite my desire for it, I found that the visions I had for revolutionary change or even for more simple reforms were often overly utopian (and recall from the introduction how such utopian visions compose their own sort of authoritarianism). While I and the majority of the people who took the classes I taught wanted reformation in our community and, in fact, gravitated toward theologies and practices that were atypical in relation to broader cultural norms, our labor nevertheless ended up being engulfed by wider ecclesial equilibrium, channeled for its own use. In fact, our sites of atypical theology and practice were often the exceptions that held the rules in place and, consequently, as with my own experience of complex desire at my ordination ritual, we frequently found ourselves to be cogs in the larger institutional machine. I argue this ecclesiology not because I want to construct status quo theologies, however, but rather because I hope that a more accurate picture of what kinds of theological transformation are actually possible in a particular context might facilitate actual—rather than idealized—strategies for genuine innovation.

No Plodding Reformism

We saw in the last chapter how Sherry Ortner calls for a more activist type of ethnography, a form of research that recognizes the slippage and potential for social change as cultures reproduce themselves. Academic theology, as Kathryn Tanner has argued, tries to contribute to that ongoing reform within Christian social practices in particular, reshaping those practices in which it participates directly. In accounting for the ways in which my own bodily, theological agency participates directly in my field of study's processes of cultural production and reproduction, I am trying to ask with Tanner, what are the possibilities and limitations when an academic theologian partners with other Christian practitioners with an interest in ecclesial reform?

Influenced in part by postliberal theologies, as well as by scholars like Bourdieu—all of whom have been accused of constructing research methods that contribute to maintaining rather than dismantling the social status quo—Tanner clearly feels the burden to demonstrate the more liberationist impulses in her methods. She argues that specialized, academic theological discourse does not preserve or even simply build on what came before; rather, it seeks to take apart inherited theologies—both everyday and academic—to reconfigure them in new ways.[5] This is precisely the type of activity I attempted to perform through the ecclesial practice of theological conversation that I guided. Nevertheless, in trying to bring Tanner's model to life in this way, I often found it difficult to substantiate her hope that a theological creativity that works through existing ecclesial conditions need not entail a "plodding reformism."[6] Plodding, it seems, is exactly the kind of reformism such creativity yields.

Tanners argues that "small changes" can "have a major effect," and that small tinkers to an ecclesial system really can "make the whole construction wobble and threaten it with collapse," at least in terms of the unjust marks of that construction.[7] But in seeking to bring her model to life, I learned that the very fact that small changes can threaten a whole system with collapse is precisely what makes even small changes so difficult to effect. It is a rare tool that wields the precision to remove the unjust or even simply problematic marks from a system without irreparably wounding it. Tanner is certainly right to say (echoing Certeau) that the "established meanings and rules" that govern a system "have no power of themselves to resist alteration"; rather, they are "held in place through the exercise of human power—by the will of the participants"[8] But as we saw in the previous chapter, with my objectified account of my own theological agency, this is only part of the story. In addition, we find that the pleasures of belonging can easily make one into a participant willing to deploy one's power in ways that inevitably, even sometimes paradoxically against one's will, perpetuate the unjust regularities of a given social system.

As much as anything else, this relationship between my desire for belonging and the consequent limits it put on my ability to catalyze social and theological change might primarily reveal my own struggles.[9] Alternately—or additionally—these struggles might reveal a problem in Tanner's model as theory that is abstracted from practice.

Theological reflection in her mode necessitates some sort of implication of the academic theologian in the everyday Christian practices she wants to affect. But to be an insider can entail a sense of group membership that at least complicates, if not diminishes, any desire to overthrow the whole system. Even the insider who draws on other forms of theological agency, like the ways in which I am shaped also by more progressive and radical academic theological discourses, might feel the ambivalence of a simultaneous desire to both resist *and* invest more deeply in the system. Performing a loose integration of the competing and cohering habitus I embody and roles I play with regard to this ambivalent desire might entail moves toward reform and revolution at various points. But for the most part, it seems this might not be how everyday life together works.

This chapter suggests that atypical spaces often enable the wider ecclesial system's flourishing, even when those spaces are created by people who interpret themselves as "insurgents," as those in our Sunday night group tended to do. At the very least, this chapter functions as a minority report that complicates Tanner's more idealized claims for the possibilities of revolutionary social and theological change. Working with everyday theologies does not by necessity entail plodding reformism but the possibility of revolution can be much more difficult to attain, and even desire, than her work suggests. By arguing that conversations between everyday and academic theologies cannot necessarily be directly correlated with movements of social reform, we must ask what theological goods they can produce. And here is where Tanner's insights into such goods are particularly helpful. Like her, I want to highlight the goods of the process—that is, a process that enables mutual understanding of difference and deepens participants' shared commitments to the materials over which they are debating, thereby deepening their commitments to each other.[10]

As this chapter demonstrates (in agreement with Tanner's claims to the same), when academic theology enters the everyday environment, it can only be heard if it works with that context's particular ways of being together—that is, it can only be heard if it can connect in some way to the community's own embodied and explicit theologies, its doxa and its articulated heterodoxies and orthodoxies. As a result, such academic theological interventions into the ecclesial sphere do not necessarily manage to create pockets of atypical practice that easily overthrow unjust systems or revise problematic theologies, precisely because those systems and theologies have also participated in creating those same pockets of atypical practice. Change is therefore more chastened when Tanner's model is brought to life in concrete practice. It happened in the classes I taught at FBC first as agents experienced tension with the wider ecclesial system; second, as they more consciously affirmed their integration with it; third, as their more conscious affirmation of their integration created small ripples of effect that nevertheless enabled the wider system to flourish. The small tinkers that *have a major effect* are few and far between in the mostly plodding reformism that makes up ecclesial life. But that plodding reformism is, for better or for worse, part of the life of faith.

The Intersecting Subcultures of FBC

I have already begun introducing FBC in earlier chapters, but now it is time to draw out some of its more particular flavors. In this section, I engage some of FBC's primary identity markers, particularly its denominational affiliation and, more fully, the relationship between its racial homogeneity and its understanding of mission. I demonstrate how each contains a minority report, a trajectory of belief and practice that functions atypically in relation to the whole. The classes I taught, in fact, create a space in which both the dominant and atypical concerns find voice. Still, as we will see, by having their own spaces within the larger whole, alternative viewpoints are kept from creating conflict, precisely because their own ways of directing their "moral energies" are not quashed.[11] They are kept in line, as pockets of resistance inevitably become cogs in the larger machine, their flourishing likewise enabling the flourishing of the wider ecclesial system. There is no revolution at FBC, only the daily—indeed, pleasurable—grind of trying to make and remake church together.

As a result, our community is a fairly moderate Baptist congregation. Its dominant culture is certainly less conservative than the broader Southern Baptist Convention (SBC) with which it affiliates but it also not quite as progressive as the more left-leaning Cooperative Baptist Fellowship (CBF) denomination, for example.[12] The fact that the congregation is open to—and excited about—ordaining women (both as deacons and, more rarely, as clergy) provides a key marker of this moderate stance. On other hot-button issues, however, the dominant culture adheres more closely with the SBC's mainline practices. For example, traditional middle-class and more conservative Christian family structures (i.e., heterosexual, monoracialized, and predominantly white, married partners with children, with the husband frequently functioning as primary wage earner and "spiritual leader" of the family) are the norm.

At the same time, there are pockets of characters within the community who see themselves as much more liberal than that dominant culture. Peter, for example, who was introduced in Chapter 1, and Gloria, who will be introduced more fully in Chapter 4, describe themselves as "sneaky liberals" and "insurgents." In both of their interviews, Peter and Richard, another class member, each expressed with fatigue, but also maybe with a little pride, that they always feel more liberal than those around them. Also recall from the introduction to this book Joan's side comment to me that she and Harlan are "that D word we don't say around here," indicating that they, in contrast to their perception of the rest of the congregation, are not Republicans. Another class member similarly referred to the "Democrat enclaves" hidden away within the community with which she preferred to affiliate. And so most of our group, in one way or another, tended to self-identify as being atypically progressive in relation to broader FBC norms.

When it comes to FBC's relationship to the SBC, members of the more dominant culture reflect broader American trends of what R. Stephen Warner calls, "de facto Congregationalism."[13] In my experience, most members seem to have neither strongly positive nor strongly negative feelings about the SBC; not exhibiting a particularly conscious pride at denominational affiliation, they seem mostly disengaged from the larger denominational body.[14] Indeed, most FBC members of my acquaintance do not refer to the "conservative ascendance," or "conservative resurgence," to use more neutral language to refer to the denomination's ideological and theological struggles of the late 1970s, at all. If they were not in some way personally involved with it, they tend to know little about it. The wider ecclesial norm at FBC is to go with the flow of being an SBC church, with little conscious acknowledgment of that fact.

Occasionally in our class, someone would mention "The Conservative Takeover" in the SBC—complete with the tone and eye rolls that my capitalization of each word suggests—which would prompt various members of the group to offer knowing glances at each other. Not only by referring to this shift in denominational leadership as a "Takeover" but by simply referring to it at all, these class members held their primary congregational affiliation in a more polemical way than members of the dominant FBC culture. They intentionally distanced themselves from the convention, marking FBC as a faithful outpost for the "way things were before things went bad," as they often described the power shift.

Continuing to go with the flow of being an SBC church, at the same time this group consciously resists that larger identity. Yet they do not affect any significant social change with regard to the aspects of that identity they dislike. For example, FBC ordained women long before the SBC changed its formal policies to exclude women from the practice of ordination. It is, therefore, a continuation of a practice that has longer historical roots than the denominational practices that would deny it. The somewhat nonefficacious resistance that the group exhibits therefore aligns with our more historical practices. Moreover it contributes to FBC's ability to maintain its affiliation with the SBC without repelling new members who might initially be put off by that affiliation from joining. And in this way, pockets of resistance end up contributing to the health of the broader ecclesial system.

Given the general lack of awareness most FBC members evince in relation to the larger SBC, a much larger identity marker, in my view, is the homogeneity of the congregation's racialized and class makeup, and the way that homogeneity relates to the community's sense of mission. FBC is not bucking any national trends with this homogeneity. As Martin Luther King Jr. is frequently cited as saying, Sunday morning at 11 o'clock is the "most segregated hour of the week." Sociologist, Michael Emerson in fact describes American congregations as "hypersegregated," as only 2.5 percent are made up of a "stable, long-term ethnic mix," as I already mentioned in the introduction.[15] FBC is not one of the rare churches that intentionally cultivates a more heterogeneous community out of a commitment, theological or otherwise, to diversity.

Rather, the primary mission focus at FBC is on creating an atmosphere and programs in which "our friends, family and coworkers who do not know Christ," an oft-repeated phrase, will feel comfortable. In other words, the congregation is concerned with witnessing to and drawing people who members already know into the community. As people tend to associate with others who share their similar experiences, Ammerman argues, one's friends, family, and coworkers tend also to share one's racialized, economic, and class traits. It is not that people "set out to make a choice based on class and race, but the results are often just that."[16] And in this way, as with many American churches, the primary mission focus at FBC unintentionally contributes to the perpetuation of the congregation's homogeneity.

The Fourth of July parades, at which the Frisbees mentioned at the beginning of this chapter were handed out, offer one of the flashpoints where these evangelistic practices are debated at FBC. These Frisbees caused an underground stir within the community. They enabled an evangelistic activity directed toward those who, like the majority in attendance at FBC on Sunday mornings, were coming in from neighboring suburbs for a particular purpose. FBC members engaged those visitors' bodily needs (free bottled water to quench the thirst of Southern summer heat) and potential bodily wants (Frisbee toys with which they could enjoy leisure activity).[17] But these material needs and wants were much more frivolous than a safe place to sleep or food they might not be able to provide for themselves. And so, the question of why water was handed out at this event to people who could afford to purchase it from the street vendors themselves when the streets are full of thirsty homeless people every day was muttered about among church members whose understanding of mission does not cohere with using resources in this way.

Within this primary way of framing missions, however, there runs another current of belief and practice. FBC's social outreach programs focus less on drawing people in to broader church life, and more on reaching toward the needs of the people living on the streets of the downtown core. They are not directed toward members' immediate, more homogenous social networks, but rather are directed toward a group that tends to be more racially diverse than FBC's general makeup, even as they are held together by shared class status of economic and social disadvantage. For this population, needs and wants are seen to be more basic than bottled water and Frisbees; this community needs and wants a place to sleep, a hot meal, and to be treated with dignity.

The desires motivating this "outreach" are complex. On the one hand, many who lead and volunteer with these programs intentionally avoid linking the social services to a call for conversion, or any pressure for our guests to attend church services. Guests to the programs have shared that they do not like this common evangelistic strategy, and most church volunteers try to respect that preference. Not wanting to be evangelistically coercive, leaders in these programs speak using terms like *hospitality* and *guest*, rather than *conversion* or *evangelism*. Their words are shaped by themes of welcome to the other, rather than themes of changing or assimilating the other.

Yet at the same time, these practices and language of reaching out rather than drawing in, of positioning these populations as guests, further affirms that *they* are not one of *us*. Quite a few of the people who volunteer with the church's programs on a more ad hoc basis, maybe only once or twice a year when their Sunday School class is signed up to bring the food, admit their need to get over their fear of the guests in order to serve them. In this way, one must wonder if the language of guest—while endeavoring to be hospitable—also consciously and unconsciously seeks to protect our vibrant, treasured FBC family from disruption. In this way, we once again discern and provide what we think others might need. The sense that we might all partner together in a shared ministry remains mostly foreign to our practice.

While members from across FBC's culture tend to participate in these programs on this ad hoc basis, almost all the people who take the classes I taught volunteer or have volunteered in some larger capacity with one or more of them. In addition, class members Miriam and Gary (with their children), Gloria, Joan, and I all serve in some official, volunteer capacity that is central to one or another particular program's functioning. Many of our class members also exhibited outright disdain for programs like the Frisbee distribution when I interviewed them. It is not the case that the group is uninterested in witnessing or evangelizing, but they are more interested in their witness being part of a larger, social justice framework.[18] Indeed, as Ammerman argues, most American Christians have "not learned the ideological lesson that if they believe in promoting social justice, they should place less emphasis on witnessing; or—at the other pole—that if they believe in witnessing, they should be wary of calls for social justice."[19] In lived practice one tends to imply the other, and at FBC most members are involved in some way with both. As Gloria frames her own involvement, "I think I'm probably more social gospel . . . you gotta do what you say you believe. You gotta do things to make the world better . . . help the poor."

Despite not being the primary missions focus of the church, the work FBC does in social programs is nevertheless diverse. The church participates in Room in the Inn, a Nashville-wide ministry for homeless people. It founded The Next Door ministry, which helps women transition back into society out of prison, rehabilitation, or homelessness. Then once this ministry became independent, FBC leased a valuable downtown building to it for its offices and residences at one dollar per year.[20] The church works with the Christian Women's Job Corps, which offers classes and training to help prepare socially disadvantaged women for gainful employment. Sunday School departments participate in Habitat for Humanity builds. Finally, the church's clothes closet, which hands out clothing to homeless people, and conversational English classes for immigrants seeking to bolster their language skills, were both instigated by members who saw a need that was not being met in the broader community. Even though this work is not a part of FBC's dominant mission narrative, it fulfills a significant aspect of who the congregation understands itself to be.

By maintaining these pockets of practice that skirt the dominant narrative for mission at FBC, the church creates spaces for alternative understandings of mission to flourish. At the same time, in so doing, these spaces continue to support the homogeneous makeup of the congregation. Ministry to immediate social networks tends to draw people in; ministry to people with different racial and class characteristics tends to look outward. In fact, tension seems to erupt—with little to no effect—when this balance is disrupted. One class member told me about how she attended a meeting to strategize for church growth. A consultant had been hired to help with this strategizing, and he was instructing the gathered on how to attract a "particular type of congregant." The consultant did not name who this "particular type" was, although his advice to install big-screen televisions in Sunday School departments, renovate the classrooms, and use full-color printing in worship bulletins indicated that he was referring to middle- and upper-middle-class congregants. "If you want to get the homeless to join," he said, "all you need to do is fling open the doors."

The way my friend tells this story, the consultant was not necessarily making a judgment between these two populations; he was simply outlining the appropriate tactics for attracting each (although, one might question whether or not his plan for attracting homeless people would actually work). Nevertheless, the class member tells this story with anger in her voice: "I shouted 'Amen,'" she said, "and I said to the people around me, 'don't we want the homeless to join? Let's save this money and just fling the doors open!'" Her outburst was greeted with silence. The narrative she wanted to tell fit neither the ways our dominant or our atypical practices perpetuate homogeneity. Her view was thus too radical. The silence with which it was greeted revealed that there are limits to the social change that atypical beliefs and practices and, particularly, more radical beliefs and practices can accomplish in this context.

Atypical Practices in the Classroom

The classes I taught on Sunday nights tended to attract FBC members who are disposed to associate themselves with a "more social gospel" undercurrent to church life both in terms of their strong sense that the SBC's conservative ascendance was a "Takeover" and in terms of the way they understand mission. For the most part, they also saw the classes as another one of these atypical spaces within congregational life. In this section, I establish that these classes functioned like FBC's other atypical practices I have described here, both in the sense that they functioned differently—or, at least, were viewed as functioning differently—than other FBC classes and in the sense that their atypical nature was easily incorporated into the larger ecclesial equilibrium.

The official enrollment for each course hovered between 22 and 25 members, which is high for one of FBC's Life Change University courses. On any given night, there were approximately 18 to 22 members present. Overall, both classes drew slightly more men than women. Yet while men in general seemed to be more comfortable talking than women, among those who talked the most, the gender division was equal. A core group of ten people took both classes—six men and four women. Of the six men, four had previously been employed in ministerial work, three as senior pastors, and one as a music minister.[21] None of the women had previously been employed in ministry leadership. All ten did, however, participate in some form of lay leadership at FBC, as did almost every member of both courses. When I conducted interviews after each course, eight of the ten core members agreed to be interviewed.[22] Of the ten, seven had perfect or almost perfect attendance across the two courses. Of the ten, Miriam, Gary, Peter, and Joan and Harlan have already been introduced; Elaine, Richard, Gene, Rickie, and Mike will figure in subsequent stories.[23]

A few exceptional details stand out from the course demographics. First, while many (but not all) education classes at FBC are divided by gender, marital or family status, and age group, these Sunday night classes were intentionally coed, mixed family status, and intergenerational.[24] These were all aspects of the classes that members said they appreciated, particularly with regard to the intergenerational component. People who attended the courses also tended to be leaders within the church. For example, the classroom would feel strangely empty whenever a deacons' meeting was scheduled at the same time as our class because many of our classmates would need to attend that meeting instead.[25] As a somewhat more elite group of leaders within the broader church structure, it might seem strange that they would think of themselves as insurgents, but they also tended to be leaders within more atypical areas of church life, and/or alternative voices within larger power structures. Finally, with regards to demographics, the people who attended our Sunday night classes were largely highly educated. All of the retired ministers had some form of advanced theological training. But in general, nearly everyone had a bachelor's degree, a few had master's degrees, and at least four members had PhDs.

The roster of Sunday night course offerings previously mentioned indicates its broadly evangelical appeal. The classes I taught fit within this roster atypically, not only because they were studies of doctrine, but also because of their style and goals.[26] This atypical nature became especially evident when, on the final night of the "God as Trinity" course, I set aside 15 minutes for everyone to write responses to questions like the following: What had worked? What did not work? What surprised you? What challenged you? Following a comment from another class member, "it [the class] has been a[n intellectual] stretch," Joan responded to much agreement from others:

> And I think that's atypical. What I'm trying to say is that it's unusual to have—in a Baptist church—a course where you have to think [*She says this with such a dry type of humor that is not innocent in its execution, and everyone starts laughing*]. No, seriously, it's like you're spoon-fed, you know? Read this. Fill in the blank. That kind of thing. Although some of what we've discussed has gone way over my head, I still would do it again. It was [*she pauses to find the right words*] you're learning, you're stretching, you're seeing what other people think. And also, that there's just not conclusions to everything.

According to Joan, our classes were *atypical* in part because they allowed authority to be questioned. People were invited to come up with their own answers and leave theological questions open rather than tie them up with neat conclusions. Departing from the more typical fill-in-the-blank format of much of the curriculum used elsewhere in FBC's life, these courses endeavored to help members see fresh avenues of theological thinking and doing, from among which they might choose to try something new.

Joan's comments, and others offered like them, are not necessarily criticisms of the other courses on offer. She and others describe other LCU courses they have enjoyed immensely. Rather, it is a direct, focused, positive appraisal of the rarer (in their experience) kind of critical reflection—the very type that an academically trained theologian is able to lead—engaged in our time together. Indeed, it was this desire for critical reflection and deeper, broader thinking—the very aspects that made the class feel atypical—that bonded the group together more than their demographics. For example, while these courses tended to attract church members who gravitate more toward social justice concerns and left-leaning politics, they also had some conservative members. Some of these members drifted away after a couple of sessions. But one of the more active members of both classes, Mike, was among those of a more conservative bent who stayed.[27] As he put it one night, regarding the diversity of our group and his own place in it: "I've been surprised to realize that I'm sitting with fellow Baptists, with the different backgrounds and the different beliefs and interpretations of beliefs . . . And we've enjoyed hearing each other, I think . . . And it causes you to leave with the idea that maybe I need to search just a little more."

Whether so-called liberal or conservative, the people who took these classes all wanted to engage in processes of being opened up and challenged in the Christian beliefs and practices they already embodied. They expressed dissatisfaction with the types of courses that give them simple answers, and instead wanted help to develop not only their own answers but also their own questions. This desire called me to a certain sort of responsibility with my research methods. My own goals for social and theological transformation had to be negotiated in relation to theirs. My own atypical beliefs and practices had to be articulated in ways that were intelligible to theirs. I may have experienced a longer leash with this Sunday night group than I would have with others, but in many ways I was still on a leash.

Like other atypical spaces within church life, the classes I taught caused their members to experience more conscious forms of tension and coherence with the broader church structure. These forms are not, of course, necessarily bad nor good. But at the same time, similar to how the ministerial authority I was given was channeled and instrumented to the larger system's use, the tools acquired by members of these classes were integrated into the ecclesial structure in a way that enabled that system's flourishing more than its disruption. In this way, the intervention of academic theology into everyday theologies—at least in the mode of intervention I attempted—did not disrupt, but rather served the broader ecclesial life.

New Tools for the Tool Kit

It is worth noting that the theories of culture with which we have so far been working support such diversity within and not just beyond the borders of particular identity groups.[28] Multiple fields of practice can intersect in one local place as they compete and cohere with each other within a larger field of power. It is not the case, for example, that so-called nontheological or nonecclesial logics should be viewed as foreign to an ecclesial environment, as clean distinctions between fields of practice only exist at the level of theory. As a result, multiple social forces have the potential to shape different ways of evangelizing, doing social outreach, or even being Christian within the same community—all of which nevertheless remain faithful to the overarching commitments of that community. The question at hand here is,

How can academic theological interventions into such communities contribute to and even redirect some of these processes of communal formation? And what types of social and theological reform do such interventions have the potential bring about?

Here, Christian Scharen's theological ethnographic insights into the relationship between ecclesial practices, community identity, and moral formation prove most helpful. As Scharen has demonstrated, the so-called secular social forces (so often misinterpreted as competing counterformations to theological formation) are frequently turned into social resources by church members seeking to direct their moral energies. Church members, therefore, draw on all their "gifts, knowledge and abilities gained through their upbringing and family, education, connection and skills on the job" and, we might add, the forms of power and privilege with which these forces imbue them to orient their action in their church and wider world.[29] There are times when ecclesial practices might play a larger role in identity formation. But for the most part, Scharen argues, their relevance for social formation is always interactive with the broader sociocultural context and individuals' personal knowledge and abilities.[30] So both the FBC members who choose to hand out the Frisbees and those who serve food to our homeless guests are experiencing *sufficient resonance* with the broader community identity as it interacts with the social forces that have shaped their own lives and, concurrently, the social resources on which they find themselves able to draw. Therefore, as the examples from FBC in the subsequent sections will demonstrate, the intervention of academic theology into the everyday offers yet another resource to interact, compete, and cohere with these other social forces.

The degree of impact these interventions can have depends on the openness of their context to receive them as much as any other factor. As Scharen points out, theological practices may have more formative power during what sociologist Ann Swidler refers to as "unsettled" times—that is, during periods of dramatic change as with religious conversions or when standard, accepted ways of doing things no longer work.[31] These are the times of crisis Bourdieu talks about that have the power to disrupt a culture's doxa precisely because they expose the need for new strategies of action to be formed from the very cultural elements that seem to have failed.[32] As Swidler argues, culture is less like "a unified system that pushes action in a consistent direction" and more like "a 'tool kit' . . . from which actors select differing pieces for constructing lines of action."[33] When one tool ceases to work, we pick up another to engage the task at hand. When academic theology intervenes in the everyday environment, it is poised to add new tools and new ways of using old ones.

In this way, Swidler's approach resonates with Tanner's idea that theology works with materials already on the ground, assembling and reassembling them into new theological configurations. During these times, the use of new tools or of old tools in a new way could lead to genuine change in the ways people's habitus are constituted and, thus, in the ways they are oriented to their worlds. It is possible that transformation can result from such minor shifts, as Tanner argues. But as Scharen notes, and as I will demonstrate next, shifts typically happen "in ways that 'fit' the dominant ethos of a congregation, the acquired habitus of the members," even during such unsettling moments.[34] In the narratives later in this text, class members draw on life experience, education, and social status to introduce ideas they claim to be heretical into our theological conversations. They do so in order to shake things up or, to use Swidler's language, unsettle us. Yet even with such bold claims to heresy at play, the shifts that happen in the group member's thought and action is slight, and it only sticks where it also coheres with their other personal stories, ways of being, and the broader ecclesial context.

Then, of course, the majority of ecclesial practices happen during what Swidler calls, "settled" times. Settled lives are marked by periods of normalcy when culture seems so "intimately integrated with action" that it becomes difficult to see the role of agents in the reproduction of social structures.[35] The agency of characters is particularly difficult to recognize in these moments precisely because culture and action seem so firmly integrated. Theorists like Ortner and Swidler, who focus our attention on agents rather than systems, thus help us recognize agency in modes that might conform to the broader culture and that might eschew outright resistance. Like Ortner, Swidler stresses the agency produced by habitus. Just because agents are using an old tool doesn't mean they aren't doing so in a new way. Moreover, even if they are using an old tool in an old way, they still might be doing so consciously, attentive to its impact on their own self and the world around them. Therefore, whether we focus our attention here on moments of flux or stability, for Swidler, it is clear that even when it seems like cultural practices are merely reproducing particular beliefs, those who are implicated in the processes of reproduction still can do so with conscious agency. In the subsequent stories that tell of class members accepting, reaffirming, or renewing a particular Baptist belief, it is less relevant to our discussion *that* they do so than *how* they do so.

Deploying Heresy for Theological Change

As argued earlier, one way in which crisis might be able to catalyze social and theological change is by articulating a field's doxa as a heterodox view. In this way, opinions that have gone unsaid come to the fore in the form of their negation: people make claims that do not correspond perfectly to everyone's collective sense of what feels right. As a result, there is a crisis in the doxa that presses people to talk about it and tease out what they really think. In these moments, culture can be unsettled, with new ideas and strategies for living rising to the surface of consciousness and action.

When we fail to see such internal difference, Tanner argues, voices that differ from the dominant, consistent view are silenced.[36] The effect is a distortion rather than a description of the realities of lived practice.[37] Attuned to poststructuralist understandings of power, Tanner asserts the importance of listening to these more marginalized voices and bringing them to audibility as legitimate contributors to group identity. In other words, she encourages the articulation of heterodoxies in order to bring doxa to light. In this light, the types of changes to dominant practice that marginalized voices can foster is not encountered merely as threat or failure, as a vision of culture that interprets communities as firmly bordered and bounded suggests, but rather is able to be viewed as a location of possibility.[38]

This kind of heterodox articulation occurred through the classes I taught at FBC in two key ways: through deploying it and through resisting it. Each of these methods reveals ways that academic theologians might participate in ecclesial life fruitfully by helping to foster the conversation that arises and is often shut down around such heterodox speech. It is important to note, however, that class members never used the language of "heterodoxy" during the course of my study, most likely because it is a more technical, less colloquial term than the more common one: *heresy*. The concept of heresy, therefore, was used to draw heterodox views into common speech with safe cover, as class members would label their own controversial ideas as "heretical" precisely as they were introducing them for group reflection. It was as if the speaker was saying, "I, of course, don't believe this, but you guys might find it interesting . . ." Through discussion, these ideas would become refined to the point of marginal acceptance or, at least, a more thoughtful, sometimes even tenuous rejection. And in so doing even initially controversial thoughts were able to contribute something new to our shared conversation—if, of course, in a somewhat muted way. While these so-called heretical ideas did not create moments of outright crisis, then, they did create what we might call moments of unsettling. These moments of unsettling, in turn, created space for class members' life experience, prior knowledge, privilege, and so on to help make ideas typically unpalatable by the community cohere, if only for a moment, with the more established broader community ethos.

It would therefore be overly idealistic to say that we always made it to open and honest discussion of the differences between us. We needed these strategies to test new ideas out. Moreover, more than one participant admitted in one-on-one interviews that they were sometimes scared to say what they were really thinking in class in case others viewed them as a "heretic" or worse, "not really saved"—as I discuss more fully later. In this way, some form of a border remained erected between acceptable and unacceptable Christian belief. Yet that border also seemed to be permeable as more confident class members would actually deploy the language of "heretic" as a self-description that permitted them to draw more controversial views into the discussion. This language complicated the difference between beliefs that were acceptable versus unacceptable and who was an insider to our group versus who was an outsider.

Richard was particularly fond of this tactic. Over the course of my ethnographic interviews, I asked everyone to name who they thought was the wisest class member.[39] By a strong margin, Richard received the most votes. Class members described him as humble, someone who waits to speak until he truly has something to say, and open-minded in ways toward which they strived. Whenever I was unable to come up with an answer to a question, the group would turn to Richard for help. Yet he never imposed his views on us or attempted to usurp my position as teacher. He always couched his comments carefully, framing them in ways that invited discussion rather than agreement.

On numerous occasions, he would jokingly begin a point by stating something like, "Y'all are going to think I'm a heretic, but . . ." One night in particular, Richard wanted to argue for more fluidity among the persons of the Trinity than our conversation was inviting, and he admitted that he "used the same terms" (that is, *Father*, *Son*, and *Holy Spirit*), only "to prevent being condemned as a heretic," but that really, "the older I get, it's an elusive thing." In this way he designated between the orthodoxy he expresses publically, and the heresy he might actually believe. Yet by labeling it as heresy, he undermined his own belief, giving himself a sense of safe cover to play with the terms. Later, having opened up this fluidity with the safe cover, Richard introduced the idea that *Father* could be encountered as *Mother*, thus once again drawing an idea that is heterodox within Baptist life—that is, a feminine Divine—into public discussion and consideration.

Richard actually used the strategy of labeling himself a heretic enough that others felt comfortable applying the label to him as well. One night when he named a desire to expand Baptist theology by putting it into "more open dialogue with other denominations, groups with whom we agree and with whom we disagree," someone else in the class jokingly inserted, "You are a heretic!" While this insertion could be perceived as language policing and, in one sense, it probably was, it also offered a form of encouragement to Richard. Most class members expressed their appreciation for engaging theological difference, and the group bonded to each other around a sense that they shared this value that they saw the larger church system not sharing. The man's declaration that Richard was a heretic bore an implied "and so are we!" Richard, without missing a beat, responded, "Well that's all right. I have been for fifty years now," as he continued his point. Once again, safe cover was granted.

Such "heretical" joking around thus allowed Richard and others to introduce ideas into our conversation that seemed foreign to our context but that were, in fact, in various ways coherent with it. Other more quiet class members, bolstered by the place of authority Richard occupied within the room, could then respond that they too sometimes subscribed to such supposed heresy with safe cover. In these moments, as the teacher and academic theologian, I had the capacity to draw on multiple aspects of various Christian traditions in order to bolster Richard's views, as well as the views articulated by those seeking to go along with him. In this way, multiple new ideas were introduced into our conversation. And still others felt authorized to disagree with these avenues of thought because, at least in their view, *the tradition* was on their side. As a consequence, voices typically marginalized were heard and affirmed, revealing the diversity internal to our group, while differences were still maintained, thus stimulating conversations across friendly conflict and competition.

Richard's willingness to lift up ideas that were heterodox within our community in fact would bolster my courage to attempt the same. His use of feminine language for God offers one such example. I admit that I experienced tensions around gendered language for God. In my own personal practice, as well as in academic theological contexts, I use primarily female gendered and gender-neutral language in description of and address to the Divine. But speaking feminine language for God is not within the realm of acceptable practice at FBC. Frequently when I used gendered pronouns, my language would falter. I would try to use feminine language, but my lips would trip at the last moment and I would fall back on neutral or masculine language. Then, when I used masculine language, I always felt a twinge of guilt that I was betraying my own commitments in order to fit in, and I wondered if the group could see my teeth clench slightly as words like *he* and *Father* slipped through them.

I do not know if certain class members sensed this strain for me, but as we discussed gendered language for God during our engagement of feminist theologies, I felt a few of them open space for more expansive language. This was the context in which Richard shared that he sometimes prays to a "Mother God." As the person in the room so many saw to be wise, his education and social status opened the possibility that others could do the same. Other class members like Maureen and Gene both shared that they wanted to try praying to God in this way too. Gene even wondered aloud if the term *Father* in the Lord's Prayer was only there because Jesus was praying it in a "male-dominated culture." Expanding these insights with personal narrative, Jerry, a gentle, soft-spoken, retired minister shared that his image of God had always had a female dimension to it because, as he put it, the "most loving figure in my childhood was my grandmother . . . she was the person who took time to sit with me and read and draw birds with me and so forth." After articulating this point, Jerry started slipping female gendered pronouns into the conversation, trying them on for size. At first, he and we laughed as he did it, all sharing in how jarring the language sounded to us. But as he repeated them, in the context of the particular conversation on gender, they came to feel more natural. Finally on our last night, when I asked the group what they had learned and which ideas still lingered, Gene volunteered that he had continued to think about God's gender and his own potential "idolatry" at imaging God only in the masculine. A few brought this same point up in interviews.

Their willingness to play with new language helped me do the same with them, even though I never really pushed the conversation about gender and God much past what they were willing to open up for us. So I joined with Richard to say that I also pray to a "Mother God," and shared that I even change the words to hymns sometimes when we are singing them in church because I find the onslaught of masculine language in those situations difficult to take. Like Jerry, I slipped some female gendered pronouns in for naming God in our conversation. And like Jerry, I did so awkwardly at first, but with growing comfort, at least within the context of the conversation about God's gender. But I never led us into a conversation that deconstructed gender binaries in general or moved us to consider female images for God that weren't tied to motherhood. In this way, we tested each other's limits, pushing against them only enough for slight shifts in our thinking and doing, but not for any revolutionary overhaul to the ways we name the Divine. Our so-called heretical speech unsettled each other a little more than it led us into crisis and, in so doing, shifts in class members' thought and action happened in only very humble ways. As Scharen puts it, they continued to "fit" with the congregation's "dominant ethos."

I should also note that all these examples of someone in the class opening up our conversation for more controversial ideas involve characters around whom quite a bit of power accrues. In this way, academic theological interventions attached to other social forces being deployed as resources by certain class members. Because Jerry is a retired minister, not to mention an older, white man, the group automatically imbues his theology with a certain modicum of trust. Richard was roundly viewed as the wisest person in the room. Also an older, white male with theological training, a history of vocation in ministry and theological education, and a frequent and favorite Sunday School teacher at the church, Richard had the authority and consequent confidence to pull off these tactics of heresy. It was easier for me to partner with older, white men like Jerry, Peter, and Richard in deploying our shared power to draw more marginalized voices into conversation. But as the teacher, I had the added responsibility to consistently seek out the opinions that were going unsaid because less power accrued to those who had them.

Resisting Heresy for Theological Change

The second way in which heterodox speech opened up our theological conversations then relates to how certain, less confident class members would shy away from articulating their heterodox views. These class members would circle around their view until someone else—usually me—could help draw it out. In these cases, the fear seemed less about whether or not other class members would reject them (although it was certainly about that too), and more about whether or not a heretical view would cause God to reject them. Here, my role as teacher took on a distinctly pastoral hue, as it was crucial to help people articulate these fears. Once the fears were articulated, we found that the tension would break for new theologies to be explored.

An example from an early night in the "God as Trinity" course helps illustrate this second way in which heterodoxy opened up theological conversation. I found this second class much more difficult to teach than "Jesus Christ and Salvation" as I struggled to find the prompts that could get conversations going, and when those conversations did start to get traction, students would often shut them down by claiming "it's just all a mystery." I lacked the tools to understand why they were so dismissive, so willing to disengage from rather than engage with mystery, just as they lacked the tools to understand why I was pushing them to try. We needed to figure out how to find our way toward each other in conversation. Their silence and resistance would make me nervous for teaching. My fear then compounded the problems further as we all struggled to find the motivations and words to get us back into dialogue. In one particularly awkward moment of silence, my pedagogical instincts directed me toward a practice on which I often rely when students seem unwilling to talk in the academic classroom: I offered an impromptu lecture.

So I launched into the following as a somewhat frustrated response to another conversation foreclosure:

> The way that I think about mystery is that mystery is not the thing we have when we run out of things to say, because mystery is so much better than that. And mystery is actually the place where we start. We can do ourselves a disservice when we make mystery the place where we run out of answers to our questions. God is mystery from beginning to end. And even when we think we've caught some sort of glimpse of understanding, all we're still doing is walking through mystery when we're talking about God. And so as we go through, it will be interesting to notice the places where we do think we know something about God, and to realize that those are actually places of mystery as well. And the places where we don't know something probably aren't all that different from the places where we do. That no matter where we are, we're walking through the mystery of God. Because I know that the Trinity is difficult and frustrating. But I think that if we hold on to that idea of walking through the mystery of God, it will make it a little more pleasurable.

This speech functioned as a turning point because it articulated an unnamed tension hidden in our conversation, therefore unearthing some new tools with which we could work. Our disagreement had not solely been over appropriate and inappropriate ways of describing God. It had also been over the concept of mystery. Naming that disagreement allowed the tension—a tension we were not understanding—to break. My academic theological intervention thus attached to my pastoral concern that fear was keeping class members from engaging the material to the degree they might actually wish to do so. Recalling Anne's desires for what academic theology could do among the everyday, this intervention did not introduce a radically new idea so much as it helped nervous class members draw on tools they already possessed with greater confidence.

The following week, as I opened the class, Richard offered the comment, "I think where you ended last session was really appropriate, talking about the mystery that must remain." My words—which had grown out of their words—had lingered, causing a shift in the way our discussions were approached. This tiny shift contributed to the ongoing process of opening up our theological conversation. Fulfilling one of the things teachers should do, I had helped hear them into speech. Other class members noted agreement with Richard's consideration. My confidence with teaching began to return as it seemed I too needed to overcome certain fears and be heard into speech. Class members began to catch themselves when they turned to mystery as a way of halting inquiry. Indeed, the desire to use mystery in this way even became a point for humor in our discussion, with people saying things like, "It's all just mystery [*pause*], but I know that means keep going." Thus the ground was cleared for us to begin experimenting with what we did and didn't know about God—that is, we began experimenting with what would constitute acceptable theological speech for us.

This mini lecture also became something I needed to build on continually to maintain its efficacy. As something new, still nevertheless drawing on Christian intellectual and practical traditions, these words introduced more instability into lives that were already unsettled by the situation in which they had placed themselves. We might not have been starting from scratch, as aspects of the wisdom we pursued together were grounded in traditions that the group—to varying degrees—already embodied with varying degrees of consciousness. Still, as Swidler points out, when lives become unsettled, even though agents might draw on the cultural resources they have long had at their disposal, it is a slow process to articulate a newly formed idea out of those resources and then move to its acceptance as common sense.[40]

With the conversation thus opened up, I still wanted to know why we were struggling so much to talk about God. Why had they wanted to disengage from rather than engage with mystery? Employing an intentional pedagogical strategy, I asked them in a direct way to reflect on the difficulty they were experiencing:

> So sometimes when we're thinking theologically, I feel like Trinity is the hardest one [i.e., doctrine]. Jesus Christ, no problem; salvation, not that difficult; Holy Spirit, I'm all over it [*with these last few words, I leaned back in my chair and mimed a dismissive "no problem" gesture with my hands. Then, leaning forward again and clasping my hands together on the table . . .*] But the Trinity feels like a difficult one to me, and it feels like a scarier one too—something about thinking my way into the mystery of God feels overwhelming, and I wondered if others felt the same way. It feels like there's a lot at stake. It feels different.[41]

Peter responded, with his usual willing openness to the new: "I agree, and I think it's the temptation to say, 'Well I can't understand that,' and go on to other things. But there's something about the mystery of God that is like a magnet. It's not that I don't want or that I want to solve the mystery—that's not it. It's that I can't leave it alone. I keep coming back and, well, OK, I'll never know it all, but I wanna know more."

Drawing on knowledge I knew had been inculcated into me through reading for my doctoral exams, the origins and specific references for which remained beyond my articulation and, even, awareness in the moment, I responded, "I do think of theology as the words that move us between God and God." The image sufficiently resonated, to use Scharen's language again, with a few class members' larger theological views as they repeated it in subsequent classes, as well as in one of my postcourse interviews. Peter's openness invited us all to follow, and we began to delve deeper into the dangers we sensed were associated with theological speech.

Miriam, who at that time was working on reading the entire Bible in a year, and was finding herself shocked by the violence of stories she had never read before, brought up God's wrath against idolaters in the Old Testament. Miriam's close friend, Elaine, who attended both theology classes (though sporadically), responded, "I think that's what makes the Trinity such a kind of scary concept to wrestle with. You don't wanna get it wrong [*people laugh quietly and somewhat awkwardly in agreement*]. You don't wanna give Jesus too much credit and not give everybody his due. And so you have this prism to look through and you don't know how do I address my prayers? What am I supposed to do here? I think there's just more at stake. You remember that vengeful God!"

Others resonated and murmured notes of agreement with Elaine's description. In that moment, a theological distinction rose out of our shared practice. The group might laugh in the face of heresy, and even deploy it as a theologically productive tool. It seems they have no problem experimenting with a belief that does not jibe with the authoritative beliefs of others. We have even seen that there is a sense among some in this group that truth sometimes lies in the places of resistance to authority. The radical individualism of American evangelicalism and the Baptist affirmation of self-determination invite such resistance.[42] But in such a schema of resisting worldly authorities, there remains one final arbiter of truth in this group's understanding: God. So getting God wrong becomes a key place where theological freedom hits a wall. Mystery isn't inviting in such a paradigm; it is terrifying.

Naming this fear out loud loosened its grip on us, however. Finding the grace and space to converse, the group cultivated more and more tools for talking about God, and I continued to learn how to frame conversations that invited freer speech. Drawing on the social and theological resources of the people gathered in the room, our atypical practices and academic theological interventions created a space in which we could experiment with contentious ideas and, in some cases, take on those ideas as our own. But this freer speech never really made it outside of our classroom walls in any substantial way—as far as I know. In the next section, we see just how difficult it is to move those ideas out into the broader ecclesial sphere.

Singing the Trinity for Theological Formation

Stories of deploying heterodoxy and heresy reveal moments of unsettling where theological change—though slight and individualized—might occur. When it comes to the possibility for those slight moments of change to ripple out into the broader ecclesial sphere—to *topple the whole system*, as Tanner puts it—we saw something even less dramatic take place. Here we turn our attention away from how conversations across theological difference might inspire small personal transformations and direct it toward the wider processes of ecclesial formation with which even our unsettled constructions of theological agency so frequently found their fit.

Even when what we were doing in the classroom created tension for participants with their broader church life, our ability to impact that life remained limited. For example, one Sunday morning, about half way through our "God as Trinity" semester, we sang a Trinitarian hymn in worship—but the music leader skipped the third verse about the Holy Spirit to save time for the larger medley. Without my prompting and, in fact, cutting off my opening activity, Gloria—a feisty, outspoken woman in her midsixties—interjected a discussion that night on the topic of the hymn. A number of class members immediately expressed shock at what we had done, but with the simultaneous admission that "I probably would never have noticed it though if I weren't taking this class." What they were learning in class thus unsettled their experiences of the rest of church life, causing moments of incongruity that led to their deeper reflection on why we do things the way we do. "I wanted to know what you guys would think of it," Gloria exclaimed as she arrived that evening, eagerly noting that she had been thinking about the hymn all day.

Her experience, which resonated with that of others in the class, myself included, had involved first noticing the disruption, as she might not have done before studying Trinitarian questions explicitly. Then, periodically throughout the day, she had mulled over the disruption, thus stimulating her desire to hear what others thought about it too. Finally, she introduced the recollection of the disruption into the evening conversation and conversed with others about it. In this way, her experience in the class had impacted her interaction with Christian practice, which simultaneously gave rise to a personal and corporate pursuit of wisdom in order to understand that new experience in light of the rest of her faith experiences.

Some sort of change in larger social practices could certainly be possible in this instance. Perhaps a choir member from the class would report our conversation to the music director and he, in turn, would shift the time-saving practice of cutting the verses about the Holy Spirit out of hymns. This could create the ripples of effect that Tanner mentions. As the congregation sang about the Holy Spirit's power more often, our deep, embodied understanding of the Spirit's importance would be confirmed. This could have a cyclical effect, such that removing the verse about the Holy Spirit from hymns would come to seem completely unnatural, as it might in a church that more intentionally affirmed the Trinity. And with time, the congregation could be inculcated with a more powerful pneumatology that further impacted other ecclesial practices.

All this is certainly possible. Indeed, Mike—a choir member—commented that he would speak with the choir director about the hymn and report back to us, but he never did. This might be because once he left our atypical space, any attempts to rock the boat alone elsewhere felt less possible than they had seemed when bolstered by twenty other people calling for the rocking. Indeed, as Mike had been the one defending the possibility that the verse had been cut "only" to save time, perhaps he did not bring it up with the choir director later because upon further reflection he had seen the other class members' point, and had decided that asking what initially felt like an innocent question would instead come across as critique. Or maybe he simply forgot. It is possible for the recognition of cracks in the system to produce social change, but it is also rare, as it is also difficult. And it might require a more focused plan for integrating theology's work into the broader system. Even the force of a good, communicable argument does not by necessity create strong effects.

Based on the way that I tried to introduce academic theology into the ecclesial environment—a way, I have argued, that makes it able to be intelligible in the ecclesial environment—it seems that the majority of social and theological changes that are possible and that are, indeed, more common, are not particularly dramatic. But that does not mean that they are not worth pursuing. Indeed, what it reveals is that inasmuch as social and theological change might be a goal for academic theologians to bring about in ecclesial environments, the process of making and remaking our theological agency together through theological conversations across difference might be its own type of good.

Deacon Devotions for Theological Coherence

Just as group members experienced moments of tension between what they were learning in class and the broader church life, they also experienced moments of deeper coherence. Harlan, for example, noted that his belief in the Trinity was more consciously affirmed as he sang the doxology benediction one morning in worship, a chorus that is sung as often as any other hymn but has no standard, repeated liturgical function at FBC. The fact that no social or theological change can really be perceived in these moments, however, when the fit between culture and action seems so *intimately integrated*, as Swidler puts it, does not mean that the academic theological interventions had no effect on class members' theological agency.

Moments of social or theological change associated with unsettled moments, we have seen, were largely limited in scope to individual lives and in-class conversation. When these moments had the potential to leave our space for broader impact, the risks associated with doing so seemed mostly too great. Without a detailed plan for dissemination, new ideas remained firmly held within our atypical space. Moments of theological coherence, however, associated with settled lives, had the potential to leave the classroom, in large part because those who experienced them had the theological agency to intuit their acceptability and intelligibility beyond the borders of our classroom. While any impact by our class on the larger church structure remained at best largely imperceptible, therefore, our shared conversational practices, as atypical practices, were nevertheless able to reorient participants to the larger structure in fresh ways. In that reorienting, the ripples that were sent into the broader community may not have changed it, but they contributed to its flourishing anyway.

Joan, for example, shared a story about one such ripple: "One thing this course did for me: I had an assignment to do a devotion for the deacons, and in keeping with the [FBC's] theme for this year—Worship and Prayer—I chose to think of hymns to sing that we sing specifically to God, Jesus, or Spirit . . . this class triggered that thought in me that I developed for that devotion."

While devotions based on the Trinity might be atypical for deacons' meetings, they are certainly not disruptive, or even controversial. By carrying a little piece of our class to another room in the church, Joan did not disrupt or dismantle anything. But she did remind FBC's crucial leadership team, whether they were aware of it or not, of a belief they hold but rarely articulate. Like a missionary from our field, arriving to a place she finds needs no converting, Joan was able to share in a collective remembering that affirmed the coherence of our community. The very tool she had picked up from our atypical space was put to work for the larger institution's use.

No Plodding Reformism?

So where do we find ourselves with regard to Tanner's claim that doing theology as a form of cultural production does not by necessity maintain ecclesial status quo or entail *plodding reformism*? While I found it possible to generate and contribute to unsettling moments that had the potential to engender social and theological change, there were limits to what those possibilities could proliferate.[43] As I mentioned previously, my inability to produce or contribute to producing large-scale, sustained social and theological transformation might have more to do with my own failures in the field—or the fact that my field was a conservative church—than with the possibility of such transformation per se. Yet, as I have also noted before, the documentation of similar struggles within more progressive churches reveals the latter claim, at least, is questionable. As for my own failure, which was certainly a factor, I hope I have demonstrated the ease with which other academic theologians who love their churches might find themselves in my shoes. I have endeavored to engage reflexive testing of the limits and possibilities for transformation throughout the fieldwork process, and that testing has revealed few situations in which I felt like I could push the group much further than I did without losing their acceptance (which was required for continued teaching) or becoming unintelligible (a certain degree of intelligibility is also required for teaching).

I am not arguing here, however, that academic theologians should give up on trying to generate social and theological change and begin valuing the status quo. More so, I want to reveal the idealism inherent to theological projects that imagine they can overturn social, theological, and ecclesial norms with ease. I want to question radical notions and revolutionary ideas that remain in the realm of ideas and that never actually manage to hit the ground running. The view from above the fray is certainly useful, as I have already argued, but perhaps it is only useful insofar as it can plan for its own reimmersion into the practices of everyday life. There are certainly goods inherent to the plodding reformism (and even plodding stasis) that is associated with much of church life. There are also certain pleasures associated with being a cog in the machine, as I hope this chapter reveals. More to the point, though, I hope that my own failures open space for other academic theologians to reflect on how to deploy their own theological agency within their communities of spiritual practice more boldly. This concluding section looks to my own experience to try to open that conversation up.

First, with the stories about how heresy or heterodoxy can unsettle communal norms to open up a theological conversation across difference, we saw how important it can be for an academic theologian to partner with others who inhabit the sphere she wishes to influence. Bolder ideas I attempted to introduce on my own typically fell flat. For example, my own attempts to introduce expansive language for God into conversation faltered until others like Richard, Peter, and Jerry were willing to deploy their own social resources along the same lines.

When academic theologians write theological texts, we do so with the sense that a well-researched and articulated argument—no matter how avant-garde—will be convincing enough to keep an audience engaged (whether or not they agree). To a certain degree, this is how effective communication functions in academic theology. But when we extend that principle to the ecclesial or everyday sphere, we can run into problems. No matter how supposedly "accessible" we make the textual missives that we lob into "The Church," without a rich understanding of the particular communities in which we imagine they'll land, their impact in those communities will remain compromised. A theological method that begins with forming deep, bodily knowledge of that ecclesial or everyday sphere realizes that it cannot lob lone missives from afar. Rather, it needs to find partners in the field whose own social and theological resources can aid in the processes of translation and transformation. Only when theology involves a reciprocal partnership from the beginning can it be mutually beneficial to those same partners.

Here we might hear Peter's insights from the first chapter: everyday and academic theologies need each other if they are to effect social and theological change together. But as he pointed out, everyday and academic theologies come shaped by and responsible to various social forces and institutions that imbue them with their power. It would be naïve for academic theologians not to pay attention to the ways in which power is deployed within our fields of study. As I found in the partnerships I forged in order to bring new ideas into our ecclesial practice, those of us to whom various forms of power accrued had a better chance of introducing something perceived as more threatening—heretical or heterodox—into the conversation. And yet, by deploying our power thusly, we opened space for those around whom less power accrued to take some theological risks as well.

Second, with the stories of liturgical formation, we saw how theology works at the level of affect and emotion, not just intellect. What people had learned consciously in class contributed to shaping and reshaping their bodily ways of being in worship. It impacted how worship *felt*. These small shifts remained localized at the individual and classroom level for the most part for us. Yet Anne's story from Chapter 1 revealed how deeply affect and emotion can remain in a person's theological agency over time—both for ill and for good. Were we to follow Bourdieu and focus our attention primarily on the ongoing production and reproduction of culture, we might miss these near imperceptible changes. But following Ortner's method, we should note that these failures at perfect reproduction—these slippages in the loop—reveal the possibility of something more creative taking place. While we might not see the whole system topple, as Tanner's hope suggests, it is worth noting that if anything is to cause it to drop, it might be the theological emotion or embodied theology as much—if not more than—the intellectual. Or at least, it might require a project in which emotional and intellectual resources share. Academic theological attention to these dimensions of theological production are thus also required if we are to have the impact on Christian practice we imagine, and hope, our work can have.

Finally, with the stories of theological coherence we see the goods of less dramatic social and theological formation leaking out into a broader ecclesial system, supporting the richness of theological engagement that occurs therein. Here we recall Joan and Harlan's insistence from Chapter 1 that theology must not just be talking but also be acting. In this chapter we see that while the activities of our class did not necessarily cause any transformation in Joan's beliefs, they did impact her actions as she tried a style of devotional leadership she hadn't tried before. Rather than focusing on *either* how practice informs theology *or* how theology informs practice, ethnographic theologians must pay attention to both sides of the equation if we are to witness the reciprocal relationship between the two.

The ways in which traditional ethnographic theology helps us with the former task are clear. An ethnographic theological method like the one being developed here, which involved the academic theologian in the ongoing life of the community within which she does her research, allows the possibility of working on the latter task as well. My concern here is not for academic theological policing of everyday Christian practice. I am not interested in academic interventions that endeavor to conform everyday theological thought and action to specific theological ends. I don't think that if people just *get the Trinity right*, for example, that they will be able to experience and foster more equitable relationships. Rather, I am interested in how these interventions can help orient Christian practitioners to their own beliefs and practices in more fully reflective ways. My hope is that this greater theological reflexivity, more so than so-called theological accuracy might help open us toward our neighbors in love.

Once again, reciprocal relationships between everyday Christians and academic theologians will be crucial in this process. But so too will be the need for the ethnographic theologian to engage reflexively with the ways in which her ecclesial and academic formation shapes both her theological agency and the ways in which she contributes to the shaping of other people's theological agency. While our actions consistently impact the field of our cultural production in unconscious ways, if we bring awareness to those actions we may become able to be more intentional about that impact.

Chapter 4

Carnal Theologies of Friendship, Sex, and Suffering

When, like Kathryn Tanner, we pay attention to the nature of theology as a cultural practice, we do not simply apply a sociological theory or anthropological method to a theological end. Rather, such interdisciplinarity actually changes how the processes of theological knowledge production work; it introduces new practices and norms, for example, new starting points and pathways, new goods and goals. When we speak of "carnal theology," then, we are talking about something shaped as much by the bodily practices associated with ethnographic fieldwork as it is by the somewhat disembodied practices of textual analysis, typically prioritized in academic theological writing. Of course, as we saw in Chapter 2, textual analysis has its own carnal comportment and knowledge too. But our theological texts typically obscure the contributions of these bodily dimensions, these habitus, to the production of academic theological knowledge. Indeed, they often obscure the production itself.

As Loïc Wacquant cites Pierre Bourdieu, the inherited intellectual history of the West "incline[s] us to see the body not as an instrument of but as an obstacle to knowledge," which in turn leads us "to ignore the specificity of practical knowledge, which is treated either as mere obstacle to knowing or as rudimentary science."[1] With carnal sociology, out of which the carnal theology is developed here, however, the researcher's embodiment is recognized as the crucial vector of knowledge out of which the academic thinking, speaking, and writing is labored. Wacquant writes: "A carnal sociology that seeks to situate itself not outside or above practice but at its 'point of production' requires that we immerse ourselves as deeply and as durably as possible into the cosmos under examination; that we submit ourselves to its specific temporality and contingencies; that we acquire the embodied dispositions it demands and nurtures, so that we may grasp it via the prethetic understanding that defines the native relation to that world—not as one world among many but as 'home.'"[2]

Likewise, carnal theology's "point of production" is in the ethnographic theologian's deep and durable immersion in the "cosmos under examination." For the ethnographic theologian, this cosmos not only is located in but also extends beyond her field of study toward the ways in which that specific location makes present a broader theological field made up of both everyday Christian social practices and academic theological practices. To be durably immersed in this cosmos requires submission to the ways its "specific temporality and contingencies" shape the ethnographic theologian's own theological agency. The ethnographic theologian's research and writing not only arises from, but also takes into explicit theological account, her embodied dispositions of belonging to and alienation from the way she experiences the field as "home."

To be clear, the field of study does not need to be the ethnographic theologian's church *home* in a literal sense, as it was for me at FBC. As I have been arguing throughout, this quality of home is shaped by the ways in which the ethnographic theologian engages reflexively with the way her field of study—whether or not that field is a site we would label as explicitly Christian—constitutes her theological agency. To recap, the organic relationship between everyday and academic theologies means that the theological agency of most academic theologians is already shaped—to varying, even fractured, degrees—by the Christian social practices that give rise to the questions we ask and seek to answer. We are, therefore, always already embroiled in some sort of relationship of belonging, even tangential belonging, to fields of Christian social practice, even if only indirectly.

These qualifications serve to highlight that the focus on embodiment in this chapter is not to narrow the fields in which an ethnographic theologian might conduct her study, but rather it is to demonstrate how she refuses and, indeed, explicitly refutes with her research methods the kinds of Cartesian epistemological dualism that still characterize the production of much theological—indeed, much academic—knowledge. Cartesian patterns of knowledge production are, first of all, notoriously individualistic. They mistrust relationality, particularly the emotional dimensions inherent to relationships, as detractors from knowledge. To reclaim the carnal dimensions of theological knowledge production, this chapter first explores some of the ways in which relationships, especially those that are emotionally charged, contributed to our practices of theological construction in our Sunday night classes.

Second, because they withdraw from the body as a locus of knowledge, Cartesian modes of knowledge production tend also to obscure the contributions of bodily difference to our ways of knowing. A methodological focus on embodiment does not automatically correct this problem, however, as Wacquant's carnal sociology well demonstrates. As I noted in Chapter 2, critics frequently accuse Wacquant of minimizing his racialized difference from the other gym members as well as of obscuring the role of women in that space. They state a desire for Wacquant to go "to more trouble to sort out the differences among the bodies at issue," to demonstrate how these bodies are "shot through with inequalities and dominations."[3] Wacquant argues, however, that in *Body and Soul*, he "deliberately brackets such differences to focus on similarities in order to capture *not diverse embodiments but the process of incarnation*" that happens as habitus comes to be structured for embodied agents in a particular social field.[4] In other words, Wacquant, following Bourdieu, is interested in social reproduction, not the slippage that occurs in the various configurations of submission and resistance enacted by agents in their social worlds to which Ortner has encouraged us to attend. To get at these questions of bodily difference, the second section of this chapter focuses on issues and theologies of sexuality that arose in our theological conversations at FBC.

The chapter's final section returns to questions of where carnal theology might produce social and theological change. If the first two sections are concerned with the contributions of embodiment to the production of theological knowledge, this final one is concerned with how theological knowledge produces—or, better, makes—a body. Here we construct a carnal theodicy, which is perhaps one of the more impossible doctrines to engage in a disembodied way given how crucial emotion, bodily pain, and relationships are to any theological reflections on suffering. In this final section, then, we see theological transformation happening somewhere beyond words, borne instead on the way one man in our class holds his body as it is pressed to absorb anew the devastating reality of suffering in our world.

A Breakdown in the Relational Cosmos

While all kinds of emotional bonds were formed among those who participated in our Sunday night classes, here I focus our attention on how they constellated around one person in the class: Ann, my friend with whom I shared Indian food, as outlined in Chapter 1. Ann died suddenly between the "Jesus Christ and Salvation" and "God as Trinity" classes. She had entered the hospital for a non-life-threatening procedure, but then her health declined rapidly as a result of complications. Toward the end, as I visited her daily in the hospital, I would linger at her side, never quite knowing which departure would be my last. And then one evening, we received a call that we should make our way to the ICU to say good-bye.

My husband Tyler and I spent a few hours that evening, holding Ann's hand, praying with her and singing hymns for her. It was the first time I'd realized just how much all those classic lyrics tell of how death is punctuated by glimmers of a life beyond. Tyler would begin to cry, and my voice would need to become stronger to keep the song going. Then he would do the same for me as I found lines too difficult even to read. I found myself hoping in these moments that the glimmers of glory punctuating the songs were true. A few times, when we were singing one of her favorites, Ann pulled her oxygen mask to the side of her face so that she could join her shaky voice with ours for a line or two. In these moments, she would return to us, and my desperate hope that this wasn't really the end for our friendship would transform into a vague belief that there might be something else beyond.

Ethnographers often form intense emotional bonds with their research partners and, as a result, have intense emotional experiences of their own.[5] While this experience of death felt uniquely painful to me, its intensity was not, therefore, unique to my own particular ethnographic theological method. Nevertheless, when such moments happen in ethnographic studies, they are usually aberrations, strange surplus fragments that hover at the fringes of the academic study. They are reported as flashes of insight that might illuminate the whole project but are rarely, if ever, incorporated as methodological guides or sites for explicit reflection throughout it. Intentionally deploying my own theological agency—which is shaped not only by academic training but also by ecclesial belonging—as a research tool, however, makes moments like this matter significantly for what I am doing.

Ann's death makes any abstract notion of relationality concrete here. Losing her, we lost a beloved friend whose contribution to our conversations had its own particular character. We lost someone who, as Gene and Gary described in interviews before her death, was someone to whom they could turn for wise counsel if they needed it. We lost someone who would "struggle her way through" a problem, Richard had said. I always encountered this struggle in her as inspiring and ferocious tenacity, but Gene described it with calmer notes, recalling how Ann was always able to "filter information and avenues and take a deep breath and reflect." Ann, it seemed, saw herself differently, as she would often apologize for "talking too much." Each person in the room connects with the others differently. The relationships in the classroom thus matter not only for how we interpret what is said therein but for shaping what actually gets said to begin with.

Ann, as we saw in Chapter 1, naturally wove personal narrative, personal loss, frustration, and joy into her theological practice. Theology for her was deeply embodied, absolutely integrated with her life experiences and with her own sense of marginalization as a woman but also with her own sense of important topics like human fallibility or social responsibility. As a result, Ann's contributions to our theological constructions were frequently grounded in different kinds of storytelling, and her classroom demeanor frequently demonstrated care toward those she perceived to be excluded. To borrow Joan's language from the first chapter, Ann was someone who not only *talked* theology but also *acted* it. In the stories that follow, Ann's talking theology helps us, as a group, open up a conversation about Divine inspiration for deeper understanding. Her acting theology demonstrates a desire for inclusivity by encouraging a potentially marginalized voice to speech. Both cases reveal how much I needed Ann to help open up both the group and me to richer theological engagement; they reveal the importance of bodies in space together, of relationships playing out in processes of theological knowledge construction.

Talking Theology

While Ann was unable to attend the first night of the "Jesus Christ and Salvation" class, she joined us for the second session, sliding into the conversation quickly and with ease. Within a few minutes of class opening, we fell into a rapidly moving conversation about how the New Testament had been assembled. A number of class members began tossing out various ideas they had absorbed and developed over the years about the interaction of oral and written tradition, processes by which events had come to be written down decades after their happening, and imaginative musings about how the early Christian communities may have engaged such a dynamic process of memory keeping.

I frequently discerned at FBC that a difference of theological opinion between a cocongregant and myself was grounded in a more fundamental difference in our biblical and theological hermeneutics—a topic that could be difficult to address in everyday theological conversation. Surprised by their openness to what I interpreted as historical and source criticism, I wanted to linger there and so offered small interjections recalled from my MDiv biblical studies classes to demonstrate that I encouraged their line of thought. No one seemed especially bothered by the idea that the Gospels were not written at the moment that their events happened or even that a complex of oral and written traditions might have been used in the process of their construction, as one might expect Southern Baptists to be. It felt like we had reached a potentially fruitful moment in our conversation where I might have the chance both to learn a little more about the interpretive complexity actually allowed by doctrines of biblical literalism and divine inspiration of scripture (both upheld at FBC, as well as in Southern Baptist and much evangelical life in general) while also having the chance to introduce new practices of interpretation to the group that I had found helpful in my own theological learning.

With this among other pathways now open before us for conversation, Ann begins to imagine various contexts and motivations for the writing of Mark's Gospel in particular: "I can't help but believe that the members of the early church, the early Christians . . . that they didn't get together in those days and say, 'what do you remember? How much do you remember?' That's human nature. You're gonna check it out." Infusing the potential process by which the Gospels may have been assembled with her own sense of curiosity, imagining that the writers and recorders must have shared that same curiosity because to her it feels so natural, Ann drew a very practical picture of how a biblical text gets written. This picture held close to a vision of Divine inspiration while complicating it with a more communal slant than typical images of a Divine source speaking directly into a writer's ear allow. Moreover, it was a picture to which the rest of the people in the room seemed not only open but also quite familiar with: "Mark was being led by the Spirit," she added, "but I don't know exactly how the Spirit works all the time, so He could easily be at work in the sharing in Christian community of what they remembered about what happened."

According to Ann, the Spirit's work directing the production of canonical texts thus occurs not at the level of the individual but rather via a process of dynamic and communal theological conversation and recollection: "So they [the disciples] share with each other their own personal experiences with Jesus, but somehow in God's own wisdom in picking Mark, He was able to sort those things out and use what he knew to do what He wanted to do in this Gospel." God is involved in the process, even guiding it toward God's own ends, and yet Mark's limitations also contribute to the text's construction in Ann's view. Closing off, she noted, "I don't know about you all, but I just think Mark was in a hurry. He had to write it down because they wanted to know what to tell the people who weren't with Jesus. He could have thought, 'I want to write it down so we don't forget.'"

I have already described some of the theological reasons the "God as Trinity" class was harder to teach than the "Jesus Christ and Salvation" one, like the disparate understandings we each had of how God is mystery or fears that a wrathful God would punish heresy. While those theological assessments grasp significant aspects of the problems we encountered, I also think we suffered simply because Ann was no longer there. Sometimes a chatty person can be helpful for a teacher, mainly because they leave little empty, dead time for us to fill. But more than filler, and in addition to her ability to be theologically insightful, Ann also called out the best in me as a teacher. Sometimes she would make points that, in my error, I might have dismissed too quickly if spoken by someone else. When she spoke them, however, my trust in her made me work harder to see the fullness of what she was saying.[6] When Ann started describing a doctrine like Divine Inspiration, I wasn't tempted to argue; rather, I'd want to hear what it meant to her, because the answer almost always was intriguing and creative.

Furthermore, whereas some class members would become quieter if I tried to question one of their ideas, allowing my authority as the teacher inadvertently to silence them, I knew that Ann would push back if I interpreted her wrongly. Our friendship could survive such scuffles. I felt the freedom to chase down her thoughts, challenge them, and engage them so that we could refine and expand them together. I could trust that she would stick with me in that process because, despite her fear that she talked too much, she also never managed to rein herself in once she got going—and this was one of her gifts. Ann and I together could model a vibrant form of theological conversation that invited others to experiment with the same. In so doing, we moved toward opening multiple ideas further together.

Thus Ann helped me avoid the quick construction of some coherent theological product, instead keeping me situated in the slow process of pursuing wisdom. She helped me practice theological lingering with ideas whose directions I could not predict or that I could see and was hesitant to engage. Similarly, she helped me relinquish control of the conversational space and follow where others led. Without her presence, I had to learn how to embody such conversational dispositions alone. This took time, as it also required the creation of new relationships and new bonds of trust. New members joined the class, and old members filled in some of Ann's gaps. Even with these new additions of conversation partners who I came to treasure, however, this new class always bore a trace of the old. Ann's absence from the room became less pressing, as absences often can, but it never disappeared.

Acting Theology

In addition to offering various insights that opened up theological imagination for myself and others, Ann also brought a pastoral presence to the room. She had a particular knack for making younger women—myself included—feel welcome in spaces from which she perhaps once felt herself excluded. Losing Ann meant we lost one of our feistier female voices; in a more particular way, we lost a woman whose presence helped other women speak out too.

Caroline was a new member at FBC and a recent convert to Christianity through her participation in addiction recovery groups. Various stories she told hinted that she had at one time lived on the streets. Her ease, comfort, and understanding with the people who were guests at Room in the Inn, FBC's ministry for homeless people, demonstrated clear familiarity with that world. Caroline, in fact, joined our class because of the friendship she and I had developed as volunteers in that work. She was not as well-versed theologically as other class members and admitted to feeling intellectually intimidated by the group to me in a one-on-one conversation.

In addition to not fitting in with the church's education and social class norms, Caroline likewise did not comply with the norms of Southern femininity also marking the bodies of most women at FBC.[7] Caroline was easily read via the lens of female masculinity, as she dressed in baggy t-shirts and jeans from the men's department that she frequently held secure with a piece of string, explaining that this option was cheaper and, hence, better than a belt. She wore no makeup and kept her hair short and shaggy, largely unstyled.[8] She worked in the US Marshal's office in Nashville and had a hardened, aggressive, yet very likable, playful demeanor once one got to know her. Caroline was fun and funny even as I was at times intimidated by her style of humor, especially when she teased me for being a bit of a "girly girl." She was clearly more comfortable at Room in the Inn than she was in a theology class, and after our first Sunday night together I had made a note to myself to try to find ways both to include her in conversations and to demonstrate to her how much her presence in the room was valued. As our conversation got flying on that second night, though, and as I tried to keep up and keep moving, I initially lost track both of how Caroline might be feeling and of my goal to be intentionally inclusive with her.

It wasn't until I listened to my digital recordings of the evening later that I realized Ann had immediately intuited Caroline's discomfort and addressed it directly. Because there were new members to the second class, I had asked the group to introduce themselves briefly again. Caroline was the only class member who Ann addressed directly in this process, offering our new church member a friendly welcome. Then in the midst of our rapidly moving conversation, Caroline interjected a short question in response to the relationship between oral and written traditions, "And a lot of people didn't read then, right?" Ann and I both picked up the point and ran with it, and then when Mike joined in, on the recording I could hear Ann—who was sitting next to me—whispering encouragement to Caroline: "That was a good point!" She quickly rejoined the flow of conversation, but not without taking the time to encourage someone she perceived as potentially marginalized within the group. In this way, Ann's contributions to classroom conversation came not only in the mode of her own theological insights but also in the ways she sought to draw quieter voices into conversation as well. Particularly because I wasn't always able to do this myself, I was especially grateful for Ann's natural pastoral presence in the room. And in this way, the bodily, relational dynamics at play in our group did not detract from, but rather contributed to our theological conversation.

Carnal Theology and Engaging Difference

Given the ways in which Ann and others were able to open the group to engaging both ideas and people who did not conform to FBC's dominant theological and social norms, I wondered where else dissonance in the communal doxa might be able to be nurtured. In the last chapter, I wrote about how this dissonance facilitates various forms of social and theological change within communal practices. Here I continue that conversation, focused specifically through the lens of bodily knowledge, through notions of what *just feels right* or *feels natural* to people in our community. Given the significance of such bodily knowledge of the *natural* to debates around sexuality (or their avoidance) in churches in general, and conservative churches in particular, I found myself both wanting to engage notions of carnal theology around this topic and somewhat fearful of doing so. Just how do you have *that* conversation at FBC?

You Might Have to Leave

Before I left Nashville, I had a good-bye lunch with an FBC friend who, like Caroline, had recently converted to Christianity and did not conform her appearance or bodily comportment to the hetero-gender norms of Southern white femininity. Perhaps it was because this would be our last time hanging out that she felt like she could raise her long-buried concerns with me. She shared that she had "a number of gay and lesbian friends" who were upset by her religious conversion, and whom she did not want to now categorize as "sinners" because of their sexual identities and practices. Throughout our conversation, I shared that I also "had a hard time" with FBC views around sexuality (this was an understatement, and I phrased it that way to pastorally echo her own language use), that I supported same-sex marriage, and that I didn't think "homosexuality" was sinful.[9]

At first, it seemed difficult for this woman to hear my affirmations of the goodness of same-sex desire, probably because they were so contrary to what other leaders at FBC had taught her. Once she began processing them, however, she expressed shock, admitting that she hadn't even realized it was possible to be a Christian—let alone a minister—and believe such things. Slowly, she began to express relief that she might not have to choose between her friends and her faith after all. I knew, however, that these weren't yet questions that she could safely explore at FBC. Raising them in the mainstream of our culture would most likely lead to an affirmation of the mostly unspoken communal belief that same-sex desire and sexual practice was sinful, and I worried that this woman would become convinced of this claim if she heard it enough. I therefore acknowledged with regret that FBC might not be a place that could help her faith flourish and that this was FBC's error, not hers. We chatted about which churches in Nashville would welcome her questions and openness, and I encouraged her to try one of them out instead.

In other words, I did a small act that ran completely contrary to the norms around not only sexuality but also mission at FBC: I tried to send somebody away. I was deeply saddened by the response I felt I needed to give, and once again I experienced a sense of regret that during my time at FBC, despite the considerable forms of authority and access to providing education I had been granted, I had not managed to contribute to a conversation that would result in this woman feeling welcome in our community in the fullness of who she was. Really, I had not managed to shape a conversation in which I could fully participate either.

Both in the moment and looking back now, I wonder if the conversation I had with this woman about sexuality, or the various passing comments that Caroline and I shared about the same topic, were either woman's attempt to "come out" to me. With both, I tried to make it very clear that I did not share the mainstream FBC view on this issue. Nevertheless, the place of authority I held within church life may still have meant that for them our shared space could not be safe enough to bear their secret if, indeed, they did identify with some form of queer identity outside of their church lives. This, indeed, marks one of the limitations on these particular ethnographic theological methods, especially as deployed within this particular context; embodying such a complicated configuration of insider-outsider status, I felt limited at times in the types of questions I could ask. My conversations with people about theology and sexuality thus remained in the realm of the general, the political, or in connection to the lives of others. They rarely touched down into the particularity of our own sexual preferences or practices.

The compulsory heterosexuality that shaped the doxa at FBC—fostered not only by the invisibility of any queer-identified folks in the community but also by the ways in which numerous programs divided participants according to marriage and family status—meant that it was difficult to cultivate safe space to talk about diverse sexualities in our Sunday night classes. While issues of sexism and racism came up in some of our conversations, issues of homophobia never did. And while I taught feminist, black, and Latin American liberation theologies in both courses, I never plucked up the courage to teach queer theologies. Putting feminist theologies on the syllabus (which was a public document, available to church members beyond the borders of the self-named liberals who actually enrolled in the class) already felt like a controversial stretch. I was quite sure that the language of "queer" would not even compute for most church members, many of whom would interpret it as a prejudicial slur rather than a term reclaimed and repurposed by queer communities in a positive way.

Indeed, for a number of class members, I wondered if the language of "queer" would register as having any sexual meaning—that is, any meaning beyond "strange or odd," which is the first entry for the term in the *Oxford English Dictionary*—at all. The phrase, "queer theology," I surmised, would be encountered at best as an oxymoron for most of those who did know of the term's contemporary usage. But these are theories I never tested. Whether or not my assessment was correct, they mark the border of what felt possible to me with regard to conversations about sexuality at FBC. Certainly, a desire to maintain my belonging—and, by extension, my privilege—at FBC contributed to the extent to which I failed to disrupt these borders. My desires for social and theological transformation in our community thus not only contributed to but were also complicit in reproducing the status quo. But at the same time my belonging—and, again, my privilege—let me experiment with where I discerned such conversations might be possible.

Homosexual Holiness

One such place was in one-on-one conversations where the topic arose somewhat organically, as happened one day with Gloria. I met Gloria for a conversation and lunch in a crowded chain restaurant near my school, Vanderbilt Divinity, and before I realized it, ninety minutes had flown by. The intense bustle of the crowd gave us some cover of anonymity, and we settled quickly into rapid-moving, vibrant conversation. Gloria, a married woman in her late sixties, with a host of grandchildren about whom she likes to boast frequently, says what's on her mind without seeming to worry too much about what others think. Because her lack of filters did tend to get us off topic quite frequently in class—in ways that were sometimes fruitful, and sometimes just seemed to get us lost—she could be a bit of a handful while I was teaching. She would frequently miss class because a grandchild had been visiting, there was football game on that night, or she simply felt she had gotten more than enough church that morning. This in itself was fine, of course, but her desire for everyone to catch her up on what she had missed the week after when we were trying to move on to something new could sometimes prove distracting.

Despite the challenges these disruptions created for me as the teacher, there was something I liked about Gloria's willingness to assert herself in this way. Women rarely presumed the right to dominate space or other people's time so boldly at FBC, and so I enjoyed her refusal to comply with such social norms. These characteristics also made one-on-one, more agenda-less time with her really enjoyable because, given my lack of power to guide our conversations, I could enjoy the thrill of having no idea where we were going to end up. Even so, with our interview, I made sure to have my questions sketched out really clearly in advance, and emphasized my desire to get through them all with her. Otherwise I feared we would never make it past the first one.

Gloria shared how much she enjoyed hearing so many opinions on Sunday nights that differed from the FBC mainstream. We talked about the topic of salvation for a while, and she outlined a more universalist soteriology than I typically heard at FBC, which she grounded in her fundamental notion that "God is love." Given her vision of an expansive, inclusive God, I sensed that she might be someone with whom I could talk about sexuality, so I brought up the topic of same-sex marriage, which was all over the news at that time.

Gloria begins slowly with her response, as if feeling me out, "On homosexuality, it's been a hard thing for so long, but I don't know." As she trails off, creating space for me to interject, I am immediately struck that this is not a new issue with which Gloria is grappling. It seems that, like a few of the other older class members who I interviewed, she's been thinking about same-sex desire for much longer than the current form of political debate has been shaping public imagination on the topic. And this means that she approaches questions of same-sex marriage, hospital visitation rights, and other contentious public debates within a larger framework of experience and understanding.

Gloria's initial examples of what has shaped her own inchoate stance begin with general, less personal types of narrative. For example, she tells me that she enjoys reading Marcus Borg—who she incorrectly believes to be gay—and that she trusts him as a "real Christian." While she is not right about Borg's sexuality, her point is that she believes that one can be a "committed Christian" *and* gay ("it's just in their DNA," she states). Implicitly drawing on the logic of "homosexual holiness,"[10] Gloria's point is that even Christians who can't accept the compatibility of the supposedly conflicting identity markers of "Christian" and "gay" must at least let the reality of someone like Borg challenge their views.

In Gloria's intuitive, carnal theology, Borg's writings demonstrate the fruits of someone living the Christian life, which would be impossible if he were living daily with some immense, unrepented sinful activity going on. Therefore, if he is also engaged in same-sex desire and practice, these cannot constitute a sin in need of repentance; or the evidence must at least make one question whether or not they are. Gloria's logic is not fully articulated here; rather, she has an intuitive, carnal awareness that things just don't add up; they just don't feel right in her bones. This incongruence marks a feeling she can neither shake nor reconcile. As a result, for her, the fruits of Borg's faith indicate its authenticity and thus have the power to sanction the core aspects of who he is, including his sexuality (once again, despite the fact that she is wrong about that sexuality). Gloria's stance is not systematic or even cognitively reasoned, however. It makes sense to her at the bodily level: "It's just in their DNA."

The logic of homosexual holiness is, of course, deeply problematic, as it requires that queer-identified people be able to justify their sexual practices according to the types of social and theological structures that already marginalize and oppress them. To claim it as a strategy for social and theological change is therefore questionable at best. My purpose here rather is descriptive; Gloria was not the only person I interviewed who claimed this type of logic as instrumental in expanding their theological views around sexuality. This leaves academic theologians with the question of not only what strategies might be better for our justice-seeking goals but, more so, what we should do when strategies that we have deemed problematic seem to achieve the goals we are pursuing. When we have enough power to do *something*, but not enough to strategize large-scale change, how can we deploy imperfect tactics to at least cause a little slippage in the reproduction of the social systems that shape our daily lives?

I Know Someone

While the problematic logic of homosexual holiness marked some of the relationships that contributed to Gloria's carnal theology of sexuality, her broader theological views had been challenged simply by proximity to queer-identified individuals, whether or not these individuals could justify themselves according to some socially or theologically determined bar. In these cases, the theology Gloria talked, to borrow Joan's language once again, was directly shaped by the theology she acted. Called to compassion for those she perceived to require it, whether or not they had earned it, so to speak, Gloria demonstrated the willingness to have her scriptural hermeneutics challenged and reshaped by her awareness of changing sexual mores.

With a somewhat hushed voice, Gloria begins to share with me how, over the years, more than one person in her peer group at the church has had a child come out as gay or lesbian (one parent actually being a former member of the ministry staff). These are church secrets she's sharing, and so she only names those people who no longer belong to the congregation, leaving descriptions of those who have hung around vaguely articulated. It seems at some point, out of love for their friends, their own children and their friends' children, Gloria's peer group had worked through these questions about sexuality together, arriving at views contrary to FBC's norm. At no point does Gloria claim the logic of homosexual holiness as a guiding principle for the group's explorations. Rather, her motivation lay in the simple fact, in her view, that God is love. "If people in this church had any idea who's sitting next to them," she added, demonstrating like Ann the significance of relational, bodily presence for theological construction, "they would be shocked . . . God has to love these people." Then, speaking of her peer group's response to that love, "It's been a process because of my generation and how we thought about it. But we've come really far."

Gloria does not articulate the biblical and theological studies conducted with her peers all those years ago with any precision, however, as she recounts the experience. Rather, she chats with that learned reasoning hanging in the background, shaping the theological structures she now brings to a variety of theological questions. As second nature, the once radical learning now structures Gloria's theological agency, a part of her own carnal knowledge. Alluding to a variety of biblical passages that most FBC members—and most evangelicals in general—would take to be about homosexuality, she describes her belief that Paul is talking about "child pedophilia and stuff," or "the orgy thing," and not about anything that looks like a contemporary understanding of committed same-sex relationships.

In the moment, I choose not to bring up the heteronormative framework that I see undergirding any sanctioning of same-sex relations that look like idealized, traditional straight ones. Instead I am struck by the fact that, like Gloria, I too could not name these scripture passages precisely without looking them up; I, too, have internalized these once radical learnings such that they are part of my embodied theological agency and, thus forgotten—at least in any precise way. Like Gloria, I know there was a time when I didn't know them, when something else felt natural. These learnings thus mark the now everyday theology out of which any academic theological reflection I might do on topics of sexuality grows. A tacit agreement thus hangs in the air between Gloria and me that passages used by our community to support homophobia hold no such power for us. Somewhere along the way, our community's doxa became heterodox to us. As a result, reinterpreting these passages is revealed not to be the goal of our conversation; rather, it is the ground.

Not Just "Homosexuality"

These conversations with Gloria were not the only ones in which I saw an accepted social norm (e.g., one should love one's friends' kids) or theological norm (e.g., God is love) disrupt our community's doxa related to same-sex desire. As a result, and given my sense that same-sex desire was not a topic that could be addressed directly in the classroom, I began to wonder if there was a way to get at the topic more obliquely. What conversation could we have that might disrupt our doxa and cause a ripple effect that made seemingly impossible conversations possible? Around the same time I was pondering this, I was also reading Kelly Brown Douglas's groundbreaking text, *Sexuality and the Black Church.*[11] Brown Douglas situates claims to homophobia in black churches in a broader, racialized understanding of sexuality. Because constructions of African American sexuality are negatively shaped within a dominant, white racist social system, she argues, it can be difficult to raise conversations about any form of sexuality at all in black churches.

While Brown Douglas's connecting of racialization to sexuality made me wonder what role the construction of Southern whiteness, specifically Southern white femininity had to play in the fact that we rarely talked about sex at FBC, especially in mixed-gender company, it was the connection she drew between homophobia and a broader sexual silence that had more direct bearing on the issue I was facing in our classroom. My intuition that we could not discuss queer theology (whatever I chose to call it) on Sunday nights grew directly out of my realization that we lacked the tools for talking about sex in general. So, as I began the "Jesus Christ and Salvation" semester, I committed myself to try to interject mature, forthright conversations about sexuality whenever the chance arose. Even with this commitment bolstered by my ethnographic observations and academic justifications, however, I found the embodied aspects of doing theology with this goal a little trickier than I initially anticipated.

The night we studied Beatrice of Nazareth seemed to me to be a perfect place to begin introducing these topics, given the more erotic dimensions to her writing. And so as I packed up my lesson plan for the evening and drove over to the church, I reminded myself to stay aware for these erotic moments so that I might direct our attention toward them. In her *Seven Ways of Holy Love*, a text shaped by literary conventions of courtly love, Beatrice outlines a pathway of mystical ascent to the Divine.[12] The charged language makes this a fun text to read and so, whereas I usually just lecture on various thinkers' theologies, with Beatrice's text I brought handouts containing sections of her writing for us to read aloud together. Just a few lines into our shared reading, however, the group's response is negative: "What is she trying to earn?" someone asks, "It seems like she's trying to gain her own salvation rather than relying on God for it!" Someone else adds, "It seems selfish. She wants to do it all. Why would you want to transcend your humanity? God made us human. It's a little selfish!"

Why was no one concerned about powerful activities of prayer when it was men we were studying? I wonder to myself, a little frustrated. As already mentioned, I experience FBC as a complex place when it comes to the construction of gender. On the one hand, I feel affirmed by the community in my ordination and teaching vocation. Nevertheless, I have also experienced attitudes I perceive as sexist. Language of men as the "spiritual head of the household" is spoken—and contested—at FBC, by both members and leadership. Various Sunday night classes affirm and even impose traditional gender roles on both women and men. I have personally experienced what I perceive as sexism through comments like those often received by female preachers, such as, "I couldn't hear a word she was saying, but I sure enjoyed watching her say it."[13] I may be oversensitive to gender issues in some contexts at FBC, but this sensitivity is well founded in others. My immediate, frustrated reaction to the group's negative comments thus made a certain sort of sense. Moreover, I sensed that if I wanted to interject a conversation about sexuality, then we at least needed to begin from an acceptance of embodied spiritual practices. If bodily practice was pejoratively associated with "works righteousness" by the group, this was going to be more of an uphill battle than I had initially realized. Surely introducing notions of the erotic would further marginalize Beatrice in the group's interpretation of her.

I attempt a number of tactics to move us along. "Mystics don't think they're doing this of their own power," I note, "but rather they are describing what it feels like to be lifted up by God. Their beating of the flesh is like us singing songs." When this doesn't work, I try describing the concept of "mystical ascent" by drawing on Augustine's experience in the *Confessions*, which I tend to take to be pretty authoritative. This too fails to convince. It seems I lack the resources to help open up this text. But then Peter, latching on to the language of "ascent," slaps the table and with a grin speaks the words to a familiar hymn, "I'm pressing on the upward way." Ann immediately catches his line of thinking, laughs and gestures toward him, adding, "New heights I'm reaching every day."

My academic theological agency had certainly kicked in there: who better to authorize a questionable practice than a foundational theologian of the Western tradition? I feel somewhat chastened by how quickly I turned to a male theologian to authorize a female one. But in the end, it was this reference to a favorite Baptist hymn that got the group to consider how Beatrice's actions might connect with Christian forms we take to be theologically authoritative in our community. Now the conversation starts to open up.

The group begins brainstorming scripture passages to support Beatrice's practice, and then they let her practice reinterpret more dramatic scriptural stories that have perhaps been domesticated by our contemporary context. When one class member wonders aloud if John's visions at Patmos had functioned with the bodily intensity of Beatrice's, it is almost too much for our more conservative class member, Mike to bear. Usually Mike's disagreements register on his body in small, restrained fidgets until he finds a way to express them verbally. But now, unable to control himself, he pushes his chair back from the table dramatically. His deep voice shoots up an octave: "You mean to say that John's visions were like THIS!" he exclaims. He emphasizes "THIS" by first smacking his palm to his copy of our handout, and then by shaking the paper in the air before slapping it back down onto the table.

Mike's body in this moment produces his theology as powerfully as do his words. A few of us burst out laughing and I smile, "Maybe Mike, who knows? They might have been!" Our shared laughter grows louder as Mike, shaking his head with a look of amazement on his face, chortles, "Well, I don't know. I just don't know." The friendly humor of the moment allows us all to feel comfortable with the drama, to rest on it and incorporate it into our ways of approaching the texts. But also, the fact that many in the class understand themselves as "progressive" or "liberal" in relation to Mike makes me wonder if his—albeit uncomfortable—willingness to link John and Beatrice will challenge others to experiment with being a little more open minded too. I begin wondering if it might be time to introduce the eros of the text to our discussion.

As soon as the thought occurs to me, I become acutely aware of my flesh. I immediately recall the comments about my sermon from the man who is less interested in what I have to say than how I look while saying it. At the same time, any class members toward whom I feel even a passing attraction all of a sudden seem to pulse a little brighter in their seats. Eroticism is an area of academic interest for me, about which I speak quite freely in an academic context as well as in life in general. But as soon as I move into trying to talk about it in this ecclesial arena, I find myself struck with something akin to the fear of God. My skin gets hot, and I wonder if I'm visibly flushed, even though I haven't yet started to speak. And while all I want to do now is take off my sweater to alleviate the sweat that is starting to form in my armpits, the idea of removing clothing as I'm about to start a conversation about sexuality feels downright impossible. And so I start euphemizing my academic interests—not to mention personal experience—with all the grace of an embarrassed teenager.

"I realize the language is violent," I begin, "but doesn't *anything* in it also sound good?" *Maybe someone else has picked up on the sexual aspects*, I hope to myself, *and will bring it up so I don't have to. Ugh, when did I become such a baby with this stuff?* But no one takes the bait. Perhaps they do not share my affirmation of sexual pleasure as a good thing; perhaps they hear that this is sexual, but don't like the sound of it. "No," someone responds, "it just sounds painful." Out of the corner of my eye I see my friend Miriam, with whom I've had the kinds of conversations girlfriends have about sex, smirk and lower her gaze. No one is coming to help me. "Really?" I continue, "There's nothing in Beatrice's bodily experience that sounds familiar?" I immediately think *what a silly thing this is to ask*—why presume this is familiar to them?—but I swear I see Gene smile now too. Still no aid, though. "OK," I try a final time, really euphemizing my way to an abstract point, "there's nothing in the panting, sweating, heat overtaking her body, and then a moment of ecstatic release that sounds good to anyone here?"

My voice is rising in pitch, and the pace of my words is now rapid. I feel the heat flush my own face; more sweat breaks out too. But this is embarrassment, not ecstasy. Someone giggles quietly, and now the class is divided between those who get my point and are not saying anything while refusing to meet my gaze, and those who are not getting it and are, therefore, protesting. If I were teaching this back at Vanderbilt, I know the students—who tend to be concerned with how to engage sex-positive conversations in church life—would certainly have caught on by now. More so, I wouldn't have felt the need to be so ridiculously oblique in my presentation of the ideas. But it's so much more difficult here! So I begin wondering how much traction those sex-positive conversations we have in the academic classroom manage to get once my students graduate and find themselves trying to navigate church life. "No! No, it sounds awful," Ann says, shaking her head emphatically while a few other older ladies nod vigorously in agreement. Exhausted and defeated by my own inadequacy to a task I thought would be easy, I let it go.

Perhaps I should have just said what I would have felt perfectly comfortable saying in the academic classroom: "Beatrice is using language associated with orgasm to describe her unity with the Divine." Indeed, I halted the conversation—silenced myself—because explicitly saying the word "orgasm" was necessary for making my point any clearer. Immature or unenlightened though it might seem, my skin felt squirmy at the idea of saying *that* word to *this* group. Simply put, these are not the people with whom I talk about orgasms. I, too, it seems, have my agency shaped in surprising ways by a church context that is unwilling to talk about sex. Therefore, I find it incredibly difficult to talk about sex in that context. At the same time, by euphemizing the subject, I created a knowledge divide between those who had ears to hear and those who did not. I felt guilty that my discomfort at saying something plainly was leading some class members, especially the older women, to a somewhat comical, unknowing refusal of sexual pleasure. I did not intend for my own embarrassment to embarrass others.

Afterward I wrote about the experience in my field notes, noting how silly I felt for not being able to simply say what I was thinking. I challenged myself in that reflective text to handle things better when I taught mysticism in the "God as Trinity" course. I wish I could say things did go better, but in the second course I overcorrected. Rather than waiting for a moment to interject the topic of sexuality, I framed my whole lesson about mystical ascent in erotic terms. I feared that the class members would be too shocked to engage; instead, they were simply too perplexed, yielding the same result.

In both cases, I realized that it is one thing to discuss a set of somewhat abstract concerns about "the erotic" in an academic environment, and an entirely other thing to talk about sexual pleasure with an intergenerational group of my fellow Baptists. The abstraction of academic theological discourse is what gives us safe cover to talk about pleasure in our liberative discourses about sexuality. It distances pleasure—as an analytic category—from our personal experience; indeed, perhaps, at most, we use coy allusions to that personal experience as provocative, carefully timed flourishes to the theory we construct. Getting close to the carnal dimensions of theology thus illuminates just how difficult it can be for academic theological notions of sexuality to attach to everyday theological practices, even for those who might wish to draw such connections. In many ways moves of abstraction help us better understand the complex dynamics of context-specific ideas, as I have been arguing throughout. Yet those moves of abstraction, it seems, help us not only understand such dynamics but also create the contexts in which they can be communicated effectively.

These carnal dimensions of theology should not be interpreted as distractions to be avoided or problems to be hidden, however. Instead, they offer crucial components of a fully robust theology. Both love and frustration can press us to create theological insight beyond where we had initially intended to go; both love and frustration can also *be* theological insight. Theology's carnal dimensions open up, limit, and produce theological possibilities—sometimes all at the same time.

In this chapter's final story, I offer an example of theological change that registers at the site of a body when words have lost their meaning.

THE SLUMP OF A SHOULDER

While the beginnings of the "God as Trinity" class were somewhat rocky, by the end of the semester the group had cultivated more tools for talking about God, and I continued to learn how to frame conversations so that they could invite more experimental speech. It continually felt like we were fumbling our way into something quite meaningful together. For one of our final nights together, as I prepared to teach about theological responses to the Holocaust, I recalled an undergraduate course I had taken on theodicy. In our first meeting, the professor had completely destabilized our young worlds by reading aloud to us the famous chapter, "Rebellion," from Dostoyevsky's *The Brothers Karamazov*. Stories of psychological horror and bodily abuse perpetrated against innocent children left us either in tears or numb. No one could launch a defense of the Divine in the aftermath of this reading; instead we all just filed from the room in silence. Theodicy, our professor realized, is quite possibly an impossible theological topic to handle logically. It is deeply carnal, connected to our greatest fears and most profound suffering. If it is not handled at the affective level as well as that of systematic reflection, then its handling is pointless.

Inspired by the memory, I wanted to bring this intensity to our Sunday night learning. I decided to try an activity I had read about that I thought might allow us to use some of our new theological tools in a more powerful way.[14] The teacher begins by inviting her class to brainstorm answers to the question, "Where is God?" She then reads to them a particularly unsettling (to borrow Swidler's language) passage from Elie Wiesel's *Night*, and asks them the same question again: "Where is God?" As with the Dostoyevsky reading, Wiesel offers a horrifying image of violence inflicted on the body of a child in a way that compels the reader to grapple with evil at the level of affect more than logic. The author of the activity thus promises that after hearing this particular Wiesel passage read, no one can offer the somewhat trite answer, "God is everywhere," likely to have been given in the first round, again. Overtrusting this author's advice, as well as his particular read of Wiesel's text, I was perhaps somewhat foolishly overeager to see how the group would respond.

I kick things off, moving from my chair, to stand at the whiteboard positioned just outside of our ring of tables. My movement causes those in the row with their backs to the board to swivel in their seats to see. Standing at the front in this way—indeed, creating a 'front' in this way—I tried to be intentional about using my own speech to encourage theirs, so that we could maintain the spirit of everyone's voice contributing to something shared. Writing their words on the board—and double-checking that I had written them accurately as I did so—affirmed the value of the group's opinions, while also keeping a record to which we could refer later. A number of class members commented in later interviews that they particularly enjoyed these whiteboard brainstorming times because they enabled them to see—not just hear—the diversity of opinions in the room. Moreover, by physically moving out of my chair to a different position in the room, my facilitation shifted the energy of the conversation. It helped focus answers for a time, as my attempts to write them down led people to condense complex ideas into short phrases. In this way, the shift in how bodies moved in the space impacted the types of theological statements we uttered.

"Where is God?" I asked them, uncapping my marker with an audible snap. The first answer came from Mike, "Everywhere." *Perfect*, I thought to myself. *This is going to work splendidly.* "Right here," said another. "Within us," "in my heart," "Heaven," called out others. Multiple spatial imaginations rapidly evoked a God who was both vast and minute, filling the expanse of everything and then squished into the ventricles of an individual's chest. And yet each answer felt somewhat clichéd. Their Sunday-School style familiarity could not conjure worlds of meaning around their utterance. As Sallie McFague has well demonstrated, theological metaphors lose their power over time, thus also losing their capacity to open out into questions and ideas that might stimulate theological imagination.[15] The metaphor of God residing in one's heart offers a prime example of this problem. While the heart could provide much fodder for a carnal theological imagination, our overfamiliarity with that image renders it a nearly fruitless metaphor—particularly in Baptist circles where the language of "inviting Jesus into my heart" is a common descriptor for the decision by which one "chooses to accept the gift of salvation." Its meaning feels ossified, no longer open for rich and varied interpretation. This was precisely the type of theological stagnation I was hoping to challenge with the activity.

When the answers died down, I handed around copies of the Wiesel passage—a brutal, infamous passage in which a child is hung in a concentration camp—and asked for someone to read it aloud. Mike fluttered his hand to volunteer, and we all began to be drawn in by his deep, rich voice. In the midst of the gruesome scene, a character asks, "Where is God," and the author, also a character in the scene, answers that God is on the gallows in the child.[16] We paused for a moment after reading. A few class members had tears in their eyes. Gloria's fingers were pinching her lips in a gesture of futility. Her usual energetic presence was stilled. The mood of the room was solemn and I worried for a moment that I had not adequately introduced the activity. Indeed, I hadn't. The transition felt jarred and so the silence hung heavily. Feeling there was nowhere else to go but forward in the planned activity, though, I asked the class again, "Where is God?"

Mike began again, "Everywhere, still everywhere." His answer shattered my expectation. *Why isn't this working? What am I doing wrong? Why don't they just get it?* For a single moment I did not register that Mike's body was now hunched over, slumped in the chair, his tone dejected and with a grasping edge to it. The words of his answer were the same, but the answer was nevertheless different. The author of the activity was both wrong and right. If we believe that the answer *is* the words, then the same words offered before and after witnessing tragedy seem foolish, even impossible to utter, the second time. But if we believe that the answer is more than the words, that tragedy changes words' meanings, then the embodiment that now accompanied Mike's words mattered.

Wiesel's passage offers an image that can amount to God's death, an image that potentially makes belief absurd. Mike's hunched, slumped torso revealed the possibility that his body had absorbed this absurdity or, at least, had absorbed his sense of struggle with the image, before his words could catch up to either. And from this unsettled place, his grasping tone indicated a desire to affirm that God is everywhere, but perhaps not an affirmation itself. In contrast to his initial confidence, Mike's response now bore a distance between body and words, a distance within which both doubt and hope had the power to compete for the chance to reconstruct Mike's theological agency into something new. Mike's *talking theology* stayed the same; his *acting theology*, however, now bore the potential, if only for a moment, to be transformed.

Others followed in with answers that picked up our shift in tone in more discursive ways: "He's where the ugliest things go on as well as the good things"; "He's where there's death"; and "He's hanging there. [pause] On the cross." "God is in silence." There was a pause after this last one, as if for a moment we were all trying to create the very silence in which we might detect the Divine. "God is in the question and the answer," someone mumbled, staring into the distance.

These answers felt richer, more intimately connected with each of our own experiences of suffering and as such felt also harder won than the first set; each was spoken tentatively as if they flowered at the edges of branch limbs out onto which we were now tentatively stepping. But then the final answer came from the youngest member of our class, Sarah, a bright college student. Refusing even to answer my question, she moved us back to the realm of disposition and pure affect. In the face of tragedy, she denied the need to interpret or analyze consciously. Instead, she sat back in her chair, let the sheet of paper fall to the table, and simply stated, "I hate that passage."

Mike, Sarah, and the others demonstrate that there is a certain kind of wisdom for us to pursue not only in but also somewhere beyond discourse, in the way discourse is held together by its writing onto our bodies. It is the tone of our voices, fingers fluttering to lips now silenced, the curve of a man's back as he slumps into a chair, and the emotive cry of a young woman. Each of these movements is as much a theological act as is the writing of these words on this page. Faced with the unsettling gravity of the relationship between suffering and God's presence in that moment, the group neither turned away nor offered panicked excuses, as they had done at the beginning of the semester. Rather, to play again with Swidler's language, we all allowed ourselves to be unsettled for a moment—they better than I—and then to pick up the words that still made sense to us out of the rubble to use them again anew. The tools we had gained together over the course of an unsettled semester were settling. New strategies of action, cultivated in unsettled times, come eventually to feel "natural," Swidler argues, like an "undeniable part of the structure of the world."[17] They become habitus, wisdom inculcated into us through our pursuit of it through the shared, ongoing practice of conversation. They become our carnal theology.

Ethnographic theology, because it is conscious of the fact that it rises from embodied practice as much as if not more so than from texts, is able to see embodiment as a vector of, not an obstacle to, knowledge. More Cartesian modes of knowledge production, as I have previously noted, eschew relationality, fear emotionality, and obscure bodily practice and difference. Whereas they do so to secure knowledge somewhere beyond doubt, a carnal theology instead sees the epistemologically productive value of doubt. In bringing a field of practice's doxa to light, we create space for doubt to bring about change, enact the gentle logics of formation, or—for ill and for good—enable theological coherence to be affirmed. Participating in an unexpected or encouraging relationship, dwelling with an uncomfortable feeling, or attending to bodily practice and difference can bring about this doubt in doxa, doubt that likely registers on the body before it is spoken in our words. As such, it's the discrete gestures—modes of affect, viscera and instinct: all the stuff of carnal knowledge—that create the moments of potential where slippage and change might happen in the ongoing processes of cultural production and reproduction that make up a theological field.

Chapter 5

My Mother's Hips

A Performance Theology of Sanctification

Throughout this book, we have explored the forms of knowledge that ethnographic theological methods can produce, using Kathryn Tanner's model of theology as a cultural practice as a frequent guide. Bringing that model to life in practice, we have also used ethnography to test and revise some of Tanner's claims: claims about the relationship between everyday and academic theology; processes of social and theological transformation; and the ways in which theology, as a practice, comes to be embodied, for example. In this last chapter, we engage Tanner's interest in theology's aesthetic dimensions to shape the particular mode of our theological production. We have studied how the academic theologian's critical self-awareness and embodiment can shape her doing of theology; now, we evaluate the role played by her creativity.

As outlined previously, Tanner rightly positions academic theologians as already implicated in, rather than external to, the Christian social practices they seek to analyze. From this perspective, whether we realize it or not, academic theologians who are engaged with culture continually try to reassemble the broken fragments of everyday Christian thought and action into a fresh aesthetic coherence. Standing in the midst of this theological detritus, Tanner argues, the academic theologian draws on the "creativity of a postmodern 'bricoleur'" who "works with an always potentially disordered heap of already existing materials, pulling them apart and putting them back together again, tinkering with their shapes, twisting them this way and that."[1] In this way, she asserts, all theological creativity, whether everyday or academic, is "expressed through the modification and extension of materials already on the ground."[2] Theological patterns are therefore not *normative* for theological reflection so much as they are *productive* of it.

Using the image of a bricoleur to interpret what I was doing in our Sunday night classes quickly reveals the concept's limitations. Certainly, the constructive theologies we produced therein assembled all kinds of viable and vexed everyday theologies into moments of loose aesthetic coherence. In this way, the metaphor of bricolage helps make sense of what we were doing. But here it also runs into some problems. Unlike the "found objects" of bricolage, the everyday theologies with which we worked were not discarded; rather, they continued to be shaped by the investment of those who held onto them, often tightly. These were not abandoned discourses, divorced from their conditions of creation and usage, waiting to be discovered by an academic theological bricoleur. Indeed, my only access to these theologies was via personal engagement with the lives of those who lived them. And those people didn't just hand them over to me. The theologies we constructed, we constructed together. They were not found; they were made.

Unlike the image of the theological bricoleur, the academic theologian using ethnographic methods to bring Tanner's model to life cannot (*ethically* at least) objectify and obscure the everyday theologies—not to mention the everyday Christians—with which she engages within her field of study. The academic theologian's agency, like the agency of her conversation partners, is always caught up in a relational dynamic in which power, friendship, conflict, and cooperation both complicate and construct the processes of cultural production within the theological field of practice. The ethnographic theologian does not, therefore, deal with silent objects. Rather, she deals with highly vocal subjects, all of whom are also exercising their own theological creativity as they bear the potential to become partners in that theological production. Unlike bricolage, here the reciprocity of competing and cohering forms of theological agency—of competing and cohering theologians—is key.

Instead of bricolage, performance art might offer an apt image for what the ethnographic theologian does when bringing Tanner's model to life.[3] With performance art, those who show up to see the artwork also communally create it. It is incomplete without them (not that it ever really becomes complete). Therefore, unlike bricolage, significant "materials" (i.e., the gathered people) of the performance artist's plan have the power to speak back to the artwork she endeavors to create. These materials, the people, interact with the artwork as it comes into being, reshaping it into something the performance artist cannot necessarily predict. What is created has the potential to comprise multiple competing agencies. This creation happens within or, at least, in relation to the vision and via the facilitation of the performance artist, of course. She is responsible for it. She gets the credit for its artistic success or, if necessary, the blame. But what she has is only a plan, a sketch of how things might go.

This description of the performance artist might feel familiar to the ethnographic theologian. On the one hand, as the academic theologian who planned and facilitated the conversations we had together in our Sunday night classes, the ultimate responsibility for them fell squarely on me. I prepared the lesson plans and, in moments when things fell apart, I was the one who had to get us back on track. At the same time, like the performance artist, the fact that final responsibility falls to me also means I get final credit. My name is on the cover of this book, whereas the ethics of research with human subjects dictate that all my research partners are assigned pseudonyms, whether they want that anonymity or not. On the other hand, as with performance art, the execution of each conversation we had was also terrifyingly—and wonderfully—dependent on the self-selecting people who showed up on Sunday evenings to chat. I needed them as much as they needed me.

These relational dynamics at play in theological production are what interest us here. Yet, because both performance art and theology can tend toward obscuring tactics when it comes to the field of power within which each operates, we pay attention to aesthetic incoherence and outright dissonance as much as aesthetic coherence in the telling of this chapter's core story. The story takes place one evening in our "Jesus Christ and Salvation" class, and it is marked by my own struggles and, indeed, failure to engage a class member on his own terms. In fact, it is a story in which I am unable even to recognize those terms, as my insecurity and frustration lead me to misdiagnose the situation at hand. Critical engagement with one of performance artist Marina Abramović's most famous performance works—*The Artist Is Present* (2010)—will help us evaluate the different dynamics of power and privilege that mark this aesthetic and theological relationality, and thus help us avoid romanticizing it.

THE STORY'S CONTEXT

There can be a moment in a performance artwork or theological conversation when the labor of the gathered resolves itself into an image or action, or perhaps an idea that captures the heart of the labor's pursuit. That happened for me in this Sunday night story, yielding a fleeting resolution around an embodied theology of sanctification, which I explore in brief at the end of this chapter. While traditional art media and theological writing would focus primary attention on such a resolving moment, performance art—and, by extension, what I am here calling performance theology—prefers to dwell in the processes of its production. Instead of going straight to this image of embodied sanctification divorced from its conditions of creation, this chapter focuses attention on the conditions themselves. It tells the story of how those of us who gathered together that Sunday night for theological conversation took my teaching plan and brought it to life. We tossed its ideas back and forth among ourselves, as each of us contributed moments of theological creativity that collided and colluded with those contributed by others.

On the night this image arose, we were scheduled to talk about Reformation theologies. Given that the group's initial negative reaction to Beatrice of Nazareth was driven by a (perhaps unduly) strict Protestant understanding of "works," as I outlined in Chapter 4, I was looking for places to unsettle our theological doxa around the topic of salvation. Luther's theology seemed a fertile site for such digging around. I wanted the group to see how an unnecessarily restricted position in one area of theological thought could cause implicit damage to another. Did Luther's concerns about *earning one's own salvation*, which they shared, undermine his theology of sanctification—a doctrine about which they cared? And by extension, did their own views of salvation negatively impact the ways they understood God to interact with their daily living of life?

I began with my typical short contextualizing lecture, being careful to guard against descriptions of indulgences and simony that would bolster any latent anti-Catholicism in the group. To accomplish this, I described both practices in a way familiar to our context: using Baptist or broadly evangelical terms to depict the pope as being engaged in a "massive capital campaign" to rebuild St. Peter's. According to the official church theology of the time, I continued, money given for indulgences and simony was supposed to be offered out of gratitude for what God had already done, not payment for services to be rendered. In that way, it was not unlike our Sunday morning financial offerings, which are given for the work of the church out of gratitude for God's work in our lives. Over time, however, as the campaign got out of hand, a practice intended as an expression of gratitude began to look like a bribe. I wanted them to see that a strong reaction to a concrete situation had led to a theological revolution of which we are all inheritors. Catholics had always believed in justification by faith, I told them; they just did not centralize the idea such that the rest of their theology was interpreted through it. Luther, I continued, perhaps overemphasized a theology of justification by faith through grace to respond to the problems he saw in Christian practice around him. But, in so doing, his understanding of sanctification was weakened. If we do nothing and God does everything, I wondered aloud, what impact does our living the Christian life have on us as human beings? Having first contextualized our Baptist beliefs within a much broader theological debate and then connected that debate back to our shared Baptist faith, I opened the floor for conversation.

If I were to imagine my theological creativity vis-à-vis the conversation that ensued as being like that of the bricoleur, I would be free to pull the ideas I like best from what was said to assemble them at my own will. Interpreting the field of study along the lines of performance art, however, requires that I take seriously the processes by which various ideas—those I liked, and those I didn't—came to light. It requires paying attention to the moments when we resisted each other, when one person helped another refine their point, and when the differences between us remained unresolved. It also requires paying attention to how the group tested, questioned, and revised the parameters my lesson plan had set.

The group begins tossing out defenses for Luther that immediately undermine the effect I'm going for: "He'd seen the extremities of works, so you can understand why he was like that." "Was [sanctification] just not on his radar because he was so focused on indulgences?" "Was he scared he might step over the line?" "Did he want to close that door quickly because we might think we can save ourselves?" As their questions challenge my plans, they call me to deeper responsibility, and I realize with a sharp pang of guilt that I have accidentally overstated the theological problem in Luther's thought for a rhetorical effect of persuasion—though it seems at least for now they remain unpersuaded. Because I also want to communicate that I don't think a responsible theologian has the freedom to let sanctification fall off of their radar even for a minute, I have to work harder to reach a more nuanced point. I want their questioning to make the ideas more precise, not inadvertently unpalatable. Yet at the same time I begin questioning myself: *When did I become so obsessed with systematicity? The episodic nature of Luther's theology is usually my favorite thing about it!*

As feelings of guilt and self-questioning swirl into insights regarding which ideas require nuancing, and as those feelings and insights mix with my desire to draw quieter people into conversation while not discouraging those who are more vocal, I also labor to track the new avenues of thought being raised, as well as how those new thoughts connect with conversations we've had and I expect will have. It seems to me that we are moving into questions of Divine and human agency, a good anticipation for the introductory lecture I am about to give on Calvin and providence. As I subconsciously begin sketching these new avenues of engagement to pursue, others in the room continue bringing up new ideas, thus continuing to increase the load of what I am trying to track as the teacher.

Gene, probably our quietest class member, draws scripture into the conversation by evoking Philippians 2:12–13: "We're told to be transformed, work out our own salvation with fear and trembling. And, we're told to submit to the will of God . . . so that would seem to hinder your sanctification if you fight that." Rickie then builds on Gene's scriptural contribution by referencing the hortatory letters sent to churches in the book of Revelation: "We get exhorted to do things . . . he [*it is not clear whether she means God or the writer of Revelation*] says 'do this, change that, you're not doing this.' I mean, why exhort people if they can't do anything about it?" When no one responds to Rickie's rhetorical question, she continues, "I have trouble saying we're puppets and God does it all and we just sit back and kind of . . . [*she trails off, pauses, and starts up again*] I think God does most of it, and we have this strange tension, paradox maybe, even doing what we allow God to do within us and how we allow him to transform us." Each point builds on what comes before while letting parts of the previous point go. The room is pulsing with possibility, only a fraction of which can be pursued.

As Rickie speaks, I feel pulled in two directions: I want to nurture her "tension" and "paradox" into the conversation, which I sense could be helpful for exploring Divine and human agency. But I also want to clarify my framing of Luther one more time. It seems I still have not rectified my initial missteps about Luther's theology. (My inability to do so would haunt me throughout the remainder of the two courses as a few times Rickie would say something like, "Yeah, that's why I can't get on board with Luther, because he doesn't have a view of sanctification . . . ," or, "Well, like Luther says . . ." Each time this happened, our context lacked the room for me to try to mend the misperception; each time, I felt the weight of teaching's authority and responsibility, as it seemed Rickie had accepted my framing of Luther as what Luther had actually said.)

Torn between this desire to nurture and to correct, I falter for yet another moment, and Ann jumps in before I have the chance to speak with a point that would direct our conversation much more than I initially imagined: "Don't you think we could stop the whole thing [i.e., the whole salvation experience, sanctification itself] as much as we can stop the whole conversion experience? I need to be dependent on the Lord to transform my life . . . I can stop the whole process by not being willing to do his will. We can stop the process anywhere we want to, but we can't speed it up by anything we do."

Because our historical contextualizing has broadened the theological terrain on which we now tread, Ann is able to introduce some ideas that are controversial to mainstream Baptist thinking, which Mike immediately picks up on. He responds to her playfully by invoking the common Baptist belief of "once saved, always saved." Grinning, he asks provocatively "if we can slow down the process of sanctification, in that slowing down, can we slow it down enough to lose our salvation?"

Establishing the borders of what we are describing, Mike reminds us that Baptists—at least, our stripe—do not believe someone who is *truly saved* can cease to be so. Once the gift of salvation has been accepted, it cannot be given back. But Mike reveals that there is a fine line between not having the power to give it back and having the power to willfully slow its progression in us. Mike's comments have connected Luther's theology to a nuanced aspect of our community's accepted belief. The guilt at the confusion I introduced around Luther's theology recedes for a moment, as the moment feels intense and loaded with the twin possibilities for either reifying or challenging some of our community's previously unquestioned theological norms.

Interpreting this theological interplay requires attending to the moments not only when participants inspired each other to richer engagement with theological ideas, however, but also when we didn't. Usually, an academic theology would be adjudicated by norms that are generated by academic theological discourse. Using the image of performance art to shift focus from the product to the process and to replace found objects with active subjects, however, likewise shifts my locus of responsibility. Seen through the lens of performance theology, ethnographic theology cares less about accounting for historical counterarguments to a claim or breakdowns in its systematic coherence than for the need to account for counterarguments and breakdowns in the theological conversation. If, with Tanner, we claim a theology's worth is in its loose aesthetic coherence, then what does that coherence look like?

A Breakdown in Communication

The night this story happened, one of our group members brought her husband to class with her. Sandra is a vivacious, middle-aged woman whose confident presence in the class I enjoyed immensely. Given that her husband, Ed, had never attended our class before, I interpreted his initial quietness as a polite deference to others. At Mike's comments, though, he jumps in to the conversation quite forcefully:

> If you're speeding up or slowing down, then you're talking about man earning his own salvation. If that's the case, obviously he can stop it and lose it. I think obedience is a matter of my surrender in following Christ rather than being the one who is given credit for having done it. I think we cannot forget the work of Christ in us when we think about our achievements. It is a work within us, not a work of our own. Therefore, we don't lose it because it's been given to us, but we have an obligation. We owe. We're indebted to Christ to be his followers and be obedient to his will.

Right away I am taken aback by the authority with which our visitor speaks. Instead of hesitating or pausing for reflection, as class members usually do when they talk, he speaks in the tone of a sermon. Rather than asking leading questions, he makes summative statements, the force of which are heightened by his use of words like *obviously* and *therefore* to draw connections. His statement thus feels closed to interpretation. Moreover, instead of responding to Mike or Ann, who have made the points he is contesting, Ed aims his words directly at me with a tone that feels like a rebuke of my teaching methods, rather than an invitation to conversation. I sense an undercurrent to what he says: *If you don't take control of this out-of-control conversation, I will.* I feel rubbed the wrong way, and his use of the gender-specific *man* to refer to what I would call humanity does not aid my patience in the moment.

I smile, trying to destabilize some of the authority Ed has claimed with a pointed question: "If we say we're indebted to Christ, then is that a debt we can pay?" I direct my gaze around the room to open the question to everyone. Mike smiles and shakes his head, perhaps recognizing that I'm keeping things in the realm of play by turning an idea that is normative for everyone—of course we cannot pay the debt—into a question. Before anyone has time to respond, Ed takes the bait that I suppose I have set and launches in: "I'm not saying it's a debt we pay. He has done the work; we can't do it. Our responsibility is to follow him and be obedient to him. It's not a matter of earning something or achieving a goal. It's a matter of believing and being obedient to his will because of what he's done for us. It's been earned for us. But it's our responsibility to be obedient."

I have made things worse: now the broader conversation is focusing into a disagreement between Ed and me. Whereas most class members offer mixtures of fragmented theology, open-ended questions and narratives that are open to interpretation when they speak, all indicating a shared sense that we are fumbling toward creating something together, Ed's speech is doctrinally focused and forceful, eschewing exploratory questions for summative statements. A theologically trained former minister, he deploys the kind of authoritative academic speech that the rest of us who share in such training have given up in order, I imagine, to allow for more fruitful conversation among us all. Rarely does someone speak in our group as if they already possess the truth, and it feels like Ed is shoring up his theological privilege rather than trying to disperse it. I worry that his speech is thus excluding others from participating, though with hindsight I realize I am equally to blame for this.

More to the point, I am annoyed by his tone: *He would never speak like this if I were a middle-aged man teaching this class instead of a young woman*, I think and, whether I am right about that or not, I don't want to let him get away with it. Right away I begin interpreting his behavior as sexist or, even, misogynist, and the thought whips me up. I am torn between trying to keep the conversation open for everyone's participation and trying to find the crucial insight that I think can chip away a part of Ed's certainty. My frustration with Ed's tone and attitude thus brings an obnoxious edge to my own tone and attitude. *If he's going to deploy his academic theological privilege, then so am I!* Whereas with Gene, Rickie, and Ann, for example, I have invited them to speak and ponder and take up class airtime whether or not I agree with the points they are making, now I'm trying to judo Ed into silence. Any ideals I had of hospitality to newcomers in our classroom has flown directly out of the window, as all of a sudden I want to limit who gets to participate in this performance theology, as well as the terms for how they can do so.

I challenge Ed's terms, *obedience* and *surrender*, pointing out that they are not as passive as we often imagine. "I'm pretty stubborn,"

I note, the irony utterly lost on me, "Surrender is the most action I could do!" "I don't like the word surrender," Ed responds. *But you're the one who introduced that word!* I fume internally. He continues, "Surrender means something different for me than for others. Surrender is when you find out that you've lost. OK, I don't want to lose, so I'll surrender and take whatever consequences come." If I were I not so riled up I would have noticed that he was actually making a really interesting point that challenged some of our communal theological norms at FBC. But I'm too busy being frustrated by my ungracious read of his statement that he interprets *surrender* differently than others do as tantamount to a self-declaration of his own superior theological reasoning. "Surrender in playing a sport," Ed continues, "is to decide that the other team is so much stronger that you're not going to put out everything you can to win." At this point, it doesn't feel like others in the room are coming along with us and, if I'm honest, I begin to sense that I'm going to lose this one because Ed clearly has more stamina to stick with it than I do; the other team *is* stronger in this case. So I play a little dirty and reference something someone else said on a night when Ed was not in attendance. Ann jumps on the invitation, and Charlie quickly joins her. Their interjection creates enough of a break that a bunch of people join in again. Perhaps I have contributed to creating a little more tension in the air than I had intended, and the group now clamors for a calmer equilibrium.

The conversation picks back up for a while, with multiple people contributing to it and it feels to me as if we are back on track—at least, we are back on *my* track. I do a time check and realize that I need to move on to my brief lecture on Calvin if we're going to avoid falling behind in our schedule—*my* schedule. A few people start taking notes, as is common practice in these moments, and it's clear that we've moved into a transitional time that will set up our next discussion. Out of the corner of my eye I see that Ed has his hand up. "I'll get to you in one second," I say, returning to the point I am in the middle of making. "Let me just respond," he interrupts me, midsentence. Once again it feels like he is trying to usurp my position as teacher, and once again I feel that his interruptive speech reveals his latent, if not overt, sexism. But this time others in the group respond to his interjection, refusing to allow him to assert his own authority over the rest of us. In the moment, I am pleased with this. It feels as if they are defending their territory against an intrusion that I interpret as shaped by privilege and arrogance. In the moment I do not pay attention to how my actions encourage such a militaristic stance, refusing hospitality to our (admittedly challenging) guest.

Once again the group falls into what feels to me like a more collaborative conversation, although I notice that Sandra is much quieter than usual, and I find myself missing her typical exuberance. I am surprised that a woman who I perceive as strong and strong-willed is married to a man who strikes me as so overbearing. Our conversation has, unsurprisingly with the turn to a focus on Calvin, moved into views of predestination. This is a doctrine with which these Baptists struggle, given the central importance of choosing Jesus at the moment of conversion. While I have little interest in convincing them to accept Calvin's theologies, I do want them to engage, rather than summarily reject them. As with other figures, I hope that getting into some of the nitty-gritty of his thought will open up our own. My formal lecture now abandoned, I adapt and begin contextualizing the concept of predestination within Calvin's larger interest in God's providence—a much more agreeable notion to the group—to try to foster engagement. Ed stays quiet for some time. But then Sandra finally settles into her typical mode of sharing, telling a story that relates God's providence to the constant presence of Jesus among us, whether we recognize that presence or not. As usual, her story is playful and self-deprecating, as she mocks her own inability to convince non-Christians into conversion. As the group laughs along with her, Ed steps in.

"There is a very good passage to support it," he says, leaving what the "it" is that is supported unclear as he begins reading slowly from Matthew 25 in his Bible, the passage distinguishing the sheep from the goats. It feels to me like he is ignoring the intervening conversation so that he can return us directly back to his own previous line of thought. "So people do the right thing often without ever knowing it's any kind of service to God," he interprets, "and to me that's what being a Christian is; it's just doing without any thought of earning anything or caring about earning anything." Ed continues with the scripture, "He also said depart from me because you didn't do these things," and then proceeds to read the entire passage. This is a passage with which everyone in the room would be familiar, and I find myself frustrated at his reading it slowly at length rather than just referencing it. Once again, it feels to me like he is imposing his voice over the rest of us, dominating airtime, and now doing so with the weight of a scripture passage that supposedly self-evidently supports his argument.

Charlie and I jump in together when Ed pauses for breath, both of us pointing out that the passage actually hinges salvation on doing good works, not the opposite point that Ed is trying to get it to make. We go back and forth a few times, with me arguing that it seems to be the works in this passage that bring salvation and with Ed arguing that the works don't count as "good works" because the people are not conscious of what they are doing. Once again he is nuancing the theological debates in ways my frustration distracts me from acknowledging. Ed speaks over me; I do the same to him. But once again I back down. I wish I could say I do so out of a desire to make space for others to enter the conversation or out of a respect for class dynamics. More so, I back down because I can feel my voice getting shrill, and I don't want to appear rattled in front of the group or as if I am attacking an old man.

Ed launches into another long speech. But though his tone is still authoritative, his content is now becoming confused. He begins repeating himself, saying the same phrases over and over again as if they are fresh points. Sandra starts shifting a little in her chair. With one of Ed's repetitions, she puts her hand on his and, in reference to me says, "I see what she's saying in that." This time when Ed stops talking, it is Sandra who jumps in: "This is the problem when we only take one passage and hang everything on it," she says, as she tries to change the subject.

Every time I reread my transcript of this moment or listen to the recording, I feel sick with regret that I didn't just take the out that Sandra was trying to offer. Each time I revisit the moment, I am struck by the level of misrecognition I brought to it as it happened, and I cringe as I hear myself use her intervention to refute the heart of Ed's argument, which in turn sets him off again. Now he confuses different biblical stories while trying to make his point, making errors that I find surprising given his apparent biblical and theological knowledge. Sandra tries again, interrupting her husband to point out that if we're going to stay on task, we need to shift to our next thinker, Descartes. This time she is quite forceful with her request, and we don't hear from Ed again for the rest of class.

All my field notes from that night record how frustrated I was with Ed's long speeches, which I perceived to be rude interruptions to what the rest of the class—or, more truthfully, I—was trying to do. In my transcripts, I have annotated some of his sections with notes like, "This is maddening. How can I get him to stop?" It is true that at various times, Ed dominated the conversation and refused to back down and go with the flow of group dynamics. But it's also true that I overreacted to him because I assumed he acted this way because of some latent sexism and misogyny. I grew frustrated and refused to back down, which also damaged the flow of group dynamics, as I effectively attempted to silence a voice whose tone I didn't like. I interpreted Ed's repetition and, what I deemed, *refusal* to engage points others and I were making as displays of privileged arrogance. When Sandra stepped in I assumed it was because she was embarrassed of her husband's behavior. It never occurred to me that Ed's repetition was taking place not because he refused to engage other ideas, but because he couldn't. It also didn't occur to me that Sandra was not embarrassed of her husband, but trying to protect him from embarrassment.

Ed joined us one more time toward the end of the course, but this time his interjections moved into confused modes of repetition much sooner in the debates. This time Sandra jumped in much sooner, again gently resting her hand atop his. It thus took me weeks to figure out that Ed wasn't the sexist jerk I was misperceiving him to be. He was actually experiencing some form of short-term memory loss or, perhaps, the early stages of dementia, the extent of which it seemed neither he nor Sandra was fully acknowledging yet and that they were still endeavoring—whether consciously or not—to hide.

In the moment when I finally realize what is going on, I am struck with a deep sense of shame. Back at grad school, I've read disability theory and theology. I have argued in my classes against theological anthropologies that rely on cognition for a vision of the human and against ecclesiologies that fail to be fully inclusive of various diversities, including those related to dis/ability. In terms of talking theology, I know all the right words. In terms of acting theology, though, it seems I'm wanting. Because here I am trying to silence and take down someone whose actions—which are infuriating me—are at least somewhat shaped by his own dis/ability. I had not yet come to embody my intellectual studies concerning dis/ability as second nature and I, thus, lacked the instincts of recognition.

Once I realized what was going on, I tried to merge my talking theology into my acting theology by endeavoring to recognize how what felt like distractions from our conversation could actually offer insights into it. Ed kept questions of grace on the table for us, for example, and pressed us to nuance our understanding of *good works* with greater precision. He raised interesting points about the concept of *surrender* and whether or not it matters if we know when we're doing good. In fact, he pursued the kind of refining insights I wanted us to achieve with our theological musings. That second night, I worked harder to find and forge connections between Ed's comments and the broader conversation, endeavoring to include (rather than aggressively attempting to exclude!) his contributions. With his insights acknowledged, Ed became less aggressive. He no longer had to attack me to get me to hear him. But perhaps my actions were too little, too late, as these were the only two times Ed attended the class—possibly because he didn't feel all that welcome. As a result, my efforts were stalled at the most cursory version of hospitality, never reaching anything even approaching mutuality with him.

Liberation theologians in particular have well established how markers of social location, privilege, and disadvantage intersect and compete with each other. We know that racialization, class, gender, sexuality and sexual practice, dis/ability, ethnic, and other social categories cannot be thought or theorized in distinction from each other without eclipsing rather than engaging our myriad differences. In a concrete way, Ed's and my conversation reveals the clash of factors such as gender, dis/ability, education, and age, among others as well, within the overlapping fields of practice and power where we construct theology. I don't want to let Ed completely off the hook. It's possible, indeed likely, that he was approaching me with some of the latent sexism I intuited. But I can't be let off the hook either. Our conversation doesn't allow me academic distance on observing these intersectional dynamics. Rather, it calls me to responsibility for the ways in which they have shaped my theological agency in ways that both disadvantage and privilege me within the communities where I live.

I failed to diagnose the intersections of difference that constellated between Ed and me accurately. This, in turn, led me to deploy inappropriate and, indeed, destructive tactics for maintaining the power and privilege that I failed to see accrued to me in spades. I relied too heavily on my intuitive analytics of gender, which as a temporarily able woman are much more finely tuned than my intuitive analytics of dis/ability. In so doing, I unconsciously deployed my own ability-privilege against Ed. In other words, I intentionally sought to outsmart someone, inadvertently using his dis/ability against him. Any story I tell about an experience of my theological transformation in the midst of conversation with my research partners is marked by this fact. Indeed, we can better understand the impossibility of a pure, utopian theological product in light of the impossibility of a pure, utopian artistic product.

THE THEOLOGIAN IS (NOT) PRESENT

From March to May 2010, the Museum of Modern Art in New York (MoMA) hosted a retrospective reenactment of approximately fifty of Marina Abramović's performance artworks from the last forty years. The title work, *The Artist Is Present*, offered the only original performance, as well as the only work performed by Abramović herself. It consisted of two chairs facing each other across a table within a sectioned off space.

The Artist[4] sat in one chair, while patrons took turns sitting in the other. Patrons were not allowed to speak to or touch The Artist, but they could occupy the chair for as long as they wished.

Because performances began before the museum opened each day and concluded after it closed, MoMA claimed that patrons were able to "experience the timelessness of the works."[5] Critics described *The Artist is Present* as affirming "moments of *presence*" by which the performer's "energetic body" would "energize spectators so that they sense the performer as well as themselves not only as intensely present, but as embodied minds."[6] Carefully curated video clips (available for viewing in a documentary about the work),[7] as well as numerous YouTube videos (many of which went viral), reveal participants weeping, smiling, and flirting with The Artist when confronted by her gaze. Abramović herself has described her various performance pieces as "establishing a dialogue with the audience through an exchange of energy, which tends to transform the energy itself." As she further puts it, "I could not produce a single work without the presence of the audience, because the audience gave me the energy to be able, through a specific action, to assimilate it and return it, to create a genuine field of energy."[8] In all these interpretations, the work is described in dramatic and spiritual terms, able to transcend not only its own commodification but also art itself into some form of genuine or truthful moment of human interrelationality.

In response to these "quasi-religious"[9] descriptions, art historian Amelia Jones rightly asks "why we continue (in the supposedly post-modern age of the 21st century) to fall back on mystifying language of presence and energy exchange" to interpret these performance works.[10] This is not to deny Abramović's artistic creativity or cultural contribution. Jones asserts her respect and admiration for Abramović as both an artist and a cultural force—an assertion with which I tend to concur. Rather, Jones wants to chip away at the hyperbolic, idealized claims made by curators, critics, and Abramović herself, to get at what the performance work actually achieves in light of the cultural matrix that shapes its meaning. Cultural engagement, rather than mystical description, would not undermine but, rather, has the potential to enhance the work's significance, she avers. Performance art cannot be judged by either the artist's stated intention or subjective responses to it alone.

As I have argued throughout these pages, theology is also constructed within fields of practice and power that require cultural analysis more than mystical description. Nevertheless, in several early attempts to write this present chapter—dealing with the aesthetic dimensions of theology, and in which I stumble toward describing a moment I personally experienced as theologically transformative—I repeatedly found myself relying on the same spiritual, abstracted language of energy exchange, relationality and the real presence of one to another that marks Abramović's descriptions of her own efforts. Something in my own theological agency—perhaps particularly as a young scholar—kept pressing me to want to make overly universal claims out of the particular, to claim theological norms out of the contingent, and to hide my own failures not only in teaching but in relational interactions as well. In fact, in earlier drafts of this chapter, I not only didn't tell the story of how I essentially bullied Ed into silence, but the idea of writing it up never even crossed my mind. Earlier drafts thus overfocused on what Gene or Rickie had to say, Sandra's insights, and my own train of theological thought running through our conversation.

So, to borrow Jones's question, why did I continue with this mystifying or (as is so often the case with theology, and ecclesiology in particular) idealizing and even triumphalist language to interpret our practice? In the language used to describe this book's methods, I would have to answer this question by admitting that in earlier drafts, my reflexivity with regard to my carnal knowledge failed. I experienced theological transformation around my understanding of sanctification through spirited conversation with the gathered. My pleasure at that experience, as well as my hope that others experienced something similar, caused me to fail to recognize at whose cost it came. On some level, I didn't want my experience tainted by my privilege. And the very fact that my reflexivity failed then means it's possible that it's failing also now, even as I endeavor for that not to be the case.

Abramović has, in fact, been accused of a similar failure of reflexivity, particularly with regard to her own power and privilege. As Jones and others have argued, rather than the so-called real or authentic relational presence that Abramović's performances claim, they are very much marked by dynamics of power and control—from the way Abramović constructs the performance, to its constant monitoring by a security team, to the modes in which it is made available to the public. In fact, argues Jones, the "literal presence" of the artist is "anything but energizing, personal or transformative," but rather it is a "spectacle—not an emotionally or energetically charged interpersonal relation, but a simulation of relational exchange with others."[11] Caroline Jones corroborates the way the participant's experience is highly controlled by noting how, after a five-hour wait in line for entry to *The Artist Is Present*'s inner sanctum, as she and others approached the "taped perimeter," the guard on duty told them that "we may not speak, place our hands on the table, bring anything with us, or ask for autographs."[12] At every level of the performance, Abramović had power to control not only the terrain in which the gathered moved but also the ways in which they moved within it.

Again, these descriptions are not offered as criticisms of the work but, rather, as insights into the creative dynamics that make it actually worth engaging. Such tight security is a far cry from Abramović's earlier performances, especially those like her famous, *Rhythm 0* (1974), in which she allowed participants the freedom even to harm her body if they so desired. Some critics romanticize these more dangerous performances as if they captured something more authentic than the recent ones. But it is worth noting that the location of a museum, rather than a small, experimental gallery space, as well as the cult of celebrity[13] now surrounding Abramović, both call for these heightened security measures. Rather than inviting us to romanticize earlier performance works when the romanticizing of recent ones falls flat, what Amelia Jones and Caroline Jones press us to see is that these faltering and failed social moments do not detract from but rather actually shape the communally created artwork. Despite many people describing being seated in the chair opposite The Artist as some form of authentic relationship, their subjective reporting is undermined by the fact that the artist's branding, the tight control of the space, and even the artwork's commodification all contribute to the power—or the frailty—of that interactive moment.

When we shift from thinking about theology as bricolage to thinking about it in terms of performance art, we are pressed to take seriously all these tricky dynamics of intersubjective—and failed intersubjective—relations. For every intimate moment of *presence* I experienced with, say, Ann, Sandra, or Peter that enabled theological flourishing, there remains a moment of tension with Ed that reveals the ways my power and privilege shaped what could happen in our classroom. Just as many participants in *The Artist Is Present* were able to have meaningful subjective experiences in the midst of the rules in place to protect the artist, so too many class members flourished by following the plan I had created for our time together. But at the same time, just as those who broke the rules of Abramović's performance were forcibly removed from participation in it,[14] my minimal sense of threat from Ed created the conditions for his exclusion from participating in our conversation on his own terms. In so doing, I shut down—or at least, tried to shut down—the mutual learning and creating that could have taken place not only between him and me but between him and me and the rest of the group as well.

Moreover, just as Abramović has some artistic privilege to interpret her work for a broader public, regardless of how the participants (on whom it is dependent for success) would interpret it, so too did I have the academic theological privilege of having final say regarding what happened in our classroom conversations. My privilege to shape the conversation (as the teacher in the classroom) *and* my privilege to interpret and narrate it later (as the academic theologian writing this book) afforded me the dubious option to eclipse Ed's agency in the processes of theological construction we all engaged together. In essence, I wanted to write about vulnerability without facing my own, most likely because I'm better at recognizing—and dismantling—someone else's privilege than I am at doing the same to my own. The Artist doesn't like someone pointing a mirror at her. The truth is that my privilege—just like any other aspect of my agency—also functions according to the logic of habitus. It is embodied knowledge, inculcated into my sense of self in the world so deeply that it is now second nature and, as such, forgotten. I am much more aware of Ed treating me according to his gender privilege than I am of myself treating him according to my ableist privilege. I am much more eager to chip away at his privilege than I am to chip away at my own. It is this highly learned, *natural* response that I need to engage and undo reflexively.

Misrecognizing my various forms of privilege meant that each time I tried to write a story in which my altercation with Ed was dominant, I unconsciously distorted my data to fit with some idealized vision of myself, erasing him from it. In other words, each time, as I tried to write this story, my reflexivity failed. Then, with that unconscious idealization of my self, I simultaneously constructed idealized notions of theology, community, church, and so on while falsely imagining, like Abramović, that our group's conversation could transcend itself into something like genuine or truthful human interrelationality even for a moment. Unfortunately, against my best attempts, I am sure that aspects of that problematic idealization still remain. Thus, while I have criticized Bourdieu's elevation of competition over cooperation with regard to social relations, I am equally concerned by theological notions of *relationality*, *Church* or *Eucharist*, for example, that likewise gloss over the conflict and competition that exists between theological agents constructing theological meaning together. To imagine that theology constructed *in the church* somehow arises from anything other than broken relationships is—to put it bluntly—not only naïve but also irresponsible. That is, to ignore these broken relationships is to mask our complicity in them as academic theologians.

It is to fall back on mystifying, idealizing and triumphalist descriptions that no longer make sense in light of the concrete realities of life lived together.

The more I sat with my data and analyzed it, however, the more Ed's persistence held me responsible not only to his presence but also to his insight. My failure to recognize and welcome not only the dynamics of his dis/ability into the conversation but also the interesting theological points he raised offers a more dramatic and more unjust version of a type of broken relationship that surely happened throughout all our Sunday night conversations. The perimeter of our classroom might not have had a visible and guarded tape around it to limit and block entry to our shared creative space; it also did not have security guards who could forcibly remove anyone who "broke the rules." Nevertheless, as we saw in Chapter 3, the types of theological conversation we had produced a self-selecting group from which it seemed various church members felt excluded. Furthermore, as we have seen throughout these pages, even within our group there were moments where members—including myself—did not feel we could be honest with others for fear of rejection.

As with performance art, our inability to achieve some impossible ideal of authentic presence—whatever that might mean—does not negate the theologies created out of our conversations. Demystifying these conversations means that moments of theological transformation are now recognized as tragically flawed but not worth throwing away, as marred but not destroyed by the contestation and conflict that gives rise to them. Here we see a theology that is, as all theology always is, both compromised by and created out of human vulnerability and failure as much as—if not more than—human wisdom and love. Theology's secret is thus unveiled: it always contains marks or traces to keep us from idealizing it. And these traces keep our conclusions open for continued refining, for the continued spiritual practice of pursuing wisdom together.

My Mother's Hips

In my frustration with Ed, I understood myself to be fighting to get us back on track. Of course, my actions excluded his contribution to what that track entailed. As a result, once I had effectively silenced him, it was easy to return us to the line of conversation we had been exploring prior to his contributions. This was a fruitful line of conversation for the group, perhaps particularly for me, as it led to one of the more powerful moments of personal theological transformation

I experienced over the course of both classes. This is the moment of resolution mentioned previously: the image of a bodily theology of sanctification. As it happened, my exertion of my own privilege helped me win the fight, and my winning conferred blessing upon me. I wish I could say that it didn't. I wish I could claim that excluding Ed irreparably harmed our subsequent theological creativity. Instead, I have to own up to how much I enjoyed the kind of advantage that infuriates me when I see others gain similarly at my expense. And I have to admit that it took a long time before I even recognized—in this story, in particular—my participation in and benefit from the systems of injustice I supposedly want to undo.

After I silenced Ed, we fell quickly back into a productive theological rhythm. So here we are now, tossing ideas around about sanctification, drawing on Ann's earlier metaphors of slowing down and speeding up to engage metaphors of movement and growth in general. Rickie, blending the theological musings that were circulating between us all with her own personal experience, picks up the thread: "As I have lived my life, I have grown and changed physically, emotionally—everything in my life changes me in some way." "So how," she continues, "if I'm letting God work in my life, how is that not changing me?" If everything we do has the power to change us, how much more so does God have the power to do so? "We open ourselves up to allow God to come in and change us," she continues, "to get rid of the old and change it into new." Responding to a number of the issues we had discussed all at once, Rickie's comments develop a picture of sanctification as a process of maturation: "We must change and grow as Christians. The Bible is replete with needing to grow. Paul's idea of eating meat and maturing. Encountering God changes us. We keep moving toward what we'll be at the end of time."

While Rickie is speaking her whole thought, her opening line, which is comparing physical growth to God's work in her, begins percolating for me. And I pick this one up and start to run with it in my imagination while half listening to the rest of what she is saying. Notions of sanctification and the body begin to swirl together, and a new theological articulation starts rising out of my own embodied knowledge. Caught in the flow of the conversation, I forget for a moment that I am responsible for leading the class and instead dive into more simply participating in it. In Rickie's comments, I see an image of a God who continually fills us with her image until we look more like her. And this evokes for me a body memory of my mother. Without really thinking about how it is my own feminine vision of God that is allowing me to make this connection—a gendered image that is at best experimental and, worst, heretical in this context—I begin to share it with the class.

I tell them how my mother has this stance where she puts her hands on her hips and leans to the side. The stance is loaded with communicative meaning via its repeated performance over the course of her life. Childhood photographs reveal that she took it on as her own at an early age, and we frequently see it still at family functions, sometimes even as intentional self-parody. Everyone in our family knows the pose. It is cheeky, an assertion of my mother's self. Never angry or imposing, it indicates that she knows she has just lost whatever game we were playing but she is going to hang on for a minute more with grit. "As soon as I put my hands there," I say to the class, and instinctively I sit upright in my chair to make room for my hands to find my hips, "I can feel my mother in my body like I'm incarnating her. I feel her in my body and I feel my body become hers."

I laugh; I did not even realize my hands had made it to my hips to tell the story, but now feeling them there, I can feel my mother in the room with me. *It is amazing how a posture can incarnate a memory.* My thoughts are buzzing and I feel my face scrunch a little as I try to interpret what I am feeling in this moment deep under my skin in my muscles and bones. It is like my thoughts are searching through my body, coursing my veins in search of the words for articulation. My body is becoming more and more explicitly necessary in my performative articulation of a theological idea.

I push my fists a little harder into my hips, as if I can find what I am looking for there. But as soon as I do so, I have directed my consciousness to myself. As fast as a flash, I am fully myself again. My mother has left the room. But the flash creates a space and I realize that the reason my body becomes my mother's for a moment has something to do with the continuity of our relationship through time. "It's through deep relationship with my mother," I add then, searching for it, but not quite grasping it, "Maybe something [*pause*] something similar is happening with God working through me. Maybe sanctification is something like an evoking of that relationship I've had with God over a lifetime." *Perhaps it's not the movement from somewhere to somewhere else*, I think, *but a movement that takes us deeper . . . deeper into our own bodies . . . deeper into what makes me me.* I stop and exhale. Reading my body aloud to the group was hard work, but good work, and I am smiling at my hands still on my hips. The room is quiet. It seems as long as I hold my hands there the floor is mine. I let go.

As soon as I let go, the silence of the room still hanging, I worry that I have said too much, and I feel grateful then that I avoided speaking my final thoughts about the relationship between bodily transcendence and immanence aloud. I have just crafted a bodily image of the Divine feminine, based on my mother's hips, as some sort of exuberant performative utterance. We had all been tossing around snippets of everyday theology, personal narrative, biblical allusions, and more among ourselves, not as found objects for any one of us, particularly not me, to assemble alone; rather, these snippets were offered as agential contributions to a shared, building, messy conversation. The image of my mother's hips functioned for a moment both as my subjective incorporation of those swirling contributions into my own theological agency and as my own contribution to our continued activity. It somehow fit into the conversation's flow while also disrupting it, just as most other images had likewise done.

Time moves slowly when you are nervous. But after what felt like an aeon, Sandra laughs joyfully and exclaims, "I think that's part of this whole thing we're talking about!" She pauses and, gesturing with her hands because she is an animated speaker, continues, "When you allow God to be as much a part of your life as your mother, that does change you, and we do begin to reflect what he's doing in us. That's a good thing!" Sandra meets me in common ground, highlighting the parts of what I had said that could be acceptable to the group and relating them back to the conversation as it is flowing, while couching it all back in masculine language for God and replacing my metaphor with simile. She makes my story a little safer and more accessible. As a result, the description becomes able to be integrated into our continued conversation. Nods circulate the table, and I notice how late it is getting. "OK," I say, "now some of you have said you want to be Calvinists. Let's finish up our reading of him and see how you feel then!" The group laughs, and we move on.

Reflexivity, Carnality, and Performance

I could tell this story naïvely as a story of spiritual or theological transformation and energy exchange, reciprocity, and genuine presence of a group of people to each other as they create fresh theological action and thought. Some aspects of that story might even be true, if only in the most fleeting of ways. In my personal relationships I would make the claim that cannot be made here—because there is no way to justify it academically—that this moment of realization about my mother's hips, hard won through theological conversation, has forever transformed my personal experience of sanctification. I now perceive or, at least, conceive God's sanctifying work in me in deeply bodily terms.

More significant for our purposes here, however, is the awareness that any theological thinking or academic reflection on the concept of sanctification I do from here on out will always be irrevocably transformed by this bodily experience, whether I acknowledge it or not. This is why the story cannot be told naïvely and why it can't just be claimed as a theologically transformative narrative. The social and theological fields in which we all participated together, as well as all the ways these fields confer disadvantage and privilege each in unequal measure on those living within them, all contribute to the meaning of that moment. The ways in which we hurt and heal, exclude and include, and shut down and open up each other are all a part of the theologies we create together.

Would my own theological musings that night have become so gendered and embodied had I not been so acutely aware of my own female embodiment in my battles with Ed? Would I even have pursued such a self-focused line of theological creativity had I not just wrested the floor from someone I perceived as trying to do the same? And would I have allowed that creativity to become so intimate had I not just experienced a feeling of group cohesion with the other class members, which was made possible through our shared exclusion of our unruly guest? Despite my repeated attempts to exclude Ed from our conversation and, indeed, from this text, his agency remains in the theologies constructed through both, if only at times as traces. Whatever beauty holds together this image of sanctification and whatever aesthetic coherence it achieves, it nevertheless remains vulnerable to the ugly fault lines of my own abuse of power required to bring it to life.

If Tanner is right that academic theologians ask and seek to answer the questions that bubble out of everyday theological reasoning—and I think she is—then the performance theology I have articulated here reveals what that bubbling looks like. As other chapters have demonstrated, the academic theologian must bring a certain reflexivity to these processes of theological construction and representation (even if, as I demonstrated in this chapter, that reflexivity kicks in a little too late). And the performance theologies in which we participate and that we guide are just some of the practices by which we might come to embody our carnal theologies. Reflexivity, carnality, and performance are thus three potential markers by which an ethnographic theology's normative dimensions might be adjudicated, as I argue in the conclusion to this book. But these are not the only three. Multiple conversation partners of an interdisciplinary ethnographic theology would produce different markers. Engaging theology as an art form rather than, say, a science, thus alerts us to the wide diversity of what theology can be, what questions it can ask, and what types of knowledge it can produce.

It is fitting that Sandra helped make my final and perhaps controversial point palatable to the group. She had been working all evening to restore the equilibrium that Ed and I had been disrupting together. She found few opportunities to contribute her own personal theological insights to our conversation that night, instead speaking in ways to protect her husband and then, it seemed, to protect me too. It is to my own shame that I never really reconciled with Ed after our battle in class. But when Sandra affirmed my maternal divine image, while also chipping away some of its bite, she smoothed out the tensions that had been erupting all evening long. Despite my conscious efforts to get us back on track, and my unconscious sabotage of that same goal, it was Sandra's efforts that actually made the return to cohesive group dynamics possible. Not that such cohesion is the ultimate goal. As Tanner points out, our ongoing making and remaking of ourselves as Christians entails engagement, not agreement.

With performance art, each participant leaves with a different spin on what happened, even as each also contributes to the experience of the others. That process is the artwork. The artist might try to capture or convey what happened to a wider audience after the fact, but that attempt at re-presentation will be a whole new thing, shaped by the agency, power, and privilege of the one who gets to tell the story. Likewise, the performance theology in which this chapter is based has long vanished. It happened in a church basement on a Sunday night among a group of people who will never assemble again. Some have died and others have moved away; anyway, much as you try, you really never can return home. I can try to tell you what happened, do my best to represent it without idealizing it, even though doing so requires the shameful admission of my own failures. But it wouldn't be wise to trust me completely.

Framing our conversations as performance theologies resituates this theological text. It cannot capture what we did, or re-present it to you. Such goals are too lofty for what I have attempted here. Rather, the theological text in this model marks one more moment of tossing a theological claim, a personal narrative or eruptive image out onto the table so that someone else can pick it up, incorporate what they want from it, reject it and reshape it, and then toss it out again. And again. And again . . .

Conclusion

Ethnographic Theological Normativity

The use of ethnography for theological reflection is not particularly new. For the past several decades, practical theologians, liberation theologians, and theological ethicists alike have claimed ethnographic research methods as crucial for producing the types of thick descriptions that ground their projects. With such models, theologians and ethicists seek to establish "what is" before they engage theological resources to argue for "what ought to be."[1] What is new with the current theological ethnography movement, however, is its insistence that a field of study can have "*embedded and embodied* within its life substantive contributions to theology and ethics."[2] As Christian Scharen and Aana Marie Vigen put it, "rather than pairing ethnographic facts to universal theological truth," these newer methods apprentice the theological ethnographer within her field of study so that she becomes able to articulate "those embedded theological convictions as primary theology itself."[3] Historical, traditional or textual theologies are not dismissed from this reflective process, but they "do not automatically have privilege over the local theological understandings operative in the lives of those studied."[4]

These shifts in how ethnography and theology are methodologically related to each other thus raise questions anew about theological normativity. As Ted Smith observes, the newer model of theology using ethnography "holds description and prescription more tightly together."[5] Smith is sympathetic to the goal of holding description and prescription (the *is* and the *ought*) more closely together, but he articulates important objections to their "easy synthesis," including the well-known critiques from Stanley Hauerwas and John Milbank that social science methods are far from value-neutral. Instead, Hauerwas and Milbank argue that these methods have an antitheological bias that undermines their capacity to describe theological reality accurately. As a result, these "distorted descriptions" produce "equally distorted norms."[6] Hauerwas's and Milbank's critiques are far from the final word on this topic: as new theological ethnography rightly demonstrates, their work tends to rely on idealized ecclesiologies to provide their normative theological content and would clearly be bolstered (or revealed as untenable) by thick descriptions of concrete practice.[7] Leaving aside this rebuttal, however, Smith notes that it must also be admitted that theological ethnography has not dealt adequately with the allegation of an inherent antitheological bias in social science methods. While some of the new theological ethnographers "start to *perform* an overcoming of these objections," Smith argues, for the most part "they do not explicitly argue with them."[8]

Particularly in the early methodological chapters of this text, I sought to launch such an argument. I have done so, however, not on the basis of the terms set by Hauerwas and Milbank, but rather on the terms of the theoretical and theological problematics that animate my own inquiry. My chief concern in these pages has been theological epistemology: how is theology produced—and how might it be produced or how ought it be produced—when the organic overlap between everyday and academic forms of theological knowledge is made apparent and nurtured? Social science methods not only have served but also have been thoroughly critiqued by this question. While it is not *doctrinal*, as Hauerwas and Milbank might wish, it is nevertheless still *theological*. My understanding of the nature of theological knowledge, for example, guided my critical engagement with Wacquant's carnal sociological methods, which are deeply concerned with the bodily dimensions of knowledge production. Reflexive engagement—through my own knowledgeable theological agency—shaped (and was shaped by) my critical use of reflexive ethnographic insights. Via this back and forth critique between ethnographic and theological forms of knowledge production, I sought not only to retrieve the former from its antitheological bias but also to resolve the potential idealism of the latter. In other words, I have sought to produce ethnographic knowledge in a theological way while simultaneously producing theological knowledge in an ethnographic way.

In addition to the objection that social scientific modes of description are inherently antitheological, concerns about normativity in ethnographic theology also often threaten it with the charge of relativism. Does the theological thought and action of a small, self-selected group of Baptists in Nashville have any necessary, normative import for the broader body of Christ and the theological academy—or any other social sphere for that matter? The tension here is less between the *is* and the *ought* and more between the *local is* and a *broader or more universal is.* Once again, such questions are not particularly new. Ernst Troeltsch raised them with regard to the historical turn in theology; James Gustafson, drawing on Troeltsch, raised them with regard to the theological turn to culture; and Smith raises them, once again, now drawing on Gustafson and Troeltsch in relation to theology's current turn to practice.[9] In sum, Smith asks, what is the nature of theological ethnographic claims, how are they justified, and what is the extent of their authority?[10] Can the theological ethnographer make claims about the Divine, salvation, or the Holy Spirit or only about what her research partners *believe* about such things? While social science methods provide criteria for establishing the validity of the latter, how would we justify the former? Whether an ethnographic theologian wanted to argue that her research partners were right (or even wrong) in their beliefs, on what grounds would she do so? Who gets the last word?

The questions raised by Smith are not, and never have been, the types of questions that can be answered in the abstract, but they do require an answer. The difference between ethnographic and other forms of theology is not that the former needs to justify the nature of its normativity and the latter does not. Rather, the difference lies in how ethnographic theology will justify itself, and because the nature of ethnographic theology is descriptive, these questions should be answered in a thickly descriptive way. In this conclusion, I therefore argue that ethnographic theologians should ask and answer questions about normativity in relation to the theoretical and theological problematics that animate their particular projects, and I do so by recapping the normative dimensions of the project at hand in that way.

Theological Normativity in This Project

Throughout this text I have drawn on ethnographic and theological methods that highlight issues of epistemology in order to consider how everyday and academic theological discourses might compete and cooperate in the production of theological knowledge. The nature, justification, and authority of this text's normative claims thus all hinge on this issue. This in fact means that I make few or perhaps no claims about Divine life itself, or even what my research partners believe about Divine life itself, for example. Rather, the tension in this text comes down to the extent or reach of what I can and cannot say about the production of theological knowledge. I then focused the *what can be said* through the lenses of reflexivity, carnality, and performativity in the three constructive chapters. I did not draw on traditional and textual theologies to judge these processes of theological reflection and production but used the processes themselves to debate and test the textual and traditional theologies. No one of these theological aspects, however, took precedence—not traditions, nor texts, nor the local and everyday theologies. Rather, we sought what erupted from the interactions between them all in practice. In this way, we not only tested Tanner's theological epistemology but debated numerous theological concepts as well, producing fresh questions and insights for further theological thought and action. In the end, I sought to write theological stories that avoided being, in Mark Jordan's words, "violently simple or demonically final."[11]

Ethnographic theologians acknowledge and accept that there is no theological "view from nowhere" that we can access, and that all theological claims are embedded in and produced by particular contexts, practices, and systems of power and privilege. This acknowledgment should place ethnographic theology in a posture of epistemological humility, thereby situated in the well-established lineage of theologies that work with "disconnects, ruptures and paradox," as Scharen and Vigen put it, seeking to negotiate, as Jordan suggests, "theological lessons of contradiction, repetition, unsaying and silence."[12] In this way, an ethnographic theology invites its reader into an ongoing theological conversation more than it tries to convince its reader of a theological argument. As I have tried to frame it here, ethnographic theology has the potential to invite the researcher and her research partners, the writer and the reader all into the doing of theology as a spiritual practice together.

Reflexive Ecclesiology: Locating Myself in the Theological Field

The *what can be said* of each constructive chapter in this book is framed by the interaction of three factors: (1) a particular local understanding of the relationship between everyday and academic theology derived from the field of study via interviews (as outlined in Chapter 1), (2) some aspect from Tanner's academic theological understanding of the relationship between everyday and academic theology to be tested, and (3) a particular facet of the ethnographic methods being deployed. For example, Chapter 3 was framed by the interaction between Peter's broad historically and geographically defined theological landscape, Tanner's vision for how academic theologians might nurture social and theological change and practices of ethnographic reflexivity that attend to the researcher's reflexivity with regard to her field of study. By constructing a frame out of pieces that do and do not fit together easily, the three aspects were able to engage, expand, and challenge each other. Theological claims that arose from this interactive framework are thus justified by it as well as authorized to speak back to it.

At the same time, neither the local, the textual, nor the theoretical components took precedence within this interactive framework. As a result, theological claims justified by it have their authority in an *interactive*, not imposing way. For example, Peter's warning that theological innovation is perhaps more likely to happen on the frontier than in the institution butted heads with Tanner's vision by which academic theology might introduce more radical notions into an everyday status quo. I, in my particular roles as researcher and minister, was called to responsibility for the ways in which I am complicit in, privileged by, oblivious to and, even, grateful for an ecclesial equilibrium I purport to wish to undo. The moments of tension in these interactions were therefore, at least potentially, theologically productive as each component of the framework functioned in relation to the other two.

This complex framing allowed a number of questions related to theological epistemology to come to the fore of contextual analysis in the third chapter. I hope other ethnographic theologians might consider testing these questions in their own fields of study. How can academic theologians deploy their theological agency for the production of hybrid everyday and academic theologies? How can academic theology contribute to reshaping everyday Christian practices? How do and how can everyday Christians and academic theologians partner with each other (consciously and unconsciously) to maintain and/or disrupt a social and theological status quo? Does the current cultural turn in academic theology and turn to practice necessarily entail a *plodding reformism*, or is more radical change possible?

While these questions were answered in the context of FBC, their import was not limited to that sphere. By testing Tanner's vision, which is grounded in a broader academic theological conversation, FBC becomes the interlocutor with whom—not the standard by which—those claims were evaluated. Our theological practices of mission, adult education, and so-called heretical speech, for example, all reveal the disconnects and contradictions in a particular academic theological coherence. They rupture that coherence and press it into a moment of *unsaying and silence*, so that it can revise itself anew. They do not, and cannot, replace that false coherence with their own coherent vision of "The Church," as formal ecclesiologies might have us do. But they can sway false academic theological coherence away from the *violently simple or demonically final.*

Tanner's argument that everyday theology produces the questions that academic theology seeks to ask and answer can thus be reimagined in light of this chapter, as well as others. Throughout this text, I have endeavored to maintain that everyday and academic theology should ask and seek to answer such questions together. For this reason, I would reframe her argument slightly by noting that a number of questions arise from this particular field of study, shaped by everyday and academic theology competing and cohering with each other within it, which could provide fodder for further academic (as well as other) theological reflection. Given the likelihood that particular Christian communities hold various competing visions for mission in tension within their own practice, for example, as FBC demonstrated, how might academic theologies of mission be revised to allow for the same internal diversity? Or, how might the dynamics of theological conversation in this particular community invite more "heretical" moments in the so-called Christian tradition(s) to function as contributors to academic theological understandings of doctrine? These and other debates articulated in this field of study all have the potential to intervene in academic theology, just as academic theology intervened in them through the classes I taught. And in this, Peter's insistence that the frontier and institution need each other if both are to flourish once again rings true.

At the same time, following Tanner and deploying practices of reflexivity, I also did not set up a situation in which everyday theology had precedence over academic theology. Alongside using the everyday to challenge the academic, I sought to allow academic ways of thinking and producing theological knowledge to challenge our ecclesial equilibrium on various theological topics. The historical theologies I introduced into our classroom context were not meant to become the standard by which everyday theologies were evaluated but rather they too functioned as interlocutors with whom my research partners and I could dialogue. They were the catalysts for various potential versions of social and theological change. So, for example, by exploring a more historical and systematic understanding of God as Trinity, some of the people who took our Sunday night classes reported a variety of ways in which their broader participation in and leadership of worship at FBC was impacted.

Carnal Theodicy: Embodying a Theological Field

Chapter 4 focused more closely on how academic theologians might even have access to everyday theological questions and insights, as Tanner describes it. In so doing, it took seriously the carnal dimensions of knowledge production (as articulated by Wacquant) and theological knowledge production in particular (as demonstrated by Ann's personal stories, outlined in Chapter 1). Here, we asked the following: How do bodies and bodily differences produce and bear everyday theologies? What in a theology makes it more or less difficult to theorize in a disembodied mode? What ways of doing theology might contribute to dismantling the Cartesian epistemology that characterizes so much theological knowledge production? We also looked at the question of carnality from both sides: how embodiment gives one access to theological reflection, or shapes it, and how theological reflection might be borne on embodiment.

This chapter challenged academic strategies of theological dissemination in particular. We saw notions long critiqued and rejected in academic theology, which nevertheless have the impact that the same theology might wish to have in an ecclesial sphere. We also saw theology *happen* somewhere beyond or prior to cognition, as the words articulated were unable to keep pace with their embodiment. And we saw the impact of academic theological texts in everyday life function differently than we might imagine. Once again, these findings were specific to my particular field of study. And yet, because they were in conversation with broader theoretical and theological structures of knowledge, they once again have the potential authority to speak back to those structures.

Performance Soteriology: Relational Dynamics in a Field of Study

Of course, none of these constructive chapters deal solely with reflexivity, carnality, or performativity. Each is focused through one of these lenses simply to explore a particular dimension of the ethnographic theological method more fully. Yet, as I have tried to make evident, the ethnographic theologian must maintain practices of reflexivity and pay attention to the carnal dimensions of knowledge, as well as how that knowledge is produced relationally, throughout the whole process of framing, researching, and writing her project. The themes of reflexivity, embodiment, and performance are all present in each chapter, including Chapter 5, even as it engages a new analytic for describing these relational dynamics in what I have called "performance theology."

This final chapter gets playful with Joan and Harlan's idea that theology can be something we act out, even as that play reveals—at times painfully—the disconnect that can happen between one's *talking* and one's *acting* theology. In so doing, it expands Tanner's notion of theological creativity as bricolage. If the ethnographic theologian's goal is not to mine information out of a field of study, but rather to nurture the places where everyday Christians and academic theologians are already cocreating theological knowledge, then a less individualistic metaphor for theological creativity is required. Research informants can become, or at least have the potential to become, research partners in the production of theological knowledge—as a critical analysis of performance art helped me to demonstrate. Just as ethnographic theology has challenged how we perceive the nature and tasks, authority, and normativity of traditional theology, so too has performance art challenged perceptions of what art is and can be. At the same time, both ethnographic theology and performance art run the risk of promising overly idealized pictures of what they can accomplish in their respective disciplines. That each claims to value, represent, or directly involve the voices of nonspecialized participants marks a claim to egalitarianism or grassroots participation that should be evaluated carefully on a case-by-case basis rather than simply being presumed.

Critical engagement with a performance artwork that is aesthetically creative, culturally engaged, yet also complicated with regard to its ethical and relational claims thus helped produce questions and insights out of our Sunday night classroom practices that are suitable for consideration in other ethnographic theological fields of study. This framework helped us ask how forms of power and privilege—everyday and academic, social, and theological—contribute to the shaping of a theological conversation and/or product. For, from, and to whom does the ethnographic theologian speak? Is theological collaboration possible across various forms of social identity difference and across everyday/academic theological difference? How do breakdowns in the intended process shape and contribute to the final theological products created? This last chapter, perhaps more so than the other two, demonstrates the shift toward a more interactive or conversational form of theological normativity with ethnographic theology.

At the same time, as demonstrated by my critique of the analogous power dynamics animating *The Artist Is Present* and my own theological practice, such processes can fail to live up to the ideals of relationality, justice, and mutuality that we might want them to attain. Scharen and

Vigen, expanding Fulkerson's argument that the ethnographic theologian works as a seeker at the site of a wound who is looking for the arc of redemption in practice, write that bodily apprenticeship helps us not only observe that redemption but also "experience ourselves some of the brokenness and repair present there."[13] As with performance art, what ethnographic theology offers is less a way to describe a world and more a way to "inhabit the world," such that we can participate in its ongoing making and remaking of itself.[14] We do this with the hope, but certainly not the assurance, that our participation in this making and remaking can help orient the world we inhabit to more just ends.

Last Words

On the final night of the two courses, in the final minutes of class, the group asks how my academic part of our work together is coming along. They know they will be characters in my dissertation (and by extension, this book), and they want to know how they are going to come across to these specialized publics. I share a few stories about the writing process, and one of the women, Maureen, asks me, "Do things get contentious at Vanderbilt? What do people think about your project?" Her implication is disbelief that people at a university would care about what a group of church people have to say: that people at a university would care what *she* has to say. I tell Maureen that my colleagues and professors really seem to like to hear what our class has been doing together. In fact, I tell the whole group that "a few of my colleagues have gotten a real kick out of the image of me floundering, trying to teach Kant to you guys." They all start laughing. "Yeah, you really did struggle there," someone comments. I hang my head and lift a hand in a futile gesture of holding back the mocking.

As the laughter dies down, Joe, Maureen's husband, who's usually a quiet guy, speaks the final words of our time together: "We need a historic plaque put up in this room," he smiles. "What would it say?" I ask curiously. I think he might be referring to something with the names of our classes and their dates, but I have to wonder why he is smirking so mischievously. Gesturing toward the back wall, he grins and marks out each word with punctuated emphasis, "She. Tried!" Everyone starts laughing again as Maureen swats her husband for his cheekiness. I shake my head and, smiling, gather my papers together and prepare to hug everyone good night.

Appendix A

Topics in Theology

Jesus Christ and Salvation

Taught by Natalie Wigg-Stevenson

In this course, we'll think together about two of the central doctrines of Christian theology: the doctrine of Jesus Christ (Christology) and the doctrine of salvation (Soteriology). We'll look at what different Christians throughout time have believed about Jesus (who he was, what he did, how he was both human and divine, how he is still present to us today, etc.), and how they connected those beliefs to the workings of salvation (what we are saved from, to, and for; how Jesus makes that salvation complete; what it means to say we are justified by faith; the role of the cross and resurrection; etc.). We will pay particular attention to how Christians connected their beliefs to the ways in which they worshipped God, as well as to how Christian beliefs throughout history relate to our own beliefs and practices of worship.

2/14 What do we believe? How are our beliefs derived from Scripture?

What do we as Baptists and as individuals believe about Jesus Christ: his person, work, humanity, divinity, time on earth, ongoing presence, return, etc . . . ? And how do we relate our beliefs about Jesus Christ to our understanding of salvation, our practices of worship and our practices in everyday life? What are we saved from, to and for, and what are the implications for the Christian life? What Scriptures inform our views? What Scriptures are we overlooking when we form our Biblical views?

2/21 I am working Room In The Inn—we can discuss whether or not to have a make up class

2/28 Theological views in the Bible and the Early Church

How was Jesus Christ both human and divine? How do his humanity and divinity relate to our salvation? If God came in the flesh, what does that mean for our own bodily lives?

Figures: Jesus and Paul, Justin Martyr, Origen, Arius and Athanasius

3/7 Early Church views *continued . . .* (1 hour class tonight for church business meeting)

How do the early church controversies set the 'rule' or 'regulations' for future understandings of Jesus Christ and salvation for Christians? What early church issues are we less concerned about now? What role did practices of worship play in early church theologies of Jesus Christ and salvation?

Figures: Arius and Athanasius, Augustine

3/14 Medieval Theologies and Practices

How did atonement theologies develop in the Medieval period? How did practices of worship relate to theologies of Jesus Christ and salvation in the Medieval period? Are there any surprising connections between Medieval theologies and our own contemporary Baptist beliefs? How do female Medieval Christian mystics approach questions about Jesus Christ differently? What can we learn from their spiritual theologies?

Figures: Anselm, Peter Abelard, Beatrice of Nazareth

3/21 I am working Room In The Inn—we can discuss whether or not to have a make up class

3/28 Reformation Theologies

How did Reformation theologies reframe Christian ways of understanding who Jesus Christ was, his divinity and humanity, and what his significance was in relation to salvation? What did Reformation theologians believe human beings needed to be saved from? What did the life of salvation look like according to Reformation theologians? What is "justification by faith" and how did it become a central topic for understanding salvation in the Reformation? How did worship practices in the Reformation relate to the understanding of Jesus Christ, salvation and the life of faith?

Figures: Martin Luther, John Calvin

4/4 Easter Sunday—no class

4/11 Views from Modernity—17th-19th centuries

How did Enlightenment views of rationality, history, science and truth shape and reshape Christian beliefs in miracles, Christ's resurrection, the existence of God and our ability to know/have faith in God? How was Jesus Christ understood in relation to these issues, and how did that impact the Christian view of salvation in the 19th century? How did Jesus' humanity relate to notions of human embodiment, knowledge and the emotions in this time period? How do our own contemporary Baptist beliefs and practices relate to and diverge from these beliefs in expected and surprising ways?

Figures: Rene Descartes & Blaise Pascal, Friedrich Schleiermacher, Soren Kierkegaard

4/18 20th Century Interpretations of Jesus Christ, Salvation and the Problem of Suffering

How did theologians in the 20th century pick up, critique, continue and depart from the views of Modernity? How did the tragic events of the 20th century shape theologians' understandings of Jesus Christ and salvation? How did a renewed interest in the problem of suffering impact how theologians understood the relationship between Jesus Christ and the triune God to be configured?

Figures: Karl Barth, Karl Rahner, Jurgen Moltmann

4/25 Contemporary Theologies—The Role of Context in the Shaping of Theology

How have the particular contexts in which theology has been written in the late 20th century—particularly in North and South

America—shaped the ideas contained in the theologies? How have American revolutions in race relations and gender relations impacted theology and led theologians to new interpretations of Jesus Christ's person and work in salvation? How have movements of liberation in Latin America contributed to fresh understandings of the same? What is the relationship between politics and theology in all these different views? How does our own context shape what we believe and do in ways we might not even notice?

Figures: James Cone, Gustavo Gutierrez, Darby Kathleen Ray

5/2 A Return to Our Own Context, Beliefs and Practices (1 hour class tonight for church business meeting)

How have our own views shifted, expanded or been affirmed throughout the course of this class? What new ideas did we find ourselves surprisingly open to? What ideas or theologies connect with our own practices of worship and other church practices? How has our faith been impacted by the historic faith of other Christians?

Figures: Ourselves!

Appendix B
Topics in Theology
God as Trinity

Taught by Natalie Wigg-Stevenson

In this course, we'll look at one of the key doctrines of the Christian faith: God as Trinity. We'll look at the Biblical basis for this doctrine, as well as its more systematic formulation by early Christian theologians. And then we'll study how the doctrine has changed shape throughout Christian history depending upon the period in which it was reconceived. We will look especially at how different Christian theologians throughout history have understood God's ways of relating to creation, how it is we come to know and experience God as Trinity, how God is revealed to us and how God's acts relate to our own actions. We will ask questions about how God is both transcendent to the world, and present within it with particular attention to how God as transcendent father relates to the historical presence of the crucified Christ and the ongoing presence of the Holy Spirit among us. Throughout the course we'll look at how historical beliefs and practices of the Christian faith with regards to the doctrine of God as Trinity relate to our own beliefs and practices as 20–21st century Baptists.

9/12 What do we believe? How are our beliefs derived from Scripture?

What do we as Baptists and as individuals believe about the Trinity—the three persons and their relations to each other, God's relationship to the world, how it is we come to have knowledge of God, etc . . . ? And how do our beliefs about God as Trinity relate to our understanding of salvation, our practices of worship and our practices in everyday life? What Scriptures inform our views? What Scriptures are we overlooking when we form our Biblical views?

9/19 Theological views in the Bible and the Early Church

What was the historical & theological process by which early church leader's came to an orthodox view of the Trinity? What Biblical stories were relevant for their formulation? What were the central debates and problems? How did the relationship between Judaism and Christianity play into the debates in this time? What early church issues are we less concerned about now? What role did the practices of worship play in early church theologies of God as Trinity?

Figures: Early church creeds, Arius and Athanasius, Eastern Fathers

9/26 Class is cancelled because I will be out of town

10/3 Transitions: Early Church to the Medieval Period (We'll dismiss at 5:50pm for church business meeting)

We will use this week to wrap up whatever material we didn't manage to get to from the first two classes. We will also look forward to next week by asking what is at stake in the shift from the central question of the early church (what is God as Trinity?) to a central question of the Medieval period (how do we know God as Trinity?).

10/10 Medieval Theologies and Practices—How do we *know* God?

How do we as 21st century Baptists understand ourselves as coming to *know* God? What is the relationship between knowing God personally and knowing God intellectually? How did Medieval theologians understand that relationship? What spiritual disciplines or practices did they and do we engage to come to know God more deeply? How do you know you know God?

Figures: St. Anselm (Ontological Argument), Marguerite Porete (Mysticism), Thomas Aquinas (The nature of theology)

10/17 Reformation Theologies—Where is God and what is he like?

If God is three in one, and Jesus suffers on the cross, does that mean the Father and the Holy Spirit suffer too? What would be the problems

with that? What would the nature of their suffering be? What is the character of God? Is God beautiful, terrible, wrathful, forgiving . . . ?
Figures: Martin Luther, John Calvin

10/24 Class is cancelled because I will be out of town

10/31 All LCU classes are cancelled

We will find a time to schedule one make-up class from these two cancelled weeks

??? Theologies of Modernity—How did the rise of scientific rationality shape our views of God?

What are the limits of human knowledge, and how does knowledge of God relate to those limits? How does philosophical thought play a role in the ways Christians understand God? How is God both inside the world and outside it? How is God revealed in history? Where does the Trinity fit in all this?
Figures: Immanuel Kant, GWF Hegel, Friedrich Schleiermacher

11/7 Theology in its Historical Context (We'll dismiss at 5:50PM for Church Business Meeting)

We will take some time to finish up the thoughts we didn't get to from the previous few weeks. In so doing, we'll ask how the particular historical and geographic contexts in which these theologies were formulated impacted the shape they took? We'll also discuss the historical, cultural shifts that took place in the 20th century, and how those impacted the theologies we'll study next week.

11/14 20th-century Theology—Why does an all-powerful God permit an unjust world?

With the cutting edges of theology located in Germany, how did the Holocaust impact the way Christians thought about God? Where was God in the Holocaust? How did the Holocaust impact the relationship between Jews and Christians in their image of God? How did the complicity of Christians with the Nazi movement impact our view of

God? What should the Christian relationship to political powers be? How did the cultural revolutions of the 1960s and '70s impact the ways in which American Christians think about God?

Figures: Elie Wiesel, Karl Barth, Jurgen Moltmann, Elizabeth Johnson

11/21 A Return to Our Own Context, Beliefs and Practices

How have our own views shifted, expanded or been affirmed throughout the course of this class? What new ideas did we find ourselves surprisingly open to? What ideas or theologies connect with our own practices of worship and other church practices? How has our faith been impacted by the historic faith of other Christians?

Figures: Ourselves!

Notes

Introduction

1. This ethnographic study received Institutional Review Board (IRB) approval from the Vanderbilt University IRB. All names used in this text for members of FBC are pseudonyms, except for references to myself, to my husband (Tyler, a member of the congregation), or to the church pastor (Frank). Tyler's name has not been made pseudonymous because his identity as my spouse is on the public record. Frank's name has not been made pseudonymous because his identity as the pastor of the church is also on the public record.
2. That I left FBC within a year of finishing my study there has nothing to do with my affection for the church. I left because, having finished my doctorate, I needed to pursue employment elsewhere.
3. Fulkerson, *Places of Redemption*, 3.
4. Sequentially, this process involved (a) worshipping as a separate community in FBC's building, (b) being led in worship in a separate building by a white pastor as an FBC mission church, (c) and finally worshipping with an African American pastor in an FBC-governed mission church before founding their own congregation.
5. FBC is not bucking any national trends with this homogeneity. Sunday morning at 11 o'clock, as Martin Luther King Jr. famously stated, is the "most segregated hour of the week." Michael Emerson in fact describes American congregations as "hypersegregated," as only 2.5 percent are composed of a "stable, long-term ethnic mix." Therefore, FBC is not one of the rare churches that intentionally cultivates a more heterogeneous community out of a commitment, theological or otherwise, to diversity. See Ammerman, "Congregations," 568. Ammerman is citing Emerson and Woo, *People of the Dream*.
6. Warner, "The Place of the Congregation in the Contemporary American Religious Configuration," 76.
7. Farnsley II, "Judicious Concentration," 47. A single Baptist church has an autonomous, democratic governance structure. That church can choose to affiliate with other organizations, such as local (e.g., the Nashville association), state (e.g., the Tennessee Baptist Convention), and/or national (e.g., the SBC). An association can disfellowship an individual church (in recent years, this has usually happened in more conservative local bodies over female ordination). Because local bodies have no

formal ties with state and national bodies, however, disfellowship from them does not immediately imply disfellowship elsewhere. Likewise, membership in the local body does not immediately imply membership with state and national bodies. For a fuller explication of this structure, see Ammerman, "After the Battles," 305.

8. See appendixes A and B for the syllabi of both classes. Each syllabus was used for publicity prior to each course's beginning, and students used it as a guide throughout. Both classes engaged a historical survey of Christian theologians. I guided reflection on the ways in which these particular doctrines had changed shape throughout time, as well as how they related to the beliefs and practices shared by FBC's community.
9. At least four people I interviewed referred explicitly to the theology classes I taught as a welcome alternative to what they called "the Beth Moore–style theology," which was often offered on Sunday nights. Moore is a popular Christian writer who writes curricula primarily for women. For more on her, see http://www.lproof.org/aboutus/bethmoore.
10. Hemphill currently serves as an SBC strategist for "Empowering Kingdom Growth." He previously served as president of Southwestern Baptist Theological Seminary. For more on him, see http://www.empoweringkingdomgrowth.net.
11. For more on The Truth Project see http://www.thetruthproject.org. The Truth Project, as the name suggests, offers an authoritative view of what truth is, which by extension is a particularly conservative—and as with many contemporary fundamentalisms, a surprisingly modernist—view.
12. Like the one I taught, this final course did not follow a purchasable curriculum, but it was a discussion-based learning module designed by the pastoral counselor who taught it.
13. While the main goal of the Crescent Project is evangelism, it has a significant subconcern for fostering healthy and civil interreligious dialogue between Muslims and Christians. While I question the possibility for genuine interreligious dialogue alongside proselytizing, this series was taught during the time when feverous national attention was directed toward the so-called Ground Zero Mosque, Qur'an burnings, and other forms of American anti-Islam sentiment. It therefore offered an Evangelical alternative to this anti-Islam fervor. For more on the Crescent Project DVDs used in this course, see https://www.crescentproject.org/bridgesdvd.
14. For more on Courtney, see http://vickicourtney.com.
15. In the first hour of each class, Pastor Frank leads a martial arts–based exercise routine, and in the second half the men do Bible study together. This focus on physical health is fairly atypical within SBC life. Even more atypical, this course paved the way for a yoga class also to be taught at the church. In line with broader SBC views, there are some at

FBC who express concern about these so-called Eastern influences in our church life. But for the most part, these practices are accepted with an attitude of "if you don't want to go, you don't have to."

16. The flip side of my frustration with this chivalry hit me—quite literally—when I moved away from the Southern United States after five years of living there. While I never lost the frustration I experienced with this doorway dance, during my first few months living in Toronto, Ontario (a much less patriarchal and, by extension, less paternalistically chivalrous location than Nashville, Tennessee), before my bodily instincts reacclimatized to their new location, I frequently bashed my face off of doors swinging closed in front of me, dropped by whichever male figure had preceded me through them. It turned out I had become much more used to the bodily practice of having a door held open than I had realized.
17. This point actually resonates with Baptist polity, which is democratically structured, with church-wide voting practices determining most major decisions within a congregation. Individuals are responsible for interpreting scripture for themselves and making "personal decisions for Christ." These beliefs and practices point to a particular Baptist ideal that each person's voice has authority for themselves and value for others. Of course, this ideal gets obscured as other practices limit whose voice counts and how. Nevertheless, they foster an environment in which conversation, even difference of opinion—within certain limits, of course—is seen as good for the community. We might rarely arrange our space accordingly, but elements of the same values are inherent in some of our other shared social practices.
18. For information on liturgical and ritual practices associated with the first community I considered studying—IKON—see Rollins, *How (Not) To Speak of God*. BDSM refers to erotic practices associated with bondage and discipline, domination and submission, and sadism and masochism. For an introduction to the connection between Christian communities and BDSM, see Brown, "Dancing in the *Eros*."
19. These questions of ethnographic ethics are perhaps brought home most powerfully by indigenous critiques of ethnographic research methods. See Smith, *Decolonizing Methodologies*; and Brown and Strega, eds., *Research as Resistance*.

CHAPTER 1

1. For a comprehensive study of different theological perspectives on engaging culture, see Brown, Davaney, and Tanner, eds., *Converging on Culture*.
2. For more on the relationship between ethnographic theology and reflexivity, see Scharen and Vigen, eds., *Ethnography as Christian Theology and Ethics*, 20ff; and Ward, ed., *Perspectives on Ecclesiology and Ethnography*, 7ff.

3. See Tanner, *Theories of Culture.*
4. I borrow the phrase "research partners" from feminist ethnographic epistemologies and use it rather than "research subjects" or "informants" because I want to emphasize our community's coproduction of social and theological knowledge. See Oleson, "Early Millennial Feminist Qualitative Research: Challenges and Contours."
5. Bourdieu and Wacquant, *An Invitation*, 97.
6. Thomson, "Field," 66.
7. Bourdieu and Wacquant, *An Invitation*, 98.
8. Ibid. For more on the difference between rules and regularities, see Bourdieu, *Logic of Practice*, 37–41.
9. I explore this notion of tacit, dispositional knowledge more fully in the second chapter, engaging Bourdieu's use of the concept *habitus*, which for him is intimately connected to *field.*
10. See Bourdieu, *Outline*, 3–16.
11. Deer, "Doxa," 120.
12. Bourdieu, *Outline*, 167; emphases in the original.
13. Ibid., 168.
14. Ibid., 169.
15. Bourdieu, *Outline*, 168–70; Deer, "Doxa," 124–25.
16. Swartz, *Culture and Power*, 136. See also Bourdieu and Wacquant, *An Invitation*, 76.
17. It should, however, be noted that a field can never be fully autonomous. In fact, Bourdieu names any description of fields as fully autonomous as a scholastic fallacy; scholars impose autonomy onto a set of practices for the purpose of academic interpretation, thus misconstruing the "fuzzy" borders and interpermeability of fields at play. See Bourdieu, *Pascalian Meditations*, 50ff.
18. Sanks, "*Homo Theologicus*," 516–17.
19. Tanner, *Theories of Culture*, 72.
20. Ibid.
21. Ibid.
22. Ibid., 57.
23. Ibid., 81.
24. Ibid., 71.
25. Bourdieu, *Pascalian Meditations*, 188.
26. Ibid., 80.
27. Ibid., 15.
28. Ibid., 17.
29. It is difficult to know whether or not their answers would have been the same had I asked my question *before* I taught one of the classes. Surely, having just participated in a class that an academic theologian taught in the church impacted their view of what an academic theologian should do in the church. Even so, the fact that they support their points with narratives and histories that are distinct from the class

indicates that their desires rise from a broader spectrum of practice than only that class. It is also quite telling that I didn't ask them explicitly what they thought they had to offer to academic theological inquiry. Consciously, I framed my questions as I did because my initial research question asked what methods *academic theologians* might employ to foster these types of conversations. Unconsciously, I have to wonder if this oversight belies an instinctual devaluing of everyday theological insights on my part, despite what I might say to the contrary. My fieldwork helped me learn just how mutually beneficial practices of theological construction can be.

30. This is perhaps an obvious point. The question of what constitutes an appropriate source for academic theology does not bubble up organically from everyday theological reasoning about faith. Nevertheless, it is worth noting that the primary mode academic theologians tend to think about everyday theology in for our work (i.e., as source) frequently bemused the everyday Christians with whom I worked.
31. Heterosexual marriage is the presumed norm at First Baptist Church, a norm that easily censors public speech about sexuality. Some of the people I interviewed, however—Peter included—wanted to use our one-on-one conversations to tackle hot-topic issues like abortion and same-sex marriage from a theological perspective. Those who brought up same-sex marriage seemed to presume (rightly) that I supported it and wanted to share that they thought they did too. A few of them brought it up specifically because they wanted me to give them theological justification for their hunches in this direction. Given the conversational nature of my methods, I would give them theological tools to deal with their questions and share aspects of my own views when asked. For better or for worse, these conversations remained focused on the question of marriage. Only with a small circle of friends who also happened also to be research partners did I reveal my larger desire to disrupt the heteronormative, monogamy-normative focus of the debates.
32. Before I moved away from Nashville, he interviewed me in order to tell my story as one of few women ordained in FBC's history. FBC is willing to ordain women, but broader social practices within the church's life, as well as conservative Christian life in the United States, do not tend to give rise to female leaders.
33. This phrase "ivory tower" has particular meaning for Peter. A few times, now, when he has asked me to describe my research to him, we reach a point in the conversation where he says, "So you're taking theology out of the ivory tower!" For him, this designates types of theology he thinks are irrelevant or a waste of time. The first time he asked me this question, I responded, "Yeah, I guess so." Each subsequent questioning has made me rethink my position a little more, though, and has even incited a desire in me that surprised me to defend this

ivory tower. And then one day I answered, here in a paraphrase because I was not recording this conversation, "Yeah, but also no. I want it to come out, but then it needs to go back in, and come out again, and go back in. I want it to interact with the world outside, but it always needs to go back inside if it is to keep training in the gifts of the academy to offer them to the world." With each subsequent answer, his smile has faded a little. With this last one, he clasped his chin in his hand, a look of disappointment tinged with curiosity fluttered across his expression, and he simply said, "Hmpf."

34. My friendship with Ann was forged before this study began when she served on my ordination committee. One of her expressed reasons for serving on my ordination committee was so that she could be a part of something she would have wanted for herself, a statement she offered, incredibly, without a hint of bitterness.
35. Cone's influence on Harlan's theological thinking, in particular, was evident in our classroom conversations. While other class members would narrate how their experiences during the civil rights movement in the South had shaped their understanding of racial prejudice when the focus of our conversation was specifically on race relations, Harlan would bring race-based critique to bear on language around darkness and blackness as negative images in our theological constructions. When he did so, I bolstered his point, expressing agreement with him in an effort to open up such conversation, but other class members who stated explicitly that Harlan and I were overthinking things quickly shut it down.
36. Bourdieu, *Pascalian Meditations*, 142.

CHAPTER 2

1. See, for example, Farley, *Theologia*; Fulkerson, *Places of Redemption*; Scharen, *Public Worship and Public Work.*
2. Bourdieu, *Outline*, 167.
3. With action research methods, the researcher participates actively in a community of practice, with the whole group working together to reflect on and respond to a particular set of problems or concerns. For more on action research, see Stringer, *Action Research.* For more on the relationship between action research methods and theology, see Cameron et al., *Talking about God in Practice.*
4. Maton, "Habitus," 49.
5. Ibid., esp. 57ff.
6. Ibid., 61.
7. Bourdieu, *Outline*, 86.
8. Bourdieu and Wacquant, "The Purpose of Reflexive Sociology," 121.
9. Ibid.
10. Fulkerson, *Places of Redemption*, 35.

11. Bourdieu, *Logic of Practice*, 69.
12. Ibid.
13. Ibid., 56.
14. Althaus-Reid, *The Queer God*, 9ff.
15. Bourdieu, *Logic of Practice*, 69.
16. Tanner, *Theories of Culture*, 57.
17. Bourdieu, *Logic of Practice*, 53; Maton, "Habitus," 50.
18. Maton, "Habitus," 52.
19. Ibid., 58.
20. Ortner, "Making Gender," 1.
21. Ibid., 17.
22. Ibid.
23. Ibid.
24. Ibid.
25. "Subaltern" is the language Ortner uses to describe her methods, even as she tends to put it into quotation marks and question its appropriateness. For a critique on the use of the language of "subaltern," see Spivak, "Can the Subaltern Speak," 271ff.
26. Ortner, "Making Gender," 2.
27. Bourdieu, *Outline*, 2.
28. See especially Bourdieu, *Outline*, chap. 1.
29. Greenfell, *Pierre Bourdieu*, 227.
30. Wacquant, *Body and Soul*, 60.
31. Ibid., 4n3.
32. Wacquant, "Carnal Connections," 457.
33. Ibid.
34. Ibid.; emphases in the original.
35. Ibid., 446.
36. My treatment of texts in this way resonates with Wendy Farley's description of nonacademic ways of relating to texts. See Farley, *Wounding and Healing of Desire*, ix–xiii.
37. The texts my friend and I explicitly referenced in our conversation are the following: Brock and Parker, *Proverbs of Ashes*; and Jones, *Cartographies of Grace.*
38. The relationship between agency and submission has received renewed attention in feminist scholarship. See Coakley, *Powers and Submissions*; and Mahmood, *Politics of Piety.*
39. See, for example, Foucault's discussion of "Docile Bodies" in Foucault, *Discipline and Punish*, 135–69.
40. de Certeau, *Practice of Everyday Life.*
41. Ibid., 149.
42. See Bourdieu, *Outline*, 4–5, for his discussion of Lévi-Strauss's objectivism; and Bourdieu, *Outline*, 73–76, for his discussion of Sartre's subjectivism.
43. de Certeau, Practice of Everyday Life, 149.

44. Ibid., 149.
45. Ibid., 65.
46. Wacquant, "Carnal Connections," 448.
47. Ibid., 449.
48. Ibid.
49. Wacquant, "Carnal Connections."
50. Lloyd, "Sentimental Education," 538–41.
51. Wacquant, *Body and Soul*, 4. Emphasis original.
52. Tanner, *Theories of Culture*, 71ff.
53. Wacquant, *Body and Soul*, 122.
54. Ibid., 99ff.

CHAPTER 3

1. Wacquant, "Habitus," 145–46.
2. Ibid., 147.
3. Ibid.
4. Ibid., 146.
5. See Tanner, *Theories of Culture*, 83.
6. Ibid., 166.
7. Ibid.
8. Ibid., 167.
9. Therein lies one of the limitations of my particular method: it requires that other academic theologians corroborate my findings for them to be convincing. It might also reveal the limitations to performing this model in a conservative congregation. Although, here Mary McClintock Fulkerson's findings that a more progressive community also struggled to sustain social change, particularly with regard to racial reconciliation, point to the possibility that I might be tapping into a larger ecclesial trend that transcends the differences between conservative and progressive congregations. See Fulkerson, *Places of Redemption*, particularly chapter 7. See also Moon, *God, Sex, and Politics* for a descriptive analysis on how debates around sexuality and politics share themes across a conservative and a progressive congregation (see especially pp. 229ff).
10. Tanner, *Theories of Culture*, 175.
11. As Nancy Tatom Ammerman argues, people tend to join congregations that offer them a way to put their "moral energies" to work. See Ammerman, *Pillars of Faith*, 268.
12. CBF was formed in 1991, when a number of churches withdrew from the SBC largely over the issue of women's ordination. For more, see http://www.thefellowship.info.
13. Warner, "The Place of the Congregation in the Contemporary American Religious Configuration," 73. As Ammerman's research also shows, at least half of Southern Baptists sense that the national body

of the SBC has little to no effect on their local church practices. See Ammerman, *Baptist Battles*, 258–71.

14. The rare occasions I have heard some form of explicit "denominational pride" have occurred around budget questions, in which there is an annual push by a small but outspoken group to increase FBC's giving to the denominational missions fund. Of course, denominational pride is expressed more unconsciously in the ways that church members emphasize their congregational belonging, a distinctly Baptist kind of pride in itself.
15. Ammerman, "Congregations," 568. Ammerman is citing Emerson and Woo, *People of the Dream*. More recent studies are beginning to reveal a growth in multiracial churches, with claims that these communities have doubled in the last ten years (see http://www.faithcommunitiestoday.org/fact-2010). This increase is, in part, due to broader demographic shifts in American culture, but has also been stimulated by a rising intentionality on the part of congregations and denominations to integrate their communities.
16. Ammerman, "Congregations," 568.
17. Of course, these toys also had "the plan of salvation" and our contact information printed on them, but even that constituted a perceived spiritual need and want. While I have mentioned the ways in which church members experience dissatisfaction with this model, it also produces effects that we as a congregation celebrate. At least one of the adult baptisms we celebrated in my year of study was related to someone receiving a Frisbee at the parade and following up on its instruction.
18. I use the term "social justice" somewhat loosely here. While the programs do not fit neatly into a charity model of church outreach (as the programs offer a more sustained practice integrated with the lives of their guests and clients and are involved with tackling a few of the broader social and political issues in a more structural way), they also do not exhibit a partnership model across the board. In many cases, those who access the programs are treated as guests, although in some cases they do work more as partners in their own care and the care of others. Official church involvement with trying to effect broad social, structural change—a key marker of social justice and partnership work—is also minimal, although involvement with the programs does inspire some participants to engage that kind of work on their own.
19. Ammerman, "Congregations," 358.
20. For more on the Next Door, see http://www.thenextdoor.org. The Next Door occupies an almost legendary status in the life of FBC. A group of women came together to pray about a building the church owned but was not using. This small group quickly grew to over a hundred "Wild Praying Women," a name that still is used when this story gets told years later. The organization has received national recognition and has opened satellite sites in Chattanooga and Knoxville.

21. FBC in fact has many retired ministers as members, enough that their integration into lay life is not strained or a significant challenge to our current pastoral team's authority. As Richard pointed out, one likely reason so many ministers and theologically educated people settle in our congregation is because of its proximity to Lifeway, the SBC publishing company, as many ministers finish up their careers there.
22. One denied my request for an interview, the other attended only sporadically and so I did not make a request of her.
23. Some other demographic details: all ten are white, middle-class professionals and retired middle-class professionals. There are two married couples in the mix: Miriam and Gary (in their late thirties) and Joan and Harlan (both in their seventies). Elaine, who is in her late thirties, is divorced. Miriam, Gary, and Elaine all have young children. Gene, about fifty years old, is single. Peter, Richard, and Mike are all retired and are all married with grown children. Peter is the oldest of the three and is in his late seventies. Rickie, also around fifty years old, is married with no children.
24. Classes divided by gender are more common in the evening programs: consider the Beth Moore classes and the martial arts classes taught by the senior pastor, both mentioned in the introduction. Divisions by marital/family status and age are more common on Sunday mornings than evenings. Sunday morning—"Sunday school"—classes, therefore, tend to attract couples enrolling in a class together. Furthermore, because there are no visible same-sex couples at FBC, Sunday evening classes designated for *either* men *or* women (there is also no formal recognition of sex or gender beyond this dichotomy) are, by default, not open to couples. For example, Harlan attended a previous course I taught, while Joan attended another on the challenges and joys of being a caregiver for an ailing spouse elsewhere in the building.
25. Both men and women can be ordained and serve as deacons at FBC, although the deacon board is made up primarily of men. Each year, only a handful of women make the ballot. This is, in part, due to cultural expectations of what characterizes a good deacon. Values of leadership, spiritual authority, and the like are not as cultured into female church members as they are into male. A small group composed primarily of women, but also men, had been working hard in the years when I attended FBC to bolster female participation, working toward this goal at every level of the political process from recruitment to various versions of campaigning for those women who do make the ballot.
26. A brief note on how a typical class proceeded: the syllabus framed each class with guiding questions and a list of who would be studied. Some looked up thinkers in advance online or in aids they have in their personal libraries, but most did not. Each class opened with prayer, then a brief discussion on the theme for the day (if there was one). Usually I prepared a handout that included relevant or interesting

quotations from whoever we were studying, sometimes for us to interpret together, sometimes simply to give a feel for the thinker. We then moved between brief lectures by me on key figures and class discussion, with the lines between these two forms of discourse often blurred.

27. I refer to Mike as "conservative" not only based on my own assessment but also because he is repeatedly described as such by other class members in interviews. Self-described liberals point to him as an example of valued diversity within the group. One night, as we were dismissing class, I caught Mike and said, while laughing, "oh Mike, I feel like you're always saying, 'well it's this, of course, or that,' and I'm always going, 'but what about this, and what about that?'" I loosely held his wrist while saying this, and gestured on his arm the motion of picking at him over and over again. He walked away laughing saying, "but it's all good; it's all good!"
28. Tanner, *Theories of Culture*, 46.
29. Scharen, *Public Worship*, 220.
30. Ibid., 223.
31. Ibid., 221.
32. See Ann Swidler, "Culture in Action: Symbols and Strategies," *American Sociological Review* 51 (April 1986): 278ff.
33. Ibid., 277.
34. Scharen, *Public Worship*, 221.
35. Swidler, "Culture in Action," 278.
36. Tanner, *Theories of Culture*, 46.
37. Ibid., 42.
38. Ibid., 51.
39. I asked this question in large part because it opened insight into numerous classroom dynamics. I learned much about the relationships between class members outside of our time and space together, such as who taught whom in Sunday School, who had served on various service projects together, and the emotional responses certain class members had to others.
40. Swidler, "Culture in Action," 279.
41. It might be interesting to reflect for a moment on my method in order to offer a layer of reflexivity to it. With both these words (and the words on mystery incorporated above it), I am experiencing discomfort at including a chunk of my own impromptu speech transcribed directly from my recordings and placed into the ethnographic reporting here. As scholars, we tend to revise, edit, and polish our thoughts before offering them publically. Off-the-cuff speech is reserved for question and answer periods in public presentations, a genre that is by nature improvisational. We almost never put our impromptu speech into print, however. With these speeches, even more so with the latter, some of what I said is actually embarrassing: the phrase "Holy Spirit, I'm all over it," paired with a dismissive gesture, is utterly ridiculous, as I recall

thinking as soon as it came out of my mouth. Indeed, being able to get away with saying it depended on the already marginal status of pneumatological doctrines within FBC's theological commitments. I thus perpetuated what I perceive to be theological problems in my church with a flippant claim. Despite the failings of my speech, however, I am convicted by the power imbalance implicit in the ways ethnographic self-representation can become polished in contrast to the ways we represent others. Furthermore, I am convinced that study of academic theologian's own everyday theological speech can yield similar types of helpful insights as study of the everyday theological speech of our ethnographic partners. My own speech is as full of context-specific compromises—conscious and unconscious—as anyone else in the class.

42. For more on the relationship between modern American religion and the ways in which heresy is no longer a possibility so much as it is a necessity for being able to claim religious affiliation, see Berger, *The Heretical Imperative* (see especially pp. 26ff).
43. For more on the pastoral and ethical limits of this type of ethnographic practice, see Wigg-Stevenson, "Reflexive Theology."

CHAPTER 4

1. Wacquant, "Carnal Connections," 465. Wacquant cites (and translates) Bourdieu, *Pascalian Meditations*, 170. Bourdieu specifically (or, perhaps, nonspecifically) pins the problem here on a 2,000-year history of diffuse and Christianized readings of Platonism, which we might note come to a particularly crucial crystallization in the modern period via the articulation and effects of Cartesian epistemology and methods.
2. Wacquant, "Carnal Connections," 466.
3. Judith Farquhar quoted in Wacquant, "Carnal Connections," 454.
4. Ibid.; emphases in the original.
5. Consider two examples from nontheological ethnographies of Christian practice: James M. Ault Jr. describes his conversion to Christianity in Ault, *Spirit and Flesh*; and Dawne Moone experiences intense emotions at a Eucharist service in Moone, *God, Sex and Politics*.
6. In particular, I felt a deep trust in Ann with regard to issues around gender and race. She was passionate about women in ministry and had agreed to serve on my ordination committee during a particularly stressful time in her own life. Moreover, she served saying, "I would have wanted to do this myself in another time; at least this way I get to be a part of someone else getting to do it," with an utter lack of bitterness regarding her own missed opportunities. So I trusted her generosity of spirit. She would also tell me stories about how her job at the Southern Baptist publishing house was threatened during the civil rights movement because she tried to put pictures of black children and white children playing together in Sunday School curriculum for

SBC churches. Knowing she sought coherence between her words and action, and that she would take risks to do what she thought was right, I therefore trusted her.

7. For more on gender roles in the South, see Rice and Coates, "Gender Role Attitudes," 744–56. The mix of quantitative and qualitative analysis in this article demonstrates that while attitudes are becoming more progressive in the South with regard to traditional gender norms, they are not doing so to the same degree as other regions in the country. Furthermore, shifts in attitudes seem to be happening more in populations whose economic and family status does not afford them the luxuries associated with traditional norms (i.e., not working outside the home, fashioning one's appearance with expensive clothes and hair and makeup treatments, etc.). In various ways, myths of the *Southern belle* or *Southern lady* still hold sway in public imagination, at least as an ideal to which one should aspire. Because FBC is a predominantly white, middle- to upper-middle-class congregation, these norms therefore continue to dominate.
8. For the pivotal work on female masculinities see, Halberstam, *Female Masculinity*.
9. While I am more comfortable using the language "same-sex desire" (which I understand to make space for multiple modes of sexual identity) than "homosexuality," I tended to use the latter term more frequently in conversations about sexuality at FBC because it is the one with which my conversation partners seemed more familiar. It is also worth acknowledging that there are problems with the term "same-sex desire," as it risks presuming gender difference and cisgendered desirers.
10. The phrase "homosexual holiness" was popularized by Luke Timothy Johnson in his influential article, "Scripture and Spirit." Johnson presses contemporary Christians to consider whether there are narratives of "homosexual holiness" similar to those of "Gentile holiness" in the New Testament in order to construct a more inclusive ecclesiology.
11. Douglas, *Sexuality and the Black Church*.
12. I use the language of "mystical ascent" with some hesitation, as recent studies in religion have demonstrated the problematic nature of studying *mysticism*. In general, the mystical experience has been understood as some form of direct contact with the Divine, apart from any social, cultural, and linguistic shaping. Such a view has been appropriately interrogated. See, for example, Sharf, "Mysticism," 96ff. For a study on how male power has defined the borders of the concept "mystic" and, by extension, has excluded female forms of "mysticism" from its definition, see Jantzen, *Power, Gender and Christian Mysticism*.
13. A male congregant relayed this to me as another male congregant's comment about my licensing sermon, the sermon one preaches to begin the public dimension of an ordination process. Both men intended it as a compliment and would have been surprised that I didn't receive it

as such. Indeed, my response—"Perhaps he should try sitting a little closer next time so he can hear"—which was the most graceful reply I could muster, most certainly came across as rude. But as I was also aware that both men had the authority to block my ordination, I did not feel the freedom to respond in any other way.

14. Pahl, *Shopping Malls and Other Sacred Spaces*, 34ff.
15. See McFague, *Metaphorical Theology*.
16. Wiesel, *Night*, 61–62.
17. Swidler, "Culture in Action," 279.

CHAPTER 5

1. Tanner, *Theories of Culture*, 166. For more on bricolage, Tanner cites de Certeau, *Practice of Everyday Life*; Hebdige, *Subculture*; and Stout, *Ethics after Babel*. Hebdige in particular draws the connection between the concept of bricolage in anthropology via Lévi-Strauss's *The Savage Mind* and in the arts via the "collage aesthetic," which I am playing with here, theorized by André Breton, *Surrealists on Art*.
2. Tanner, *Theories of Culture*, 166.
3. In many ways, performance art grows out of artistic bricolage, as artists gradually displaced the significance of traditional media like paint and canvas with paper, cardboard, found objects, and even their own bodies. From Pablo Picasso's and André Breton's two-dimensional collages, to Marcel Duchamp's and Louise Nevelson's later three-dimensional assemblages, to Carolee Schneemann's and Chris Burden's later use of their own flesh, artists have consistently deployed the stuff of everyday life in their artistic creativity. This particular trajectory is, of course, only one way of tracing the advent and development of performance art. A fuller survey would need to include, at a minimum, a more global perspective, engagement with movements like Dadaism and Abstract Expressionism, as well as experimental music, theatre and film.
4. I capitalize "The Artist" here because, along with a number of art critics, some of whom I reference in this section, I reject descriptions of the work that interpret Abramović's bodily or literal presence to the audience as anything like a personal, intimate interaction. Viewers did not meet Marina; they met, as the title of the work suggests, The Artist—a highly constructed, highly controlled, even highly branded role being played by the artist, Marina Abramović.
5. MoMA, http://www.moma.org/visit/calendar/exhibitions/965. Accessed July 19, 2013.
6. Fischer-Lichte cited in Jones, "The Artist Is Present," 32–33.
7. *The Artist Is Present*, film, dir. Matthew Akers and Jeff Dupre (2012: Music Box Films).
8. http://www.theartstory.org/artist-abramovic-marina.htm. Accessed September 24, 2013.

9. Carrie Lambert-Beatty, "Against Performance Art," *Artforum International* 48, no. 9 (May 2010).
10. Jones, "The Artist Is Present," 42.
11. Ibid., 18.
12. Jones, "Staged Presence."
13. Anyone who wants to deny that Marina Abramović is surrounded by a cult of celebrity might want to peruse the multiple, fashion-style photographs of her that are used to publicize her exhibits now; her collaborations with actor James Franco; her guest-starring role in the HBO series, *Sex and the City*; or her collaboration with rapper, Jay-Z, on his video, "Picasso Baby," the form of which is based on the artwork, *The Artist Is Present*. For the latter, see http://www.npr.org/blogs/therecord/2013/08/03/208589809/jay-z-video-puts-hip-hop-and-art-back-in-the-same-room.
14. The documentary offers two such examples: one man pulls a mirror from the folds of his clothing and holds it in front of his face so that The Artist must gaze upon her face instead of his and a young woman enters the space and immediately strips naked, professing later that she wanted to open herself to the same vulnerability experienced by "Marina." While neither seems to pose a threat to Abramović, but rather simply interacts with the artwork on his and her own terms, they are nevertheless forcibly removed from the exhibit immediately.

Conclusion

1. Scharen and Vigen, eds., *Ethnography as Christian Theology and Ethics*, xxii.
2. Ibid.; emphases mine.
3. Ibid.
4. Ibid., xxiii.
5. Smith, "Troeltschian Questions," 3.
6. Ibid., 4. See, for example, Hauerwas, *The Peaceable Kingdom;* and Milbank, *Theology and Social Theory.*
7. See Scharen, "Judicious Narratives," 125–42; and Smith, "Redeeming Critique," 89–113.
8. Smith, "Troeltschian Questions," 4.
9. See Troeltsch, "What Does 'Essence of Christianity' Mean?"; and Gustafson, "Just What Is 'Postliberal' Theology?," 353–55.
10. Smith, "Troeltschian Questions," 4–6.
11. Jordan, "Writing the Truth," 5.
12. Scharen and Vigen, eds., *Ethnography as Christian Theology and Ethics*, 69; Jordan, "Writing the Truth," 4.
13. Scharen and Vigen, "Ethnography Audacious Enough to Witness," 4.
14. Ibid.

Bibliography

Abramović, Marina. *The Artist Is Present.* New York: Museam of Modern Art, 2010.

———. *Rhythm 0.* Naples: Galleria Studio Morra, 1974.

Althaus-Reid, Marcella. *The Queer God.* New York: Routledge, 2003.

Ammerman, Nancy Tatom. *Baptist Battles: Social Change and Religious Conflict in the Southern Baptist Convention.* New Brunswick: Rutgers University Press, 1990.

———. "Congregations: Local, Social, and Religious." In *The Oxford Handbook of the Sociology of Religion*, edited by Peter B. Clarke. New York: Oxford University Press, 2009.

———. *Pillars of Faith: American Congregations and Their Partners.* Berkeley: University of California Press, 2005.

The Artist Is Present. Film. Directed by Matthew Akers and Jeff Dupre. Chicago: Music Box Films, 2012.

Ault, James M., Jr. *Spirit and Flesh: Life in a Fundamentalist Baptist Church.* New York: Knopf, 2004.

Berger, Peter. *The Heretical Imperative: Contemporary Possibilities of Religious Affirmation.* Garden City, NY: Anchor Press, 1979.

Bourdieu, Pierre. *The Logic of Practice.* Translated by Richard Nice. Stanford: Stanford University Press, 1980.

———. *Outline of a Theory of Practice.* Translated by Richard Nice. Cambridge: Cambridge University Press, 1972.

———. *Pascalian Meditations.* Translated by Richard Nice. Stanford: Stanford University Press, 2000.

Bourdieu, Pierre, and Loïc Wacquant. *An Invitation to Reflexive Sociology.* Chicago: University of Chicago Press, 1992.

Breton, André. "Crisis of the Object." In *Surrealists on Art*, edited by L. Lippard. Spectrum, 1970.

Brock, Rita Nakashima, and Rebecca Parker. *Proverbs of Ashes: Violence, Redemptive Suffering, and the Search for What Saves Us.* Boston: Beacon Press, 2001.

Brown, Delwin, Sheila Greeve Davaney, and Kathryn Tanner, eds. *Converging on Culture: Theologians in Dialogue with Cultural Analysis and Criticism.* New York: Oxford University Press, 2001.

Brown, Lea D. "Dancing in the *Eros* of Domination and Submission within SM." In *Dancing Theology in Fetish Boots: Essays in Honor of Marcella*

Althaus-Reid, edited by Lisa Isherwood and Mark Jordan. London: SMC Press, 2010.

Brown, Leslie, and Susan Strega, eds. *Research as Resistance: Critical, Indigenous, and Anti-Oppressive Approaches.* Toronto: Canadian Scholars/ Women's Press, 2005.

Cameron, Helen, et al. *Talking about God in Practice: Theological Action Research and Practical Theology.* London: SCM Press, 2010.

Coakley, Sarah. *Powers and Submissions: Spirituality, Philosophy and Gender.* Malden, MA: Blackwell, 2002.

de Certeau, Michel. *The Practice of Everyday Life.* Translated by Steven Rendall. Berkeley: University of California Press, 1984.

Deer, Cécile. "Doxa." In *Pierre Bourdieu: Key Concepts*, edited by Michael Grenfell. 2nd ed. Bristol, CT: Acumen, 2012, 114–25.

Douglas, Kelly Brown. *Sexuality and the Black Church: A Womanist Perspective.* Maryknoll: Orbis, 2004.

Emerson, Michael O., and Rodney M. Woo. *People of the Dream: Multiracial Congregations in the United States.* Princeton: Princeton University Press, 2006.

Farley, Edward. *Theologia: The Fragmentation and Unity of Theological Education.* Eugene, OR: Wipf and Stock, 2001.

Farley, Wendy. *The Wounding and Healing of Desire: Weaving Heaven and Earth.* Louisville, KY: WJKP, 2005.

Farnsley, Arthur E., II. "'Judicious Concentration': Decision Making in the Southern Baptist Convention." In *Southern Baptists Observed: Multiple Perspectives on a Changing Denomination*, edited by Nancy Tatom Ammerman. Knoxville: University of Tennessee Press, 1993.

Fischer-Lichte, Erika. "Performance Art—Experiencing Liminality." In *Marina Abramović: Seven Easy Pieces*, written by Nancy Spector, Erika Fischer-Lichte, Sandra Umathum and Marina Abramović. Milan: Edizioni Charta, 2007.

Foucault, Michel. *Discipline and Punish: The Birth of the Prison*, edited by Alan Sheridan. New York: Vintage Books, 1995.

Fulkerson, Mary McClintock. *Places of Redemption: Theology for a Worldly Church.* New York: Oxford University Press, 2007.

Greenfell, Michael, ed. *Pierre Bourdieu: Key Concepts.* Bristol, CT: Acumen, 2008.

Gustafson, James M. "Just What Is 'Postliberal' Theology?" *Christian Century* 116, no. 10 (1999).

Halberstam, Judith. *Female Masculinity.* Durham: Duke University Press, 1998.

Hauerwas, Stanley. *The Peaceable Kingdom: A Primer in Christian Ethics.* Notre Dame: University of Notre Dame Press, 1983.

Hebdige, Dick. *Subculture: The Meaning of Style.* London: Routledge, 1988.

Jantzen, Grace M. *Power, Gender and Christian Mysticism.* New York: Cambridge University Press, 1995.

Johnson, Luke Timothy. "Scripture and Spirit." *Commonweal* 121, no. 2 (1994).

Jones, Amelia. "'The Artist Is Present' Artistic Re-enactments and the Impossibility of Presence." *TDR: The Drama Review* 55, no. 1 (2011).

Jones, Caroline A. "Staged Presence: Caroline A. Jones on Performance and Publics." *Artforum International* 48, no. 9 (2010).

Jones, Serene. *Cartographies of Grace: Feminist Theory and Christian Theology*. Minneapolis: Fortress Press, 2000.

Jordan, Mark. "Writing the Truth." *Practical Matters* 6 (2013).

Lambert-Beatty, Carrie. "Against Performance Art." *Artforum International* 48, no. 9 (2010).

Lévi-Strauss, Claude. *The Savage Mind*. Chicago: University of Chicago Press, 1968.

Lloyd, Richard. "Sentimental Education." *Contemporary Sociology* 37, no. 6 (2008).

Mahmood, Saba. *Politics of Piety: The Islamic Revival and the Feminist Subject*. Princeton: Princeton University Press, 2005.

Maton, Karl. "Habitus." In *Pierre Bourdieu: Key Concepts*, edited by Michael Greenfell. Bristol, CT: Acumen, 2008, 48–64.

McFague, Sallie. *Metaphorical Theology: Models of God in Religious Language*. Minneapolis: Fortress Press, 1982.

Milbank, John. *Theology and Social Theory: Beyond Secular Reason*. Oxford: Blackwell, 1993.

Moon, Dawne. *God, Sex, and Politics: Homosexuality and Everyday Theologies*. Chicago: University of Chicago Press, 2004.

Oleson, Virginia. "Early Millennial Feminist Qualitative Research: Challenges and Contours." In *The Sage Handbook of Qualitative Research*, edited by Norman K. Denzin and Yvonne Lincoln. Los Angeles: Sage Publications, 2005.

Ortner, Sherry. *The Politics and Erotics of Culture*. Boston: Beacon Press, 1996.

Pahl, Jon. *Shopping Malls and Other Sacred Spaces: Putting God in Place*. Grand Rapids, MI: Brazos Press, 2003.

Rice, Tom W., and Diane L. Coates. "Gender Role Attitudes in the Southern United States." *Gender and Society* 9, no. 6 (1995): 744–56.

Rollins, Peter. *How (Not) to Speak of God*. Brewster, MA: Paraclete, 2006.

Sanks, S. J., and T. Howland. "*Homo Theologicus*: Toward a *Reflexive* Theology (with the Help of Pierre Bourdieu)." *Theological Studies* 68 (2007): 515–30.

Scharen, Christian. "'Judicious Narratives', or Ethnography *as* Ecclesiology." *Scottish Journal of Theology*. 58, no. 2 (2005): 125–42.

———. *Public Worship and Public Work: Character and Commitment in Local Congregational Life*. Collegeville, MN: Liturgical Press, 2004.

Scharen, Christian, and Aana Marie Vigen, eds. *Ethnography as Christian Theology and Ethics*. New York: Continuum, 2011.

———. "Ethnography Audacious Enough to Witness." *Practical Matters* 6 (2013).

Sharf, Robert H. "Mysticism." In *Critical Terms for Religious Studies*, edited by Mark C. Taylor. Chicago: University of Chicago Press, 1998.

Smith, Linda Tuhiwai. *Decolonizing Methodologies: Research and Indigenous Peoples*. New York: Zed Books, 1999.

Smith, Ted A. "Redeeming Critique: Resignations to the Cultural Turn in Christian Theology and Ethics." *Journal of the Society of Christian Ethics* 24, no. 2 (2004): 89–113.

———. "Troeltschian Questions for *Ethnography as Christian Theology and Ethics*." *Practical Matters* 6 (2013).

Spivak, Gayatri Chakravorty. "Can the Subaltern Speak?" In *Marxism and the Interpretation of Culture*, edited by Cary Nelson and Lawrence Grossberg. Urbana: University of Illinois Press, 1988.

Stout, Jeffrey. *Ethics after Babel: The Languages of Morals and Their Discontents*. Boston: Beacon Press, 1988.

Stringer, Ernest T. *Action Research*. 3rd ed. Thousand Oaks, CA: Sage, 2007.

Swartz, David. *Culture and Power: The Sociology of Pierre Bourdieu*. Chicago: University of Chicago Press, 1997.

Swidler, Ann. "Culture in Action: Symbols and Strategies." *American Sociological Review* 51 (1986): 273–86.

Tanner, Kathryn. *Theories of Culture*. Minneapolis: Fortress Press, 1997.

Thomson, Patricia. "Field." In *Pierre Bourdieu: Key Concepts*, edited by Michael Grenfell. 2nd ed. Bristol, CT: Acumen, 2012, 65–82.

Troeltsch, Ernst. "What Does the 'Essence of Christianity' Mean?" In *Writings on Theology and Religion*, edited by Robert Morgan and Michael Pye. Louisville, KY: WJKP, 1990.

Wacquant, Loïc. "Carnal Connections: On Embodiment, Apprenticeship, and Membership." *Qualitative Sociology* 28, no. 4 (2005): 445–74.

———. "Habitus as Topic and Tool: Reflections on Becoming a Prizefighter." In *Ethnographies Revisited: Constructing Theory in the Field*, edited by Antony J. Puddephatt, William Shaffir, and Steven W. Kleinknecht. New York: Routledge, 2009, 137–51.

Ward, Pete, ed. *Perspectives on Ecclesiology and Ethnography*. Grand Rapids, MI: Eerdmans, 2012.

Warner, Stephen R. "The Place of the Congregation in the Contemporary American Religious Configuration." Vol. 2 of *American Congregations: New Perspectives in the Study of Congregations*, edited by James P. Wind and James W. Lewis. Chicago: University of Chicago Press, 1994.

Wiesel, Elie. *Night*. New York: Bantam, 1960.

Wigg-Stevenson, Natalie. "Reflexive Theology: A Preliminary Proposal." *Practical Matters* 6 (2013).

Index